# Themes in Hume

*The Self, the Will, Religion*

TERENCE PENELHUM

CLARENDON PRESS · OXFORD

192

# OXFORD

UNIVERSITY PRESS

Great Clarendon Street, Oxford OX2 6DP

Oxford University Press is a department of the University of Oxford.
It furthers the University's objective of excellence in research, scholarship,
and education by publishing worldwide in

Oxford New York

Auckland Bangkok Buenos Aires Cape Town Chennai
Dar es Salaam Delhi Hong Kong Istanbul Karachi Kolkata
Kuala Lumpur Madrid Melbourne Mexico City Mumbai Nairobi
São Paulo Shanghai Taipei Tokyo Toronto

Oxford is a registered trade mark of Oxford University Press
in the UK and in certain other countries

Published in the United States
by Oxford University Press Inc., New York

First published 2000
First published in paperback 2003

British Library Cataloguing in Publication Data

Data available

Library of Congress Cataloging in Publication Data

Penelhum, Terence, 1929–
Themes in Hume : the self, the will, religion / Terence Penelhum.
Includes bibliographical references and index.
1. Hume, David, 1711–1776   2. Self (Philosophy)   3. Religion—Philosophy.   4. Will.
I. Title.

B1499.S45 P46 2000   192—dc21   00-021967

ISBN 0-19-823898-3 (hbk.)
ISBN 0-19-926635-2 (pbk.)

1 3 5 7 9 10 8 6 4 2

Typeset by Graphicraft Ltd, Hong Kong
Printed in Great Britain
on acid-free paper by
Biddles Ltd.,
King's Lynn, Norfolk

*To Edith*

# PREFACE

THE essays in this volume were written over a period of no less than forty-five years, though most of them are quite recent. Three are published here for the first time. All deal with aspects of Hume's thought on which I have had occasion to reflect repeatedly, and now and again to change my mind. With two exceptions (Chapters 1 and 7) they make no claim to provide a general overview of Hume's system, although as time has gone by I have become increasingly convinced that Hume saw all his main philosophical positions as systematically interrelated, and that the common practice of reading and reflecting on him by discussing isolated extracts from his writings is one that misleads us when trying to interpret him, and impoverishes us philosophically into the bargain. I have expressed myself at some length elsewhere on the nature of Hume's philosophical system, however. Here I shall merely try to place the discussions in these essays in context, and make the changes in emphasis and judgement that I now feel to be necessary.

I see Hume as a philosopher who is squarely in the Socratic tradition. He is in the Socratic tradition because he sees philosophy as a source of liberating self-knowledge. On the other hand, if we think of Socrates as the teacher of Plato, and forget (for example) that the ancient Sceptics saw themselves as the heirs of Socrates too, we shall be more inclined to liken him to Democritus or Protagoras. For he certainly saw human nature as being subject to scientific understanding in the same way as the physical world, and he certainly saw our emotional lives and our practical judgements as determined by our social natures and the sentiments of our fellows. These latter features of his system account for the increasing esteem in which his thought has come to be held in the latter part of the twentieth century. But he is a Socratic figure because he is convinced that life must be examined to be fully lived; and that the philosopher, in examining it, can remove hindrances to the living of it.

What makes Hume a modern figure, indeed more clearly the incarnation of modernity than his competitors, is the way he thinks that self-understanding is to come about, and the hazards that beset us as we try to attain to it. For philosophers have been schooled, since Plato, to see themselves as able to rise above the prejudices and conventions of common life, to take or leave them after examining them, and even to forge alternative systems of thought to compete with them. As Hume sees the matter, the hubris of philosophy should be the first casualty of genuine self-knowledge, since when we come to see what we are really like we shall see that the traditional ambitions of the philosopher are vain ones. There are two strands in Hume's thought that he sees as combining to bring about this essential insight. One, the more fundamental, is the 'science of man'. This is the science that shows us how, in fact, our beliefs and our moral commitments arise; and its fundamental explanatory doctrine is that of the association of ideas. It is a mentalistic science—which distinguishes it from the naturalisms of the present day. It shows us how our beliefs, our sentiments, and our choices are causes and effects of one another; and the stories it tells leave only the most modest place for reason, which Hume sees as instrumental and ancillary: as the slave of the passions, which are the real driving forces of human nature. To suggest that philosophical reasoning could enable us to rise above these forces is to invert the real relationship between the intellect and the passions it exists to satisfy.

The second strand in Hume's thought that enables us to see the limits of reason is the sceptical strand. This is a prominent feature of Hume's thought, and those interpretations that seek to deny this cannot explain why his contemporaries found its prominence so obvious, even when Hume sought, for quasi-political reasons, to underplay it. The Sceptical tradition, since antiquity, has used philosophical dialectic to undermine our confidence in reason as a source of truth. Hume rejects the rationalist attempts to provide these justifications (or foundations, as they have been called since Descartes). But he does not follow the classical Sceptics in supposing that it is possible to adopt some uncommitted or beliefless form of life in which we manage without them. We are creatures of belief and commitment. Yet the Sceptic is right to argue that reason cannot underpin them. They are made possible by our passions, or instincts, which entrench the beliefs we need to live by and the commitments we need to mingle successfully with our fellows in society. The Sceptic is answered, but not refuted. The moral is that we must accept the purely instrumental role that reason has in our lives, and recognize our nature for what it is. If we fail to do this, we are left with one of two alternatives: one is the fairy-land of rationalist meta-physics, and the other is the anxiety-ridden attempt to follow the Sceptical formula of life without belief. Neither is viable outside the study, and each is a form of philosophical vanity. Hume shares with the Sceptics of antiquity the desire to be reconciled with the customs of common life that philosophy examines; but he rejects their aspiration to pretend to conform to them without inner commitment.

If this reading of Hume is the right one, then his science of man and his scepticism reinforce one another and are not at odds. His naturalism and his scepticism are blended, and neither undermines the other. This is a result of the fact that Hume is a post-Cartesian thinker. For him, as for Descartes, the contents of the mind are known to us. They form the data of the science of man. The post-Cartesian sceptic, unlike the sceptic of antiquity, questions only our inferences from these data to the world 'outside' them; and one of the purposes for which Hume uses his science of man is that of explaining how our natures bypass the sceptical doubts about these inferences by supplying us with the beliefs we need to function together in our world.

The essays here all reflect this understanding of what Hume is about, and although most of them deal with detailed aspects of Hume's system, I hope they play a part in supporting this understanding of his work.

On the surface, it should seem that Hume should be most at ease when he describes how our nature delivers our doxastic and practical commitments. In one way he is. In Book II of the *Treatise of Human Nature* he is leisurely, serene, even tedious, in describing the mechanisms whereby our passions come and go; in Book III he applies the psychology he has developed there to explain the origins of our commitment to justice. And even in Book I, he is at his most creative and ingenious when he tells us how our beliefs in causal necessity, external objects, and personal identity are generated by the associative mechanisms that Book II is to delineate more fully. Yet it is his views on personal identity that he singles out for what is almost a retraction in the Appendix, in a passage that has baffled many scholars. It is probably a mistake to read too much into this passage; but many have felt that his account of self-identity, or rather of our belief in it, is one of the least satisfactory parts of his system, and it is tempting for a critic to think that when Hume himself expresses discontent with it, he has come to acknowledge the error that the critic has seized upon. Whatever error he is recognizing there, his views of the self have left even his most admiring readers discontented. Chapters 2 to 6 are concerned with different puzzles that these views have raised. Chapter 2, the oldest here, was written without much recognition of the motives at work in Hume's philosophy. As its first paragraph makes clear, I was more concerned then to uncover conceptual errors in Hume's account of how we attribute identity to all changing objects, and as a young philosopher of the mid-century I felt confident that once these errors were recognized, the puzzlement that fuelled Hume's scepticism about this attribution would be largely dissipated. I still think I was right to accuse him of these errors, and to deny that our relevant linguistic practices are shot through with mistake and paradox in the way he says. His mental science tells him the truth about what makes us ascribe identity in the ways that we do, but does not support his judgement that such ascriptions are mistaken ones. And if he is guilty of these errors, then the unnamed opponents whose theories he ridicules at the outset of his discussion were guilty of them too.

In Chapter 3, prompted by criticisms of the earlier analysis of Hume's text, I had occasion to probe more deeply into the nature of Hume's mental science, and to distinguish it from other theories often thought to be latter-day versions of it. Hume thinks that his science of man enables us to see that our belief in self-identity conceals the deeper truth that our minds consist of mere bundles of mental phenomena that lack the unity we ascribe to them. Just as he supposes our common sense ascription of self-identity to these bundles is ultimately paradoxical, so he in turn is often criticized on the ground that he is guilty of paradox himself in supposing there is a unitary mind that ascribes the identity he denies. I suggest that this criticism is unfounded.

Chapters 4 and 5 address a distinct but equally baffling interpretative problem: the relationship between Hume's discussions of the self in Book I of the *Treatise* and that in Book II. In Book I he goes out of his way to indicate that personal identity as it concerns the passions is not his immediate topic; but when he comes to deal with it in Book II, what he says seems disconcertingly at odds with what he has said earlier, even when the change of theme and emphasis is recognized. I offer my own versions of the standard lame defences: that it is the real self, the bundle of perceptions that I have, that he claims to be the object of pride and humility, and not the simple and identical soul of his rationalist predecessors. But these palliative responses are not satisfying, and these two essays argue additional theses: the first, that for the actual mechanisms of pride and humility to be understood, and to be subjected, as in life they are, to moral criticism, the self whose idea is central to those emotions must have its boundaries already set and recognized; the second, that since the indirect passions depend essentially on the familiar contrast between oneself and others, what Hume tells us in his account of those passions requires him to assume the mind to have the ability to draw this contrast, when his mental science has not supplied any account of how we come by this ability.

Chapter 6, a new essay in this volume, is an attempt to deal with some problems in the earlier pieces; and it contains some (unoriginal) reflections on Hume's puzzling second thoughts in the Appendix, which I have pusillanimously avoided writing about before this.

If the arguments in Chapters 4 and 5 have weight, Hume is wrong to distinguish as sharply as he does between personal identity as it concerns the thought or imagination, and personal identity as it concerns the passions. But this sharp distinction only mirrors his pervasive and fundamental insistence that reason is the slave of the passions and cannot be their master. This is the central theme of his moral psychology, and he sees it as the primary lesson that the search for self-knowledge teaches us. It is the primary sign that we are part of nature, and that our aspirations to rise above nature are self-destructive and self-deceiving. He opposes this vision to that which Plato puts into the mouth of Socrates in the *Phaedo*, according to which the human soul is an alien prisoner in the natural order and can rise above it by following reason and shunning the bondage of the passions. In Chapter 7 I argue that Hume's vision of our natures exaggerates the truths it teaches, and that the common opinion that Hume is anxious, in the moral sphere, to support rather than to undermine, already embodies a middle way between the Platonic and Humean polarities by recognizing that the passions can themselves be reasonable.

The naturalist is usually a determinist, and Hume is no exception. The rationalist is likely to be attracted by some form of libertarianism. Hume is the major source of the claim that determinism is not at odds with common moral judgement in the way it seems to be. The purpose of Chapter 8 is to examine his 'reconciling project' and its place in his system. I argue that it is more at odds with common moral judgements than he claims it is, and that his moral psychology has us apportioning praise and blame to features of human personality that are the result of endowment and fortune, thus allowing him no response to the problem of what is now called moral luck.

One of the reasons for the distance I claim to find between Hume's moral psychology and common opinion, is the fact that common opinion has been partially Christianized. Hume, as a neo-Hellenist, is hoping to ease philosophical opinion back towards classical models, and away from Christian forms of rationalism. The most difficult interpretative question the Hume scholar faces is that of deciding whether he has any degree of real (rather than assumed) tolerance towards a diluted Christian religion based on custom and tradition, of the sort that the Sceptical Fideists might approve as their ancient forebears did. It is this question, and those allied to it, that are the topics of Chapters 9, 10, and 11. The question comes to a head when we try to interpret the calculated ambiguities of Part XII of the *Dialogues Concerning Natural Religion*. These essays, composed over twenty years, do not arrive at the same answers; but I reproduce them here essentially unchanged for two reasons. First, no one can be sure that he or she has this perplexity completely resolved. It is obvious that Hume is hostile to revealed and insitutionalized religion, and that he thinks it is the enemy of the modes of adjustment to the needs of common life with which our nature has endowed us. It is also obvious that he thinks he has undermined much of the classical Design Argument for the existence of God. But that is all that is obvious. It is unclear whether he thinks there is an inescapable core of belief that the Design Argument expresses, and unclear what the 'man of letters' should identify as that inescapable core, if it exists. And it is similarly unclear how Hume thinks the man of letters should relate to the religiousness that is clearly so much a part of the common life to which he must defer in other spheres. Hume's readers continue to differ quite radically on this. So there is an excuse for airing one scholar's uncertainty by offering differing, though equally tentative, responses to it.

The second reason for presenting these essays in sequence is that each approaches the question of Hume's attitude to religion from a different perspective. Chapter 9 approaches it through an examination of the differing phases in Hume's scepticism, from the *Treatise*, through the first *Enquiry*, to the *Dialogues*, where the proper role of scepticism in relation to religion is one of the explicit themes. Chapter 10 examines most particularly the relation of Hume to the Sceptical Fideist tradition, and some of the twists and turns of the interchanges between Philo and Cleanthes in Part XII. Chapter 11, an essay not previously published, is an attempt to view the *Dialogues* in the light of the probable import of the two Sections on religion in the first *Enquiry:* the famous 'Of Miracles', and the subtler and under-read 'Of a Particular Providence and of a Future State'. This essay shows where my views rest at present, but Hume has deliberately left us with what seem to be conflicting signals, and I have no doubt that the controversy over his detailed intentions will continue.

The final two chapters deal with Hume's debts and responses to two of his predecessors. Both Butler and Pascal are Christian thinkers with objectives Hume rejects; but both are writers towards whom he felt some degree of respect, in the latter case very grudging. I have great admiration for both of them, and have been intrigued to find how much similarity there is to be found between the details of his views and theirs, when one looks past the obvious opposition between the morals they and he would draw from these details.

Some of these essays are confined to exegetical and interpretative issues, whereas others offer critical judgements, sometimes severe ones. To some extent these differences are the result of the occasions for which they were originally composed; and I trust no one will suppose that where I confine myself to deciding what Hume thinks, I think that what he thinks is true. Most particularly, I trust no one will make this inference in the case of religion. While I have from time to time stated the common view that Hume has definitively refuted the Design Argument, I am no longer confident of this, or of much else in the philosophy of religion except of the need for those who practise it to respond to the criticisms of which he is the classic source.

It is impossible to record here all the debts I owe to fellow scholars and colleagues, but I will mention some of them. First, I should express my gratitude to those individuals and groups whose meetings gave me the occasion and opportunity to assemble my thoughts on the questions discussed here. Most prominent here is of course the Hume Society, whose meetings I have always tried to get to since it began in the early 1970s. Chapters 5, 8, 9, 10, 11, and 12 all began their existence as presentations to its meetings, and are improved by the discussions that took place there. I have found no more congenial environment for scholarly discussion anywhere. The Canadian Society for Eighteenth-Century Studies kindly asked me to speak to its 1991 Calgary meeting, thus stimulating me to write what is now Chapter 13; I also had an opportunity to present it to the Royal Society of Edinburgh in 1992, and wish to record my gratitude to them and to the Royal Society of Canada and the British Academy, who jointly sponsored a lecture and research tour of which this appearance was a part. Chapter 7 first saw the light in a preliminary version at the 1990 Hume Society–NEH Institute on Hume's philosophy which was held under the benign directorship of Wade Robison at Dartmouth College. The Royal Society of Canada kindly asked me to take part in a commemorative symposium on Adam Smith and Hume at Laval University in 1976; hence the essay that forms Chapter 1. In that same year I was able to present what is now Chapter 9 to the McGill Hume Congress that David Norton directed. My thanks to the sponsors of all these occasions.

My personal debts to colleagues are very numerous, and cannot all be listed. I do, however, wish especially to thank the following for personal kindness and for the stimulus of their work: David and Mary Norton, Donald Livingston and Marie Martin, James King, Lorne Falkenstein, Jane McIntyre, John Gaskin, Peter Jones, Charlotte Brown, and Donald Ainslie. Peter Momtchiloff of Oxford University Press has been the source of much help and wise advice.

My wife's love and support at a time of supposed retirement have been indispensable, and for this no thanks can ever be enough.

T. P.

# ACKNOWLEDGEMENTS

I wish to express thanks to the original publishers of those essays that are reprinted here for permission to reproduce them.

Chapter 1, 'David Hume: An Appreciation', originally appeared in the *Transactions of the Royal Society of Canada*, xiv, 1976, under the title 'David Hume 1711–76: A Bicentennial Appreciation'. It appears here by kind permission of the Society. Chapter 2, 'Hume on Personal Identity', first appeared in the *Philosophical Review*, 64, 1955 (copyright 1955 Cornell University) and is reprinted by permission of the publisher. Chapter 3, 'Hume's Theory of the Self Revisited' was originally published in *Dialogue*, 14, 1975, and appears by permission of the journal and its editors. Chapter 4, 'Self-identity and Self-regard', first appeared in *The Identities of Persons*, edited by Amélie Rorty, published by the University of California Press in 1976 (copyright 1976 The Regents of the University of California), and is used here by permission of the University of California Press. Chapter 5, 'The Self of Book I and the Selves of Book II' appeared first in *Hume Studies*, 18, 1992, and is reproduced here by permission of the journal.

Chapter 7, 'Hume's Moral Psychology', was first published in *The Cambridge Companion to Hume*, edited by David Fate Norton, copyright Cambridge University Press 1993, and is reprinted with the permission of Cambridge University Press. Chapter 9, 'Hume's Scepticism and the *Dialogues*', first appeared in *McGill Hume Studies*, edited by David Fate Norton, Wade Robison, and Nicholas Capaldi, published by Austin Hill Press in 1979; it is reprinted here by permission of David Fate Norton. Chapter 10, 'Natural Belief and Religious Belief in Hume's Philosophy' originally appeared in *The Philosophical Quarterly*, 33, 1983, together with a reply by Stewart Sutherland, and appears here by permission of Blackwell Publishers.

Chapter 12, 'Butler and Hume' appeared first in *Hume Studies*, 14, 1988, and is reprinted by permission of the journal. Chapter 13, 'Hume and Pascal' first appeared in *Lumen*, 12, 1993, and is reprinted here by permission of the journal.

# CONTENTS

# REFERENCES AND ABBREVIATIONS

In common with most readers of Hume, I have until now made continual use of the Oxford texts edited more than a century ago by L. A. Selby-Bigge. This volume is being prepared at a time when the new Oxford edition of Hume, under the editorship of David Norton, Tom Beauchamp and M. A. Stewart, is beginning to appear. There is no doubt that it will become standard, and no one who publishes on Hume should do anything that can hinder its universal adoption. But there is also no doubt that the Selby-Bigge editions will continue in use for a long time. Since this book is being prepared at the very beginning of the transition, I have tried to make in-text references in a form that will cause minimal inconvenience to any future readers using it who have access to the new edition when I at present do not.

For the *Treatise of Human Nature*, I have used the abbreviation *T* followed by the Book, Part and Section numbers in upper-case roman, lower-case roman and arabic numerals respectively. These are followed, wherever required, by the page number in the second Selby-Bigge edition, revised by P. H. Nidditch, 1978. An example: *T* I. iv. 6. 251.

For the *Enquiry Concerning Human Understanding*, I have used the abbreviation *EU*, followed by the Section number in upper-case roman and the Selby-Bigge page number (e.g. *EU* x. 127), and for the *Enquiry Concerning the Principles of Morals* I have used the abbreviation *EM*, plus the Section and page numbers. In both cases the page numbers are those of the third edition of the Selby-Bigge text of the two *Enquiries*, revised by P. H. Nidditch, 1975.

For the *Dialogues Concerning Natural Religion*, I use the abbreviation *D*, followed by the number of the Part and the page number in the edition of Norman Kemp Smith, published in 1947 by Thomas Nelson, Edinburgh, and reprinted by Bobbs-Merrill, Indianapolis (14th printing 1980); e.g. *D* XII. 227. The abbreviation *NHOR* stands for the *Natural History of Religion*. I have used the edition edited by H. E. Root, published in London by Adam and Charles Black in 1957 and in Stanford, California by Stanford University Press.

The abbreviation *LDH* stands for *The Letters of David Hume*, edited by J. Y. T. Greig, 2 vols., Oxford University Press, 1932. *NLDH* stands for *New Letters of David Hume*, edited by Raymond Klibansky and E. C. Mossner, published by the Clarendon Press, Oxford, in 1954.

The abbreviation *A* stands for *An Abstract of a Treatise of Human Nature 1740*, with an Introduction by J. M. Keynes and P. Sraffa (Cambridge University Press), reprint Hamden, Conn.: Archon Books, 1965.

# 1

## David Hume: An Appreciation

IT would be generally agreed that David Hume was one of Edinburgh's most illustrious citizens, and the most notable intellectual figure of the Scottish Enlightenment. The city thinks of him with pride, and its university has named one of its buildings after him.[1] But his community's estimate of him has not always been so high. One of the best-known facts of his career is the failure of his candidacy for the chair of Moral Philosophy in 1745. The position was awarded instead to a bright young man who never published.[2]

This typifies what has happened to Hume's reputation. It has taken a long time for his stature as a philosopher to be fully recognized. His own contemporaries could not fully take the measure of him; and although he was *famous*, and was lionized and vilified by turns, this was because his readers were drawn to those aspects of his work which he made easily palatable or consciously shocking. By now it is commonplace for us philosophers to say that he is the greatest of us ever to have written in English. But even though his present-day admirers will say this, they will still quite often do so on the basis of a very narrow selection of his achievements—confined usually to his epistemology. Although they owe him so much of their own doctrines and methods, they still incline to attend only to those aspects of his work which can be stated in twentieth-century idiom. Even now, Hume is very little appreciated as a *systematic* thinker.

Of course no philosopher can avoid having his successors pick and choose among his doctrines. This is the price he pays for being read by later generations. But there are special reasons in Hume's case

---

[1] Since this essay was originally written, Edinburgh has honoured Hume further. A statue was erected in his honour near the top of the Royal Mile in 1997. It was funded by public subscription on the initiative of the Saltire Society.

[2] These unhappy events are described in Chapter 12 of Mossner 1954. For more recent accounts see Emerson 1994 and Stewart 1995.

for the uncertainty of his reputation. These reasons have led his warmest admirers to feel reservations about him. They cannot quite bring themselves to talk of him in the same breath as Plato or Aristotle or Aquinas or Spinoza or Kant. They are wrong: his work can stand these comparisons; or I at least think so. But anyone who thinks this has to explain why it is so seldom admitted even by those who consider themselves Hume's followers.

## I

The first reason why philosophers have never taken Hume altogether seriously is that he does not seem to take himself altogether seriously. This is very dangerous for a philosopher. We expect *great* thinkers to manifest the accepted symptoms of profundity: to be solemn and prolix and decently obscure. But Hume's sentences can be understood at the first reading; he apportions the length of his discussions to the importance of his topics; and, most disconcerting of all, he has a sense of humour. He banters and teases, and in style and manner he is the most obviously ironic thinker since Socrates. (There are other parallels: both were accused of impiety, and both were judged unfit to teach the young.) But it is not just that he is engaging and humorous and self-depreciating in the way he writes. What he says is disconcerting. Sometimes he just gives up on a problem and says it is too difficult for him. At other times he will happily admit that an argument is unanswerable but remain quite unaffected by it. And whatever are we to make of a supposedly great thinker who concludes thirty pages of intense argument by saying 'Carelessness and inattention alone can afford us any remedy. For this reason I rely entirely upon them.' (*T* I. iv. 2. 218)? Such a person may be greatly gifted. But surely he is frivolous?

What this perception of Hume misses, pardonably enough, is that when he seems to make light of things that others treat with solemnity, this is not the manifestation of temperamental frivolity, but something quite opposite. It is the deliberate application of a doctrine. The doctrine is that of the impotence of philosophical reasoning. Hume's central philosophical message is that we should not take philosophy itself too seriously. And this message comes to us from someone who is temperamentally inclined to do this. When we gaze at the fat and complacent-looking figure who stares at us from Allan

Ramsay's portrait and think of all the stories of the charming and
irreverent and clubbable Hume, it is too easy to imagine that the
famous irony comes from a temperamental immunity to philosophical anxieties. There is plenty of evidence that this was not so.
The *Treatise of Human Nature*, which was completed by the time
he was twenty-six, is a work whose pages fairly glow with the ex-
citement of intellectual innovation. In order to write it, Hume had
to undergo financial hardship and emotional stress. He reveals the
extent of this stress in one of his most famous letters, written to an
unnamed physician in 1734, not long before his departure for
France, where the *Treatise* was finally written. The letter does not
seem to have been sent, but it was, significantly, kept by Hume all
his life.[3] In it he tells how his mental exertions had produced the
'Disease of the Learned', a 'coldness and desertion of the spirit',
accompanied by such psychosomatic symptoms as 'scurvy spots'
on the fingers, 'wateriness in the mouth', and a sudden ravenous
appetite which seems to have been the initial cause of his famous
corpulence. At the close of the letter he tells us of his resolve to deal
with these distresses by a period of activity in business. This activity was a failure, but the same pattern of anxiety and attempted release
finds expression in the famous passages with which he concludes the
first Book of the *Treatise*. Here he tells us, in prose in which I find
no trace of irony, that his philosophical perplexities have led him
into such melancholy and isolation that he fancies himself 'some
strange uncouth monster', and is 'in the most deplorable condition
imaginable'. He continues:

Most fortunately it happens, that since reason is incapable of dispelling these
clouds, nature herself suffices to that purpose, and cures me of this philosophical melancholy and delirium, either by relaxing this bent of mind, or
by some avocation, and lively impression of my senses, which obliterate all
these chimeras. I dine, I play a game of back-gammon, I converse, and am
merry with my friends; and when after three or four hours' amusement, I
would return to these speculations, they appear so cold, and strained, and
ridiculous, that I cannot find it in my heart to enter into them any farther.
(*T* I. iv. 7. 269)

At the personal level, therefore, Hume sees himself as one of a
minority who have a predilection for philosophical thought.

[3] This letter is to be found on pp. 12–18 of the Greig edition of Hume's letters
1932, and is reprinted in Norton (ed.) 1993, 345–50. See also Chapter 7 of Mossner 1954.

Unfortunately this predilection leads only to bewilderment and despair, for philosophy cannot answer the questions that it forces us to ask. The only cure for this despair is a recognition of the limits of philosophy and an absorption in common affairs and human society. Fortunately this release is available, for the philosopher does share a common human nature with the rest of mankind, and a reasonable apportionment of his time will be enough to ensure that the resources of our common nature will overcome the distempers that philosophy generates. It is interesting that Hume had a special venom in reserve when he criticized what he calls the 'monkish virtues' of the ascetic and the solitary. Such a person, he says, 'after his death, may have a place in the calendar; but will scarcely ever be admitted, when alive, into intimacy and society, except by those who are as delirious and as dismal as himself'. Such a person cuts himself off, by policy, from those very natural and social resources which serve as the corrective to theory and dogma.

So the fat and cheery Hume of tradition is real enough, but as a self-conscious *persona*. He is the deliberate achievement of a man who knows better, not less well, than his opponents what a hard taskmaster philosophy can be. Such a *persona* has to be deliberately sustained. Hume sustained it by his social proclivities, by extensive achievements in areas outside philosophy itself, such as economics and history, and by a refusal to engage in controversy with those who assaulted him in print; but, above all, he sustained it by systematic theory. It would be paradoxical if the theory with which Hume kept philosophy in its place were itself wholly philosophical theory. To a large extent it is not. It is here that we can see a profound difference between Hume's negative view of philosophy and that of Wittgenstein in our own day. Both men have the same intensely pursued deflationary objective of offering us release from the never-ending uncertainties of philosophical reflection. Both insist that the theories philosophers construct can offer no resting place. But Wittgenstein's remedies are themselves philosophical explorations in a new vein. Hume's are not philosophical at all. They derive instead from his understanding of human nature, from what we would now call psychology. It is not that Hume does not take philosophy seriously because he is temperamentally flippant. It is that he holds as a point of doctrine that it *ought* not to be taken seriously because it is a potential source of temperamental disorder. I suggest, then, that we must view Hume's mature personality and his philosophy as of a piece. But this is primarily a matter of seeing the personality as a reflection of the doctrines. He does not treat serious problems light-heartedly: he pursues light-heartedness seriously. I shall now try briefly to interpret the theory that determines the strategy of this pursuit.

## II

Hume's fundamental theoretical step is to view philosophical reasoning, and indeed reasoning in general, in the wider context of the science of human nature. His claims for that science are extreme:

Here then is the only expedient, from which we can hope for success in our philosophical researches, to leave the tedious ling'ring method which we have hitherto followed, and instead of taking now and then a castle or a village on the frontier, to march up directly to the capital or centre of these sciences, to human nature itself . . . There is no question of importance whose decision is not compriz'd in the science of man; and there is none which can be decided with any certainty before we become acquainted with that science. In pretending therefore to explain the principles of human nature, we in effect propose a complete system of the sciences, built on a foundation almost entirely new, and the only one on which they can stand with any security. (*T* Int. XVI)

This is how he begins the *Treatise*, and his language could hardly be more ambitious.

Hume was not the first to make grandiose claims like these. Descartes had also proclaimed a new foundation for the whole of human knowledge in the preceding century. The two thinkers have much in common. Both think that science can tell us only the principles that govern natural happenings but can tell us nothing about any ultimate purposes they may fulfil. Both believe that there is a sharp distinction to be drawn between the world of public physical events and the world of private mental events. But a great gulf separates them in spite of these likenesses. The foundations on which Descartes tries to build are metaphysical. Hume is inspired by Newton, and the foundations he builds upon are those of observations and experiment. In consequence of this we find an even more critical difference. To Descartes it is the metaphysical separation of the mental and the physical that dictates the limits of science: science has limits because it is confined to the physical world; and the soul, with its simplicity, its freedom, and its self-consciousness, is beyond the scope of science. To Hume, the simplicity and the freedom that Descartes ascribes to the mind are myths, and the self-consciousness of which Descartes speaks amounts to no more than our familiar ability to observe and report the course of our own mental processes. Hence there is no reason to suppose there cannot be a science of mind. There can. Indeed, it would be a thoroughly Newtonian science, in which the principles and procedures that Newton had applied with such spectacular success to the physical world would be applied to the mental. Such a science would first find the ultimate corpuscular units that our observation of mental phenomena reveal to us. Hume calls these ultimate units *perceptions*, and divides them into *impressions* and *ideas* (roughly, sensations and feelings, and the images that derive from them). Since the mental world is, by its very nature, in a constant state of change in the way in which Newton has said the physical world is, the science of man will require a principle which will account for the changes that occur within it. Such a principle will provide a mental analogue of gravitation. This analogue is *association*. The association of impressions and the association of ideas account for the many and varied ways in which the units of our mental life succeed one another. 'Here,' he says, 'is a kind of *attraction*, which in the mental world will be found to have as extraordinary effects as in the natural, and to show itself in as many and as various forms.' Hume was especially vain of this principle. In 1740 he wrote an anonymous pamphlet, the *Abstract of A Treatise of Human Nature*, in a vain attempt to boost public interest in the *Treatise*, which was not getting much attention. In it he says, 'If anything can entitle the author to so glorious a name as that of an "inventor", it is the use he makes of the principle of the association of ideas, which enters into most of his philosophy,' (*A* 31).

Today the mechanism of association is the most dated and unattractive aspect of Hume's system. But one does not have to adopt its details to grasp its radical implications, or to see that these implications can follow from other forms of the science of man equally well. What follows from the acceptance that there is a science of the mental is that what we think, what we feel, and what we will can be explained as the effects of causes and as instances of natural law— the mind of man is a part of nature, not a stranger in it. And what follows from any form of the science of the mental which, like Hume's, treats thoughts or feelings or volitions as the units of explanation is that the mind of man can have no control over its thoughts, or its feelings, or its volitions. For consider: if the never-ending changes of the physical world are all to be explained in terms of the attraction of material bodies to one another, it is clearly nonsensical to suggest that the physical universe that *contains* these bodies can exert any independent force of its own that can interfere with the effects of gravitation. It is just the place where these effects happen. Similarly, if the course of my mental history is determined by the associative attraction of my perceptions; if they cause one another; then there is no sense to the suggestion that *I*, the mind or soul that *has* them, can myself exercise any powers over their course. All the mind does is *include* them. The self or ego or soul has nothing to do: it is (and even this is wrong) just the theatre on whose stage mental events happen. So the Humean mental world is a totally deterministic world, and the denial of the independent reality of the self is not an awkward result of Hume's system, as it is often thought to be, but one of its cornerstones.

I have suggested that Hume's personal and intellectual objective was the deflation of philosophical reasoning, and that this objective was one which he pursued through the development of a science of the human mind. I would now like to show how this objective and this science combine to produce those two aspects of his system for which he has always been most notorious—his scepticism, and his proclamation that reason is the slave of the passions.

### III

It is as a sceptic that Hume is most widely known. To most students of philosophy, indeed, scepticism *is* the position that Hume adopts about induction of perception or personal identity. This understanding of him was the standard interpretation of his work in his own day also, and his only serious contemporary critic, Thomas Reid, concentrated his attack upon it—as did Reid's follower James Beattie, the 'bigoted silly fellow' who did so much to spoil the equanimity of Hume's last years. This understanding is a correct one, in spite of Hume's own protests and those of his recent admirers. It is correct, but incomplete. Hume tries in many places to define his attitude to scepticism with something approaching precision, but the fact that he makes so many attempts to do this leads to some difficulties of interpretation. It is disconcerting for an interpreter, after reading the most devastating battery of sceptical arguments in existence, to find their author saying that 'the doctrines of the Pyrrhonians or Sceptics have been regarded in all ages as principles of mere curiosity, or a kind of *jeu d'esprit*, without any influence on a man's steady principles or conduct in life. In reality, a philosopher who affects to doubt of the maxims of common reason, and even of his senses, declares sufficiently that he is not in earnest, and that he intends not to advance an opinion which he would recommend as standards of judgement and action.'[4] But there is no incoherence here. What misleads us into thinking so is our incomplete understanding of what scepticism was before Hume, and of the important changes he makes in it. He is a sceptic, but a sceptic of a very special sort.

Scepticism is not merely the doctrine that there are no good philosophical reasons to support the beliefs of common sense or the dogmas of metaphysics and religion, although this is an essential part of it. The sceptical tradition has a long history, which is usually traced back to Pyrrho in the fourth century BC. It became one of the major philosophical movements of Hellenistic times, and is best known through the writings of Sextus Empiricus in the late second century AD. Hume was acquainted with the work of Sextus, though there is no doubt that he was most directly affected by that of modern sceptical writers on the Continent, especially Pierre Bayle. Ancient Scepticism was a reaction against the pretensions of philosophical systems, especially that of the Stoics. But it shared a common moral objective with Stoicism, an objective which post-Humean students of scepticism have tended to overlook. This moral objective is peace of mind, *ataraxia*. The Stoic and the Sceptic sought this objective in different ways, though both saw it as an inner condition which the wise man could attain for himself even when social circumstances were against him. The Stoic sought it by appealing to a system of thought in which he could understand his fortunes and his duties as rooted in the divine order of things and could suppress the irrational resistance of the emotions. The Sceptic sought it through a recognition that our intellect is unable to establish the truth of this system of thought, or that of any of its many competitors. The wise man must recognize that he cannot penetrate to the inner nature of things. When this recognition dawns upon him, he will suspend his judgement on how things really are, or what things are in themselves good, or what is the nature of the gods. These things are beyond him. Of course he has to act, and he will; but he will conform to the prevailing opinion, always holding himself aloof from the assent and commitment that other men give to their dogmatic opinions. For such commitment leads to enthusiasm and mental turbulence. Superficial conformity backed by inner suspensions of judgement permits enough involvement for practical affairs but preserves inward peace. The philosophical acumen which the Sceptics displayed could not lead them to certainties, but by revealing the hopelessness of men's attempts to find certainties it offered them the release that comes from standing aloof from the dogmatic commitments that agitate men and sow dissension among them.

Hume inherits the negative thrust of classical scepticism, and as a man of his century shares the sceptical aim of seeking release from the turmoil of factional strife. But for him it is not philosophical reasoning that can provide this release. What provides this release for us, if we will let it, is human nature. Hume does not believe that suspension of judgement leads to tranquillity. Suspension of judgement is unnatural. Fortunately it is not possible for us, except for very brief periods in our studies. Our common human nature does not permit us to hold back our assent from the beliefs of common sense for more than a brief time; and if we attempt to prolong that time by over-indulgence in philosophical questioning, the result will not be *ataraxia*, but mental disorder and anxiety.

This does not mean that the classical sceptic is wrong when he says that the beliefs of common sense lack rational justification. They do lack rational justification. We all believe that past experience is a proper guide to the future: that because the sun has come up every morning until today, we have good reason to expect it to do so tomorrow. But the sceptic is right: however many times it has done it hitherto, the conclusion that it will do so in the morning does not follow in logic, so we have no rational ground for our expectation. We all believe that our changing and fleeting perceptions are perceptions of a world of continuing and independent objects. But the sceptic is right: my having these fleeting perceptions now and then gives no guarantee whatever that what I perceive has an existence independent of my perceiving it. Each of us is quite sure that he retains his identity with the being whose thoughts and feelings he can remember from the year before, and who carried his name in the past. But the sceptic is right here, too: sameness or identity, says Hume, is logically incompatible with the constant change and variety each of us encounters within when he introspects. Hume's destructive argumentation on these themes is the most widely and justly celebrated part of his system, and every philosopher since has felt obliged to find something wrong with it. But 'answering' Hume's scepticism is a thankless task, and I do not think anyone has yet succeeded in it, though there have been many glorious failures.

Hume himself says the answer is ready to hand, if only we will look in the right place. It does not lie in philosophical counter-arguments, which he subjects again and again to devastating criticisms. Nor does it lie in the stance of the classical sceptic, who acts with the common herd but who snobbishly holds back from inner assent. That does not work because it is psychologically too stressful to attempt, and because we are so constituted that we *could* not withhold agreement from what everyone else believes even if we were prepared to do violence to our social natures by trying. It is here, simply, that the only answer is to be found. The science of human nature shows us that our beliefs have causes which have nothing at all to do with reasoning, and that these causes entrench our natural beliefs long before any philosophers can be found to ask about their rational justification. So it is not surprising that when sceptical philosophers point out that they have none, their arguments, as Hume puts it, 'admit of no answer and produce no conviction'.[5] Nor is it surprising that when rationalist philosophers try to invent reasons where none have existed before, the reasons they invent depend for any plausibility they may have on the very natural beliefs they are supposed to justify. The simple truth is that we are believers by nature: 'Nature by an absolute and uncontrollable necessity has determined us to judge as well as to breathe and feel,' (*T* I. iv. 1. 183).

*How* does nature determine us to judge? What causes our beliefs if it is not that we have reasons for them? Hume offers intriguing and ingenious answers, in which he draws heavily upon the doctrine

[5] *EU* XII. 155 n. He makes this remark specifically about the reasonings of Berkeley, whom he interprets as a sceptic *malgré lui*.

of association. The details are of secondary concern. But the answers are never edifying ones. As Hume describes us we are creatures of habit, so that we are led to embrace the idea of the sun's coming up tomorrow morning through the sheer repetition of past experiences. We are lazy, so we conveniently allow ourselves to be confused between single unchanging perceptions and series of distinct but similar ones. And although the manufacture of our natural beliefs takes place in us, we do not control or direct it. It is as well for us that we do not. For if we could control our beliefs as the classical sceptics thought, we would never reach those conclusions that enable us to act. So even though belief is, as Hume expresses it, 'more properly an act of the sensitive, than of the cogitative part of our natures', (*T* I. iv. 1. 183) we are very lucky that it is. For as things stand we are provided with what he ironically calls 'a kind of pre-established harmony between the course of nature and the succession of our ideas', (*EU* v. 54).

Irony, especially Hume's, has many roles. One of its roles is that of making it possible to say something deeply disturbing by lightening one's tone of voice. This is its role here. For the sentence I have just quoted is one which expresses the very essence of Hume's theory of knowledge, and this theory is very wounding to our pride. For what Hume tells us is no less than this: that our most fundamental beliefs, in the regularity of nature, the reality of objects of perception, and the continuity of the self, are beliefs for which we can find no justification, but which our natures, through causes over which we have no control, and which we cannot evade, generate irrespective of the absence of such reasons—and these beliefs happen, by convenient Darwinian accident, to conform to our needs for survival and social relationships in much the same way as our natural propensities to digest our food or produce children. That such a deflating view of human nature and human intellect could have been evolved at the height of the Age of Reason is remarkable. It is not at all remarkable that Hume's contemporaries did not quite take it in, and refused to believe that he really meant it. Nor is it remarkable that Kant, when he encountered it, was awakened from his dogmatic slumbers to develop an alternative account that would be less uncomplimentary to human rationality. For Hume, who did mean it, the message was clear. To the man who is afflicted with a fondness for philosophical reasoning, wisdom dictates only a modest indulgence in it. The only cure for the perplexities and anxieties to which it can otherwise lead is the relaxed acceptance of common opinion and participation in the pleasures of social intercourse.


## IV


But if we consider man's social nature, Hume immediately confronts us with another blow to our self-esteem. He does not merely try to dethrone reason in the theory of knowledge, but dethrones it, notoriously, in the sphere of morality also. 'Reason,' he says, in his most shocking pronouncement, 'is, and ought only to be, the slave of the passions, and can never pretend to any other office than to serve and obey them,' (*T* II. iii. 3. 415). It is with this pronouncement that Hume shows himself to be the major theoretical ancestor of the Romantic movement. His doctrine is complex, and an accurate interpretation of it is not helped by the shock-value of the rhetoric in which he indulges as he develops it. Hume is not the first person to hold that the human intellect can at most plot the means to the satisfaction of objectives that are set for us by our desires. Aristotle had said this long before. What Hume is attempting to do is to destroy a very common understanding of human choice which his rationalist predecessors had taken for granted, which Kant later tried to reinstate, and which still has strong supporters. This understanding receives a common, if vague, expression in the popular contrast between reason and the emotions, and in the familiar idioms of common speech in which we talk of a man contending with, or mastering, or being overcome by, his passions. There is a metaphor only just beneath the surface of such talk, a metaphor which was given classic expression by Plato. It is the political metaphor which divides up the human personality into distinct and warring elements, and then identifies the true or real person with one of the elements into which the personality has been divided. The chosen candidate for this is traditionally the reason. When this division and identification are made, we have a frame of thought which treats our passions as inner but alien forces which assault the sanctuary of the self, and sometimes overcome it, and sometimes are overcome by it. Acts done from passion are acts done *in passivity*. A passion is something that happens to us, and what we do in consequence of it we do not, in the fullest sense, *do* at all. We are fully masters of our actions only on those occasions when the blandishments of the emotions are resisted and overcome.

Hume is bound to reject this metaphor. For it contradicts the very notion of a science of man. Those who still hold to some version of it today are likely to deny that there can really be any science of human action, psychology and sociology notwithstanding. For what the metaphor requires is that a man can take stock of an emotion that arises within him and decide whether or not to admit it into the inner core of his personality. And this implies a real distinction between myself and the emotions that I have. But if the mind is merely the theatre in which the succession of mental phenomena is played out, or is just the sequence of mental phenomena themselves, there is no room for this distinction and any moral psychology which depends upon it must be false. When Hume says that reason is the slave of the passions he is primarily concerned to proclaim the falsity of such a view of human personality.

The difficulty in denying this understanding of human personality, however, is that the metaphor it depends on seems to fit some of our actions very well, and the ones it fits most easily are the ones we are most vain about. Do we not all, now and then, shun the temptation of some seductive desire and pursue a higher and greater good in spite of it? We can all think of tax bills paid under difficulties, second helpings of dessert declined, and bulging briefcases opened with a sigh after dinner. What Hume has to do is to prove that these occasions do not have to be described in terms of the popular rationalist metaphor.

The account he offers is one which replaces the story of my real self overcoming a passion that arises within me by a story in which one possible cause of my actions is simply replaced by another. If I crave the dessert but decline it because I want to slim, then it is my desire to slim that initiates my action, not my desire to eat. But this is a mere matter of one desire that is in me being stronger than another: it is my desire that is operative, not *I*. So the actions that the rationalist praises are to be understood in the same way as those he condemns. But there is one discernible difference: the craving for the dessert is likely to have an aching, agitating, sensory quality to it, whereas it is well known that the desire to slim does not set the nerves tingling at all. Yet the desire to slim may win, and the craving for the dessert may lose. This shows we need to distinguish between the felt intensity of a passion, and its effectiveness. A passion can be strong, in Hume's language, that is to say it can affect my conduct, without being violent. This is Hume's famous doctrine of *calm passions.* On the surface the doctrine is paradoxical—surely we cannot be passionate and calm together? Hume would say that such a response shows us to be in the grip of rationalist theory, and to be unwilling to recognize that the prudent cold fish of a man acts just as much from desire, from passion, as the hot-blooded dessert-eater does. In each case the man's acts are determined by the strongest inner wish; in each case the wish arises from causes within the man which he does not control; the self-controlled man is no more the master of his passions than the weak-willed man, it is merely that his passions are calmer ones. Following calm passions is what we misleadingly refer to as acting reasonably. The only genuine role left to reason, on this account, is that of calculating means and results.

I have tried to represent Hume's proclamation that reason is the slave of the passions as being first and foremost a clear recognition of the implications of a science of human nature. Such a science leaves no room for those supposed forms of freedom which rationalist accounts of man are primarily concerned to preserve. The same relentless determination to carry the implications of the science of man into the citadels of human reason is the key to Hume's moral philosophy. It is well known that he denies moral evaluations to be the work of reason. In essence, his view of them is that approval and disapproval are emotions which have a causal history behind them just as all our emotions do. They are products of the natures of the persons feeling them, not perceptions of moral qualities in the actions or persons they are directed towards. Hume's account of their role and origin is at least as subtle as any of its twentieth-century imitations, and it has the advantage over them of being recognized by its author to be only a small part of the concerns of the moral philosopher. Hume's major interest in ethics is the exploration of those aspects of human conduct to which our moral approval and disapproval are directed, that is, to the question: what sorts of conduct *arouse* our approval or disapproval?

This is a psychological question, one about the causes of certain of our passions. In deciding, again quite self-consciously, to set his question in this way, Hume is taking a step that has fundamental anti-rationalist implications. If it is just a fact of our natures that we approve of some kinds of conduct (expressing this by saying they are good or right or virtuous), and disapprove of others (expressing this by saying they are bad or wrong or vicious), those forms of conduct that we evaluate in this way must already be established in human society for us to evaluate them. Our moral judgements of right and wrong cannot, therefore, be the *sources* of morally good conduct; it has to be there already. So our sense of rightness, in spite of much popular wisdom to the contrary, cannot be the motive which generates virtuous conduct—any more than our sense of wrongness can be the motive which generates vicious conduct. In each case it is merely a *response* to conduct which is already a feature of our society—though no doubt our approval and disapproval can come in time to exert some secondary pressures of their own on ourselves and our fellows. This very simple conclusion strikes at the heart of rationalist ethics, for it is of the essence of the rationalist tradition that our reason, which is said by the rationalist to be the source of our moral judgements, provides us with a motive (that of duty) which is the prime source of moral conduct. Hume admits that this motive occasionally moves us, but insists it is not due to reason, and that morally good conduct usually has other sources.

What are these sources? Hume denies the opinion of cynics like Hobbes who tell us that all our motives are selfish. Only some of them are. We are also gifted with benevolence—a desire to benefit others. And we are gifted with what he calls sympathy—by which he means a capacity to recreate in imagination the pleasure or distress of others. Self-interest, benevolence, and sympathy between them are the sources of those forms of human conduct which we approve, and in approving call *virtues*. But again a deeply disturbing consequence is drawn from this account. These motives are recurrent features of human nature. When we observe them in others we recognize that the patterns of behaviour that they generate in the people who have them are *useful* or *agreeable* to the persons who have them, and to their associates. He calls this aspect of them their *utility*, fathering in the process the most famous tradition of English-speaking ethics. It is this agreeableness or utility which is the immediate cause of our approval. But surely, one might say, other features of men are useful beside their virtues? What about their talents? Surely being witty or charming is as useful to a man, and as useful to his fellows, as being truthful or benevolent? Yet wit and charm are not virtues. Hume does not shrink here, any more than elsewhere, from the clear consequences of his own theories. In a much-neglected section near the close of the *Treatise* he cheerfully denies there is any difference between a talent and a virtue.[6] Both are equally

---

[6] *T* III. iii. 4, 'Of Natural Abilities'. See also *EM* Appendix IV, and Chapter 8 in this volume.

appropriate objects of moral admiration. The only reason we can offer for distinguishing between them is a reason which Hume declares to be manifestly false: this is the belief that we inherit our talents but help to create our own virtues. Here again, a dispassionate consideration of the science of man shows this to be a vainglorious myth. My virtues and my talents alike have causes in my nature which I cannot independently control. To say I am free to be virtuous or not is as false as to say I am free to be clever or not. Such inner freedoms do not exist; we do not make our own natures—though we may have greater or less liberty in performing those actions which our natures lead us to choose. Fundamentally, therefore, morality is the result of good fortune: the good fortune which has endowed us with natures that lead us to act in ways that are mutually beneficial, to have desires which are not mutually destructive, in short to be inherently social beings. In such a world the foolishness of the ascetic and the solitary is a criminal foolishness.

V

I have tried to offer an interpretation of David Hume the philosopher which relates some of the most famous elements in the philosophy to one another and to David Hume the man. I have suggested that the personality is itself a manifestation of the message of the philosophy. That message is one of acceptance of our nature as it is. We can understand it through observation, as we understand the world in which it is placed; and when we do we will see it to be a nature which serves and protects us by endowing us with those beliefs and those emotions and those social attitudes which we need to survive and to be content in that world. But these endowments have to be recognized as nature's gifts, and only absurdity and despair are in store for us if we pretend they are intellectual achievements, or try to fabricate intellectual substitutes for them, or adopt ethical postures which put us at odds with the social environment in which we naturally belong.

Whether this interpretation stands or not, it inevitably leaves much unsaid. Two fundamental aspects of Hume's philosophy, however, cannot be omitted.

First, I have not once mentioned *empiricism*. Hume of course *is* an empiricist. That is to say, he does hold that all our knowledge, save that of logic and mathematics, comes from experience, and all our concepts derive from our impressions. I have said nothing about this because it is the least original part of his philosophy, and also the most dogmatic. He inherits most of it, as every philosophy student will tell you, from Locke and Berkeley. What is original is his use of it. It is a most convenient vehicle for the negative side of his scepticism. Being able to begin by asserting that all our knowledge comes from experience, he is able to proceed to his sceptical conclusions by demonstrating that all our daily reflections and decisions require us to believe far more than experience can assure us to be true. This is why our intellectual powers do not suffice for our natural needs, and other resources in our natures have to supply what they can not.

But even though Hume is known to all students of philosophy as an empiricist, he is even better known as a *secularizer*. His hostility to revealed religion was the major cause of his notoriety throughout his career, and was the reason he was rejected for the Chair of Moral Philosophy at Edinburgh in 1745, and the Chair of Logic at Glasgow in 1752. Although he had many friends among the Moderates in the Scots clergy, he was always the target of clerical hostility. His 'atheism' was a chronic source of attack on his personality, as well as upon his doctrines. For example, when he was on his deathbed Boswell, preposterously, called to see him in order to determine the extent of an unbeliever's equanimity in the face of death. Hume, who expected his existence simply to terminate, and was so far managing to face this prospect with complete calm, allowed himself to tease Boswell, who was predictably shocked, and then told Dr Johnson all about it. Johnson's reply, from his own piety and fear, was this: 'It was not so, sir. He had a vanity in being thought easy. It is more probable that he should assume an appearance of ease, than so very improbable a thing should be, as a man not afraid of going into an unknown state, and not being uneasy at leaving all he knew. And you are to consider, that upon his own principle of annihilation he had no motive to speak the truth.'[7] But it was not only Hume's enemies who were affected; his friends also were on their guard. The most striking case is that of Adam Smith. He had just transferred to the Chair of Moral Philosophy at Glasgow when Hume's name was suggested for the Chair of Logic.

[7] Boswell 1906 edn., ii, 113–14, entry for 16 Sept. 1777.

Smith said to a friend, 'I should prefer David Hume to any man for a colleague, but I am afraid the public would not be of my opinion, and the interest of the society will oblige me to have some regard to the opinion of the public.' He was visited with the same surfeit of discretion when Hume, in his last days, asked him to ensure the posthumous publication of the *Dialogues Concerning Natural Religion*, which Smith had helped persuade him not to have printed during his lifetime. Smith declined to undertake this, and Hume was forced to pass the duty on to his nephew. The effusive tribute that Smith wrote after Hume died probably owed some of its warmth to a desire to compensate for this (Mossner 1970: 604).

But of course Hume's enemies were entirely right in identifying him as the most dangerous destructive critic of Christianity in modern times. Although he veils his attacks with irony and innuendo and simulated praise, the negativity is obvious and the power unequalled. Whatever one thinks of its conclusions, the *Dialogues* is beyond any question the greatest work in the philosophy of religion in English, and a strong candidate for the same title in any language. In it he destroys a whole tradition: the tradition of rational or experimental theism, that seeks to represent belief in the Christian deity as susceptible of scientific justification. To say the tradition is destroyed is not to say it is dead; no doubt it will always go on. But it is utterly discredited, and all perceptive readers, Christian as well as anti-Christian, see that it is. In destroying it Hume does not only pave the way for secular freethinkers like Bertrand Russell; he also, without intending to, paves the way for fideists like Kierkegaard. When Hume tells us, with unconcealed sarcasm, that 'Our most holy religion is founded on faith, not on reason' (*EU* x. 130), all we need to do is to say the same thing with a straighter face, and Kierkegaard stands before us.

This is not a historical consequence that Hume would have relished. His own objective is clearly that of exposing revealed religion as a pathological manifestation of fear and intolerance and bigotry, as an unnatural disturber of man's inner and social peace. The *philosophes* of contemporary France saw him as one of themselves; but he shrank from the identification, claiming that no one could seriously call himself an atheist as they did. One thing that worried him about the strident atheism of his French counterparts was that they were more confident than anybody has any right to be about what the universe does *not* contain; but, more important, he saw in them the same enthusiasm and fanaticism that he saw in their Catholic and Calvinist opponents. He might agree that it does not become a philosopher to worship, but equally it does not become a philosopher to shake his fist at the empty sky. We should not try to defeat religion with its own weapons. We should let it wither away as society outgrows it.

This is the reason why we find those baffling passages in which Hume seems to pay lip service to the very religious traditions he is attacking. There is irony here, but it is often misread. It is generally agreed now that the character in the *Dialogues* that most nearly represents Hume himself is not Cleanthes the theist, but Philo, the sceptic. Yet at the close of the *Dialogues* we find Philo, the agent of destruction, talking about preserving 'true religion', and appearing to accept the theism he has been undermining on every page before. But if we look at the theism Philo agrees to, what does it consist of? 'That the cause or causes of order in the universe probably bear some remote analogy to human intelligence' (*D* XII. 227)! This proposition is not devotionally nourishing. One can accept it without having to do or feel anything whatever in consequence. Someone who is prepared to accept it, however, is embarrassingly close to those liberal theologians who progressively remove specific doctrines from their theology and edge nearer and nearer to secular humanism in order to commend their theism to the educated society of their day. Now Cleanthes, Philo's disputant, is just such a theologian. The moral is clear. The power of revealed religion is not to be destroyed by noisy atheism. It is to be destroyed by polite social accommodation with theism, provided this theism is suitably emasculated and free of doctrinal content. The insidious, uncanny modernity of these closing passages of Hume's last work has a message for the secularizing theologians of the present day.

# VI

It is now as fashionable to praise Hume as it was a hundred years ago to attack him, though I have tried to give some reasons for thinking that he is still not seen whole even by his admirers. They stress his contributions to the theory of knowledge. The most famous of these is the discovery of a problem: the problem of induction. It takes a major philosophical mind to discover a problem where none was

seen before, and just as we owe to Socrates the discovery of the problem of self-knowledge, so we owe to Hume the discovery that there
is a problem about the rationality of inductive reasoning. His insistence that it has no answer has been the single most stimulating claim
in epistemology in modern times. Associated with the discovery of
this problem is his famous analysis of our idea of causation. This is
the most striking negative achievement in modern philosophical
thought, in that it is to Hume that we owe the final demise of the
Aristotelian philosophy of nature, with its world of essences and
natural purposes. For this world Hume substituted another, fitted
to the climate of post-Newtonian science: a world of sheer given
sequences, in which there is no way to discover what is to take place
but to observe, no way of determining a being's powers but from
its performances, and no more to what is necessary than what men
find familiar. Perhaps Hume's world is not the real world, but it is
the world that modern man thinks he inhabits, and no one has done
more to define modernity than Hume.

Another familiar feature of our modern understanding of ourselves
is our recognition of how much the inner nature of each of us colours
our experience of the world we inhabit. It is to Hume that we owe
the distinction between fact and interpretation: for it is the key plank
of his system that our interpretation of our world is the work of
our emotions and not of our intellect, and to maintain as radical a
thesis as this you have to try to tell where the data end and the
interpretation starts. It fell to Kant to offer a different account of
the contribution the mind of man makes to his experience of his
world—an account which is at once less unflattering than the one
Hume offers, and much harder to understand. But it was Hume who
showed him the need for *some* account that did justice to the inner
as well as the outer sources of our daily experience.

The investigation of the determinants of our natures is a dominant feature of contemporary culture. Since Freud and Marx we have
come to take a darker and less optimistic view of these inner forces
than Hume chose to take, even though we happily follow him in saying that reason has little or no place in them. But Hume is the first
major philosophical thinker to draw the conclusions that follow
from accepting that man's nature can be scientifically understood:
in particular the consequence that a man cannot be identified with
some locus of power or decision that is above and beyond the forces
that are at work within him. This conclusion may be false, but it

does follow from that premise, and that is why the status of that premise is still philosophically disputable in spite of the undoubted successes of those disciplines into which the science of man has diversified itself.

Hume is the first thinker to treat morality as itself a proper topic of the science of man, and in so treating it, wisely or not, he fathers both the so-called emotive theory of evaluation and the utilitarian theory of ethical principles.

These are massive achievements, and all of them are still with us and still supply us with sources of insight and controversy, more often than not in the very words in which Hume first expressed them. For who could express them better?

What are Hume's failings? There are many alleged ones, but I will pick on two. First, the experience of human nature and its effects in the 200 years since Hume's death can hardly leave us with the same optimistic acceptance of it, as it is, as an assured source of contentment or even of survival. In social terms, the acceptance Hume recommends requires an easy, even complacent, conservatism. If we cannot rest easy with this, then we cannot rest easy with the insistence on which he bases it: that we cannot change or direct or mould our natures. Perhaps the passivity that Hume finds the source of peace is instead the source of turmoil.

Second, there is an unresolved tension in Hume's system between his scepticism and his secularism. If our common-sense beliefs lack rational justification, but our nature happily requires us to hold them, why is it that when Hume shows us that our religious beliefs lack rational justification also, he expects them to wither away? If there is a pre-established harmony between our common-sense beliefs and the course of the world, why should there not also be a pre-established harmony between our religious beliefs and the structure of reality? If all our beliefs are equally devoid of rational justification, why should some be more equally devoid of rational justification than others? Hume's only answer is to tell us that the natural forces that produce religious beliefs only operate in *some* men, whereas the natural forces that produce common-sense beliefs operate in *all* men. The spread of secularity in our own time would suggest he is right about this; but it might be that the men in whom the sources of religion still operate are privileged, not disadvantaged. They at least would say so.

Whatever the failings of Hume's philosophical system, it has helped define the intellectual climate of the modern Western world

more than any other. It could have done this without being an integrated system: many of our contemporaries who acknowledge their
debt to Hume are happy to treat his writings as an unconnected assemblage of separate insights. But our greatest philosophers have all been
systematic thinkers, and I have tried to show that Hume has been
appraised less highly than he deserves because the systematic connections in his thought have been overlooked or misunderstood. When
we view his work as a whole, we can see him to have developed a
system of thought which, for all its deliberately deflating doctrines
and its self-conscious lightness of tone, is an attempt to understand
human thought and feeling and action together, and to offer us what
is, when all is said, a saving way of life. If this sounds odd, it is because
Hume does not think we are to be saved *from* our natures or *from*
the world, but saved *by* our natures *for* the world. He tells us not
to get above ourselves, but to *be* ourselves. In our day and age we
may feel we need other, more ambitious advice; there is indeed no
shortage of it. But he has done so much to make us what we are
that we are no longer able to decide with any confidence what other
advice to take.

# 2

# *Hume on Personal Identity*

I WANT in this paper to examine the arguments which Hume uses
in the famous Sixth Section of Part IV of Book I of the *Treatise*,
not primarily as a work of scholarship, but in order to assess how
good they are and to try to learn something from them when they
are mistaken as well as when they are right. Hume's discussion of
personal identity is the best there is; no one can feel the same about
the problem after reading it as he did before; and like so much that
Hume says, it is incisive, penetrating, and most unsatisfying. It also
has an additional, topical, interest: it gives us, I think, an excellent
example of how complex and far-reaching the consequences of a mistake in linguistic or conceptual investigation can be.

I

To consider first the general problem with which Hume deals: the
problem of personal identity can be roughly described as that of trying to justify a practice which seems at first sight to be strange, and
even paradoxical. This is the practice of talking about people as
single beings in spite of the fact that they are constantly changing,
and over a period of time may have changed completely. It almost
seems a contradiction to say that John Smith at two and John Smith
at fifty-two are the same person, because they are so different.

Of course the same problem could be raised in the case of other
things—think of Heraclitus and the river. It might look as though
the problem of personal identity were just one case of a general problem of the persistence of an object through change, and that any
special interest we had in personal identity, rather than in fluminal,
floral, or faunal identity, arose from the fact that the kind of thing
in question is nearer home. But this last fact has had other effects

as well: we are in a position to know that human beings have feelings and thoughts and images and pains, and that although these can be talked about by others, they cannot be *seen* or *had* by them, even though our bodily movements are open to public inspection. Now there has been a tendency among philosophers to do more than just recognize that people's lives *include* such private happenings— the tendency has been to regard them as forming a separate *thing* which has a purely contingent relationship to the body. This tendency to dualism has frequently restricted the way in which the problem of personal identity has been put. It has ceased to be 'How are we to account for the unity we assume people to have throughout their lives?' and has become 'How are we to account for the unity possessed by one *mind* throughout the changes in its (uniformly private) states?' A result of this restriction has been the invention of an entity called 'the self', which Hume very properly derides. The purpose its invention serves is this: There is a certain type of solution to the problem of the identity of changing things which consists in saying that in spite of all apearances, which it is admitted are certainly to the contrary, there in fact *is* some item in the composition of changing objects, which does *not* change in any respect. A partiality to this type of solution in the case of persons might quite naturally lead to making the unchanging item a private one; but if this partiality is combined with the dualistic view of the nature of persons, then it is inevitable that the seat of personal identity should be thought to lie in the mind, and the unchanging item be mental. This is of course 'the self', which Hume begins by attacking. I shall now turn to his actual argument, and expound it briefly.

## II

He has already maintained in the previous Section that no one has rendered intelligible the relationship of 'support' which is supposed to hold between 'the self' and the other components of our mental histories. In Section VI he opens by disposing of the view that the existence of the self can be recognized empirically—he does this very simply by denying that anyone can find it, unless of course its defenders are differently constituted from himself. Assuming that this is not the case, then the whole of mankind are 'nothing but a bundle or collection of different perceptions' in a constant state of change.

There is none of the simplicity or identity that the self was supposed to provide. This means that it is a mistake to 'suppose ourselves possessed of an invariable and uninterrupted existence through the whole course of our lives'. Yet we all do suppose it (not merely, Hume implies, the philosophers who try to justify us). How does this mistake arise?

It is based, Hume says, on the confusion between two ideas: (a) that of an object which persists throughout a length of time without change or interruption—this is the idea of identity; (b) that of a succession of related objects—this, he says, is clearly a case of diversity.

We confuse these two because the succession is a succession of *related* objects, and contemplating or imagining such a succession feels much the same as contemplating or imagining an unchanging and uninterrupted object. Having been thus confused, we 'substitute' the idea of identity for that of a related succession. And we cannot free ourselves from this confusion for long; the only result of reflecting on it is the bogus attempt to justify it by inventing 'some new and unintelligible principle', like 'substance' or 'the self', which is somehow supposed to preserve the sequence unchanged.

To prove this thesis Hume thinks he has merely to show that those things we (mistakenly) call the same even though they are changing and interrupted consist of a succession of related parts. To show this he takes various kinds of changing thing, claiming in each case that the relation of the change to the whole which changes causes us to overlook its occurrence and continue to call the object the same. (The change, for example, is small in proportion to the whole, takes place only gradually, leaves the function of the whole unaffected, etc.) The same principles are at work in the case of persons; so in their case, as in all other cases, the identity we ascribe to them is 'fictitious'.

Hume ends by saying that his whole examination of this question reveals that most of the disputes about identity are 'merely verbal'. Since, as he puts it, 'identity depends on the relations of ideas, and these relations produce identity by means of that easy transition they occasion,' when these relations and the ease of transition grow less, the tendency to believe in identity grows less too. He gives no example here, but the kind of thing I take it he has in mind is this (I shall take a simple and non-personal instance): If a philosopher were to take a particular case like the history of a building from its initial construction to its final demolition, and were to ask at what point what was originally a mere pile of bricks became the house, and at what point what had been the house ceased to be this and gave place to a mere pile of bricks once more (should we date these events by the laying or crumbling of the foundations, or the tiling or stripping of the roof, or the installation or removal of the plumbing? etc., etc.), the answer to give him would be that the tendency to ascribe identity to the changing and complex object is in this case based on the relationship which all the parts have to a central function, viz., the usefulness of the building for sheltering people, but that when this relationship is equivocal (e.g., when the structure could hold people, but only uncomfortably) we simply have a stretch of time when the tendency to say that this is a house rather than a heap of bricks exists, but with less force. At such a time we can decide much as we please which to say it is, and it does not really matter. Our decision would only matter if we invented some philosophical fiction to bolster it up.

III

I wish first to comment briefly on Hume's statement that the whole of mankind are 'nothing but a bundle or collection of different perceptions'. What is meant by this? Part of what he means is of course that human beings are not composed of something called a 'self' *plus* some other, less permanent, items, but only of these latter items themselves. So much would be a mere reiteration of what he has already said. But he is clearly committing himself besides to something much stronger and stranger than this, viz., to the view that these items of which, and of nothing-else-but, the whole of mankind are composed are 'perceptions'. Now this claim is clearly not of quite the same sort as the claim of some philosophers that material things are nothing but perceptions. For (a) this latter claim is usually somewhat to the effect that statements made about any material thing can somehow be construed as being in fact statements about some of the things that happen to observers when they look at it; and if this were the sort of thing that Hume meant by saying that *people* were nothing but perceptions, it would follow that according to him each person is composed of *other people's* perceptions, that every statement about a given person ought to be construed as a statement about some *other* person or persons; I feel confident that he does not mean this. (b) I feel confident also that he is using the word 'perception' in a much wider sense than the sense in which it is used by philosophers who claim that material things are nothing but perceptions, since they use it to mean events which might otherwise be called 'sensations', whereas he seems to include in its meaning such events as dreams, feelings, images, etc.—all those events I mentioned earlier which are not open to public view in the way in which our bodily movements are.

What Hume's claim about human beings involves, then, is that they are nothing but the series of *their own* sensations, feelings, dreams, images, and the rest. Clearly to reach this conclusion he must have been dealing not with the question 'How are we justified in attributing identity to persons?' but the question 'How are we justified in attributing identity to *minds*?' (where the word 'mind' is understood as meaning the 'theatre', to use Hume's own term, where these private events take place). It is far from trivial to notice that these two questions are not equivalent (obviously not, since the words 'person' and 'mind' are not); for answering the latter rather than the former restricts the discussion of personal identity considerably. It forces us to ignore, for example, that the most common way of settling practical problems of identification is by scrutinizing people's physical appearance; or that the gradualness of the changes in complex things which Hume claims to be one of the main contributing causes of our calling them identical is only a feature of human beings if one thinks of them partly in terms of their physical careers; or that the uninterruptedness which he thinks we erroneously attribute to them is in fact a feature of their physical lives.

Fortunately, however, this restriction does not affect the pertinence of his discussion as much as it might be expected to do. This is due to the fact that although he talks at various points as though the problem he is trying to answer is that of the unity of the *mind*, and refers to that of personal identity as though it were the same, the way in which he tries to illumine it is by putting forward a *general* thesis, which I have already outlined, concerning the *general* propensity to call complex and changing objects identical, a propensity of which the ascription of identity to persons is just one instance. It follows, therefore, that the objections I have just raised would apply rather to his view of what sort of thing a person *is* than to his *general* view of the *kinds* of factor at work when we ascribe identity to changing and complex things, whether they are persons or not. I am prepared to agree with him (a) that persons are changing and complex, and (b) that such features as the proportionate smallness of changes, or their gradualness, which he says consolidate our propensity, can be found in the case of persons (more easily, in fact, if we recognize that 'person' means more than just 'mind'), and this is all that it is necessary to agree to in order to admit that his thesis applies to the case of persons. My subsequent comments will be concerned with this central and general thesis, and are therefore independent of the foregoing criticisms of Hume's view that the life-histories of persons have merely mental components, just as the thesis itself could be stated independently of this view.

## IV

Hume's thesis turns on one central point, and stands or falls with it. This point is his contention that it is, 'to a more accurate method of thinking', a confusion to call an object that changes the *same*. The 'idea of identity or sameness' is the idea of an object that persists *without* changing. The fact that the parts of a changing thing may be related to one another does not, after all, alter the further fact that they do change, so in this case we do *not* have identity or sameness, and it must therefore be due to some ingrained tendency of the mind that we talk as though we do. From this point, which he brings in fairly unobtrusively, the remainder of his arguments follow naturally:

(1) The puzzle that remains is a psychological one, viz., what is it about us that makes this mistake possible?

(2) Any account of the relationships that hold between the parts of complex things will only be relevant to *this* question; they do not affect the question of whether we are *justified* in calling such objects the same, because we just aren't.

(3) Clearly the borderline cases, where we are undecided whether to say that what is before us is the same object or another one, as it were, taking over where the first one left off, are merely verbal and undecidable because *whatever* we decide will be groundless and mistaken. For the very fact that a change is taking place ought strictly to make us say it is not the same object, but the fact that other changes have preceded this one should have made us say that long before. There is no difference in *kind* between the borderline cases and the times of change during the previous history of the object. The only

difference is in the degree of psychological compulsion acting on us—the propensity to misapply the notion of identity is beginning to falter when the borderline is reached, but has not done so before. The only possible *standard* is violated at *all* stages.

(4) The fictions of the self and substance have arisen because philosophers have sensed the nature of our common mistake, but have not been able to free themselves from it for long. The inevitable result of this conflict-state is that they have felt there *must*, really, underneath, out of sight, be an unchanging something-or-other which is the real object, so that our strange habit is justified after all.

All of these are natural consequences of what Hume says about the nature of identity in the early part of the Section. If it is true that we make a mistake in the first place by talking of identity through change at all, then all the rest follows. But I think it is not hard to show that *he* is making an elementary error here, not everyone else, and that the facts he brings to our notice are twisted and misapplied as a result.

It is important to keep in mind as one reads him that he does think he has uncovered a *mistake*, as his language does not always lay stress on this. For instance, when talking about persons, he says:

I cannot compare the soul more properly than to a republic or commonwealth . . . as the same individual republic may not only change its members, but also its laws and constitutions; in like manner the same person may vary his character and disposition, as well as his impressions and ideas, without losing his identity. (*T* I. iv. 6. 261)

This does not, taken out of context, sound like the account of an alleged mistake at all, but it is quite clear from everything that has led up to it that it is, including in particular the fact that this passage is intended as a demonstration that the identity of the mind of a person is a 'fictitious' one. The same applies too, of course, to the identity of a republic or commonwealth. Hume is not just saying that our common practice of attributing identity in such cases cannot be justified, or has no sound reason in its favour (as he says of our belief in the regularity of nature): he is here making the less modest claim that our common practice is wrong, that the evidence points unequivocally to the opposite. We proceed not without, but in the face of, the evidence. But it would seem from the tone of the above passage, as well as from his well-known second thoughts in the Appendix, that even Hume found this odd and paradoxical sometimes.

For odd and paradoxical it certainly is. What he is actually claiming is that we are constantly making a mistake in referring to a person from day to day as the same person (in using the same proper name, for example), or in referring in this way to *anything* that has changed in the slightest. For, strictly speaking, a changed person would be literally *another* person. A little effort of imagination is enough to indicate just how much chaos would result from adopting Hume's diagnosis as the source of a prescription and using a different proper name whenever we noticed the slightest change, even in ourselves (or rather in the separate people that we would be from minute to minute). If we make a *mistake* in *not* doing this, it is a mistake we *all* make *all* the time, and a mistake of which the correction would require a complete overhaul of the concepts and syntax of our language. I suppose Hume would say this is one of the reasons why we continue to make the mistake—to avoid the desperate awkwardness of trying to live up to our moments of philosophical insight all the time. But I find it hard to believe that a mistake lies at the root of so much of our language, especially since Hume has claimed to reveal it by a piece of linguistic analysis. I want to show that his analysis is a bad one, that the 'mistake' is not a mistake at all, and that its supposed revelation is not a piece of philosophical insight, but of short sight, or rather, astigmatism.

Once the basic point is located, it is not hard to see that Hume has gone wrong. Let us consider the essential three sentences:

We have a distinct idea of an object, that remains invariable and uninterrupted thro' a suppos'd variation of time; and this idea we call that of *identity* or *sameness*. We have also a distinct idea of several different objects existing in succession, and connected together by a close relation; and this to an accurate view affords as perfect a notion of *diversity*, as if there was no manner of relation among the objects. But tho' these two ideas of identity, and a succession of related objects be in themselves perfectly distinct, and even contrary, yet 'tis certain, that in our common way of thinking, they are generally confounded with each other. (*T* I. iv. 6. 253)

It is not hard to find his error here. What he is saying is that since we would call something the same for a given length of time when it continued without any alteration, and since we would say that a succession of objects was a collection or number or series of objects, it would obviously be a contradiction to say that in the latter case we would have *one* object. In a sense this is true, but not in the sense which Hume requires. He has not noticed what is wrong because he has chosen to talk in very general terms here, and to ignore the way in which we would actually talk on particular occasions. But a rebuttal can be produced even in general terms. Let us call the unchanging single object *X*. *X*, we would say, is the same throughout. Let us call our succession of distinct but related objects *A, B, C, D, E, F*, etc. Here, if we count, we obviously have several, not one. But we can quite easily produce a class-name for the series of them, say $\varphi$, such that a $\varphi$ is, by definition, any group of things like *A, B, C, D, E, F*, etc. So there would be no contradiction in saying there are six objects and one $\varphi$; this is what a $\varphi$ *is*. Quite obviously our ordinary language works this way. A succession of notes is one theme. A succession of words is one sentence. If the succession does not form a theme or sentence, it is still a *succession* or series. There is no contradiction in saying 'There are six notes in this theme,' or 'There are six words in this sentence,' though there would be in saying 'There are six notes but only one,' or 'There are six words but only one.' Naturally *this* would be absurd, but no one ever says it (for that reason).

So, in spite of Hume, there is no contradiction in saying that certain kinds of things are composed of a succession of parts, and yet are each only one thing. Whether a thing can have many parts or not depends entirely on what sort of thing it is. Most things (including people) do.

There is another, closely related, mistake which Hume has made. This is the mistake of thinking that for anything to be entitled to be called 'the same' it has to remain *unchanged* from one period to the next. This is a muddle of two things that he himself distinguishes at one point, viz., the two distinct senses of the word 'identical' or 'the same'. These are the numerical and the specific senses, as he calls them. Two things can be the same as one another in the specific sense, i.e., exactly alike in some respect, yet they will still be two things; but if they are said to be the same in the numerical sense they are being said to be not two things but one after all. These two senses are distinct from one another. Now to remain unchanged is to remain the same in the *specific* sense, i.e., to be now exactly as one was at an earlier time. But I can remain the same in the *numerical* sense without doing so in the specific sense—I can be numerically the same but changed. In fact I cannot be said to have changed unless I *am* the same in the numerical sense. The only reason for saying that something is numerically different (something else, that is) when a change occurs, is if it is by definition an unchanging thing. When a note is played, for example, as soon as the tone is raised or lowered we have another note, not the same one at all. But in the case of most things, the words we use to talk about them are words the meanings of which allow us or require us to continue to use them throughout certain changes, though not of course *any* changes. What kind of changes can occur without our having to say that the thing has ceased to exist and given place to something else depends on what *kind* of thing we are talking about. To know what such changes are is part of what it is to know the meaning of the class-term for that sort of object. A house, or a person, is something which admits of many changes before we would say it had ceased to exist. To know what these changes are is to know, in part at least, what the words 'house' and 'person' mean.

The rejoinder to Hume, then, consists simply in saying that the pairs of expressions, (a) 'numerically the same' and 'containing many parts' and (b) 'numerically the same' and 'changed', are not pairs of contradictories. So we have not made a mistake in saying that a succession of related objects may form a unit of a certain kind, or that the same thing may undergo radical changes. Once this is admitted, the rest of what he says appears in quite a different light.

## V

(1) His *examples* point quite a different moral from what he thinks:

(a) The paragraph I quoted can hardly be said to contain an example, but if we produce examples to fit it we get quite different results from those Hume intended. There is nothing about 'an object that remains invariable and uninterrupted' *per se* which requires us to say it is the same thing throughout, and nothing about a succession of different but related ones *per se* which requires the opposite. It depends entirely on what concepts we are using when we talk about each. If we heard a continuous sound we would say it was one sound and not several; but it is not hard to imagine some situation in which we would be interested in counting the number of seconds of sound, in which case we would say there were, for example, ten of them. In the case of a succession of objects, the whole series might very well be said to form a unit: a succession of men may form a march-past. There is nothing revealing in choosing a single and uninterrupted sort of thing rather than a complex thing, and Hume has fallen into a conceptual muddle by doing so. He only makes it worse by talking of 'an *object* that remains invariable' and 'several *objects* existing in succession', because he is here using the same noun in each case, viz., 'object'; and although this is the vaguest noun in the language, the mere fact that he uses the same one in each case suggests very easily that in the two phrases he is thinking of objects of the same kind, e.g., a single and uninterrupted note and a succession of distinct notes. This would point a contrast, though of dubious value to Hume;[1] but if we took the variable-word 'object' at its face value and substituted different nouns in each phrase the contrast would disappear: where is there a contrast between 'an invariable and uninterrupted arithmetical progression' and 'a succession of different but related numbers'? If it is thought that I have chosen a favourable example here, the reply is that I am quite entitled to do so. I am quite ready to admit that we could find a contrast here by making different substitutions, but his just bears out the essential point that whether we get one or not depends entirely on what nouns we choose to work with, and not on the concepts of identity and diversity. Put generally, whether the result is logically absurd, or logically possible, or logically necessary, if the two phrases 'the same continuing $x$' and 'several different $y$'s' are used of the same thing depends entirely on what nouns we use to replace $x$ and $y$. It does not depend on the words 'same' and 'different' in themselves.

(b) There are two specific examples which Hume does offer, but misunderstands. He offers both as instances of confusion between numerical and specific identity. The first is this:

A man, who hears a noise, that is frequently interrupted and renew'd, says it is still the same noise; tho' 'tis evident the sounds have only a specific identity or resemblance, and there is nothing numerically the same, but the cause, which produc'd them. (*T* I. iv. 6. 258)

I do not think the man in this case would be guilty of this confusion. When he says it is still the same noise, he may mean one of two things: (i) he might be using 'same' in the specific sense, in which case he would be saying merely that the noise he hears now is exactly like the one he heard before; or (ii) he might be using the word 'noise'

---

[1] It would be of dubious value to him because although if we replaced 'object' by the same noun in each phrase we would get a contrast, we would quite clearly get a case where the confusion he has in mind would be altogether unlikely.

as roughly equivalent to 'an intermittent series of exactly similar sounds', in which case the constituent sounds of the noise, in this sense of 'noise', can certainly come and go.

The second example is this:

> In like manner it may be said, without breach of the propriety of language, that such a church, which was formerly of brick, fell to ruin, and that the parish rebuilt the same church of free-stone, and according to modern architecture. Here neither the form nor materials are the same, nor is there anything common to the two objects, but their relation to the inhabitants of the parish; and yet this alone is sufficient to make us denominate them the same. (*T* I. iv. 6. 258)

Here again the example does not bear out Hume's views at all. *Of course* the relationship of the building to the inhabitants is enough for us to call it the same, because the concept with which we are operating, say that of 'the village church of Muddlehampton' is simply and solely the concept of *any* structure which has the unique purpose at any period of subserving the religious needs of the people of that parish. This is why we would use the same phrase whatever building was there, and would say, both before and after the rebuilding, that we had the same thing there; for, in the sense of the concept we would be using, we *would* have the same thing there. There is no mistake in this, as there would be in saying we had the same building, in the sense of the same pile of stones; but we would not say *that*. The village church of Muddlehampton can be pulled down and rebuilt again many times over with perfect logical propriety.

(2) But Hume's error of supposing that invariance is the standard of identity in all cases, when it is only the standard in a very few (those in which invariance is part of the concept of the thing) makes him not only misunderstand the import of his own examples, but miss the point of his otherwise very revealing account of *the relations between the parts of complex things*. Factors like the proportionate smallness of changes, or the conspiracy of the remaining parts to the same end, he claims to be factors which make us overlook the fact that changes have occurred at all. But we do not overlook this fact; we are perfectly aware of it. What Hume is actually describing here in general terms are the kinds of change that are comprehended under the concepts of certain sorts of things. It is true that these are often small in proportion to the whole, that they take place slowly, and so on. But it is not true always; it is not true of

the concept of a river, as Hume himself says. It depends on the concept. As he puts it himself, 'What is natural and essential to any thing is, in a manner, expected'; that is to say, more changes are allowed in some things than others, depending on the kind. He should have added, 'and it is embodied in the concept of the thing'. This might have stopped him saying that these natural and essential changes merely make us misapply the concept of identity, and revealed instead that the standards for applying the concept of identity depend entirely on the substantives it is joined onto. The rules for using nouns (and it is the *modus operandi* of nouns to which his description is relevant) are evolved by generations of language-users, and we have to decide in terms of these at what point a noun applies to whatever we may be considering and when it ceases to.

(3) This decision is not always easy, since the rules we apply are at best very general ones, learned from experience, and not able to cover every eventuality. There are inevitable times when we do not know just what term applies. These are the *borderline cases*, the occasions when the 'nice and subtle' questions about identity start coming up. In deciding whether the roofless structure in front of us is a house or a heap of stones, we may have reached a point where the conventions governing neither expression are sufficient to tell us, and we just have to decide for ourselves and, in so doing, make these conventions more precise. We can make mistakes here, like taking a decision which has unforeseen legal repercussions regarding the status of our property. But we do not make a mistake just because we are considering saying it is the same object when it has changed. Hume would have to say that in this case we are merely repeating an error which we have made many times already during the object's history, and just happen for strictly psychological reasons to be feeling uneasy about it this time. But we are uneasy because the rules for our words are not geared to meet every eventuality, not because they ought not to meet any at all. It is true that we lack a standard, but not because we have not been following one before.

(4) It is now time to consider *Hume's criticisms of other philosophers*. He pours scorn on theories of 'the self' and 'substance', whether they claim to be empirical or not. I do not want to dwell on his criticisms of these theories, since they seem to me to be sound ones. I am more interested in discussing his account of how such theories arise. He claims that they arise because philosophers, like the rest of us, are subject to those factors which produce the

mistake of allowing numerical identity to complex and changing things, but are occasionally made aware, by the kind of argument he himself uses, that they *are* making this mistake. Being human, and unable therefore to shake off this pernicious but convenient confusion, they have eventually tried to justify it by inventing fictions like 'the self' to meet the requirement of invariance that they see could not be met otherwise. I have suggested that the factors he has enumerated do not contribute to a mistake or confusion, because there is none. But I agree that the self is a fiction. Such fictions have quite probably arisen in the way Hume describes. That is, the philosophers in question may have thought they found a contradiction between saying a thing has changed and saying it is still the same thing; and they may have tried to overcome this by saying that there is in fact some crucial respect in which the thing will *not* have changed, and inventing the self to fill the bill. But if I am right, they need not have bothered; since there is no contradiction there to be avoided, the fiction is unnecessary. What is of more interest is that Hume, in exposing the nature of their mistake, has conceded their main premise, viz., that there *is* a contradiction there, and has merely said that it is impossible to avoid it and recommended us by implication not to try to justify it. This is a sturdier course than theirs; but as it proceeds from the same starting-point, it is not surprising that Hume's solution seems to him the sort of paradoxical scepticism for which the only cure is a change of subject or a game of backgammon. This is all the result, as far as I can see, of a linguistic error, of a misdescription of the way in which certain words in the language are in fact used.

I must now try to anticipate a criticism: it might seem that I have been too severe on Hume, too keen to stress the consequences of a position which is more austere than the one he actually holds. I might appear to have missed the point of the fact (noted above) that as his discussion proceeds he does not seem to be *objecting* to the practice of calling people, for all their complexity and changingness, the same throughout their lives; in the course of several pages devoted to the psychological influences on our linguistic conventions, Hume does not seem to be *criticizing*, but only to be *describing*, the way in which we talk. He certainly says that our tendency to talk of changing things as identical is a mistake and a confusion, but he only says this at the beginning, in an attempt to discredit philosophical constructs like the self, which only occur when philosophers try to justify, or show rational ground for, a practice which is just a matter of habit and could not conceivably depend on anything *they* had to say. Hume is not trying to discredit our usage, but only to discredit misguided attempts to defend it.

This sort of view is held by Professor Kemp Smith,[2] who insists that Hume has no objection to our everyday use of the notion of identity, once this is understood to be based on custom and not on argument. It would follow from this (and Kemp Smith accepts this consequence) that when Hume refers to the identity of persons as 'fictitious', he does not mean *fictitious*, but something less censorious, something more like 'stretched': Kemp Smith suggests 'Pickwickian'. So although he begins by maintaining that 'to an accurate view' talk of the changing or complex as identical is paradoxical, Hume is not himself disposed to take the accurate view, nor to urge it on others—the fact that it is an universal custom *not* to take the accurate view makes it pointless to attempt to impose it in any case.

I have no particular wish either to welcome or to resist this interpretation of Hume's position, or to discuss how far Hume is consistent if this reading of his position is correct. For it is irrelevant to my main contentions:

(a) Whether he is saying that our habit of talking involves us in a paradox which we render tolerable by certain psychological mechanisms, or that the habit is only paradoxical when we take an overscrupulous view of it, but justifies itself pragmatically somehow and should therefore not distress us, he is in either case saying that it can be shown to involve a paradox on examination. However lightly he takes it, he believes it is there. I have denied it is there at all, whether we take an 'accurate view' or not.

(b) Whether he thinks the use of the word 'identical' with reference to complex things or changing things is a mistaken use or merely a stretched use, he certainly thinks the word is being at least mildly abused on these occasions. I have denied this.

(c) Whether his account of what makes us talk of identity in this mistaken or Pickwickian way is intended as a description of how we hide the paradox from ourselves, or merely of what enables us to talk with a (perfectly proper) lack of concern for it, it is in either case misdirected, since our apparent unconcern for the paradox is due to its

[2] Smith 1941, esp. 96–8 and 497–505.

nonexistence, and what he in fact describes are the factors governing the use of substantives, and not the *mis*use of the adjective 'same'.

In other words, however tolerant of our linguistic behaviour Hume may be, there is nothing for him to be tolerant about.


## VI

Two points in conclusion: (1) I have not paid special attention to personal identity rather than any other kind. Here I am following Hume. While his chapter and my comments might well have been enriched by descriptions of the relationships between the various stages and facets of the life of persons, such descriptions would have been incidental to the issue which is the core of his argument, viz., the analysis of the concept of identity, and in particular its compatibility or incompatibility with the concepts of complexity and change. This question is the same whatever complex or changing objects we choose to take as examples. Admittedly persons have a greater degree of complexity and a greater tendency to change than most other things, but to explore this complexity and these changes is to illuminate the concept of a person rather than that of identity.

But there is a positive danger also in laying special emphasis on persons, a danger to which Hume is very much alive: it makes one very susceptible to the suggestion that as we are persons ourselves we are in a better position in this one case to locate the unchanging particle which carries our identity with it, since we have access to human life from the inside as well as the outside. This makes it tempting to give a term like 'the self' a quasi-empirical character, as though it referred to an object of introspection. It has been suggested that when this happens it is easy to believe that certain somatic sensations are revelations of the self. If this is true it might explain some of the (otherwise very extraordinary) empirical claims of the kind Hume mentions. It is one thing to claim the self must be there, but quite another to claim you have found it. But to follow the scent of this red herring is to be diverted from recognizing that the whole purpose for which the search was instigated is misconceived.

(2) Hume's language throughout makes it clear that he thinks the error he claims to detect is committed by everyone, that is, by every

user of the language, not just by philosophers. If I am right, this is not the case and the ordinary language-user is quite innocent. He clearly holds that it is the philosophers who have invented the fictions of substances and selves. Here he is right, of course. What emerges from this is that such philosophers, in inventing their fictions, are not defending the layman at all. For they concede, with Hume, that the only chance of showing there is no such paradoxical error in the layman's language is by finding the unchanging kernel within each changing thing. But the layman does not need this sort of defence, because there is no paradox there in the first place. So any claim that the doctrine of the self is a defence of the layman or that it represents the 'common-sense position', if this means the same, would be bogus. This point is in no way altered by the fact (and it does seem to be one) that laymen beginning philosophy tend to prefer substance-type theories. For this would be the result of unclear theorizing *about* language (quite a different activity from the mere using of language, and demanding quite distinct aptitudes —rather as travel and cartography differ). Someone new to linguistic theorizing could quite well think he detected a paradox where others claimed to, and fail to notice that his own daily practice did not bear this out. Once this happened, the self might very well seem the only way of evading the paradox. But at this point we are not dealing with a layman any more, but with a philosophical novice. A view which the plain-man-newly-turned-philosopher prefers is not necessarily one he is committed to beforehand.

# 3

## *Hume's Theory of the Self Revisited*

THIS paper is in two parts. I begin the first part with a brief resumé of a previous discussion of Hume's Section 'Of Personal Identity', and follow it with a response to some criticisms of my interpretation of that Section. The authors of these criticisms consider that Hume's account of personal identity is less sceptical and more defensible than I suggested. In responding to them I look again at some difficult but important problems in Humean exegesis. In the second part I turn to some criticisms that are commonly levelled against Hume, and which I have been inclined to subscribe to myself in the past. I do not think that a proper assessment of these criticisms depends upon accepting or rejecting the reading of Hume I try to defend in the first part, so the two parts of the essay are largely independent of each other.[1] I now incline to believe, however, that the criticisms I shall deal with in the second part are criticisms to which Hume has, or could find, quite plausible answers. His critics have accused him of incoherence in his account of the self, and of saying things about it in the Personal Identity Section that are inconsistent with things he says about it in his treatment of the passions in Book II. I shall suggest that whatever weaknesses his theory has (and I am not anxious to champion it), it can deal with the usual objections raised against it on these counts.

I

A.   I begin with a summary of the exposition of Hume's Section which I originally gave, and which still seems to me the most natural reading of the text.

---

[1]   An exception is the argument I offer in B. (2) (i) of Part II, which does presuppose the soundness of Part I.

Hume begins by attacking those philosophers who hold that each of us is at all times intimately conscious of 'what we call our *self*', and are certain of its 'perfect identity and simplicity'. In opposition to them he says that the term has no idea corresponding to it, since no impression can be found from which it can have been derived. All we can find on introspection is the series of 'perceptions' that the self, on the view of these philosophers, is supposed to *own*. So each of us is 'nothing but a bundle or collection of different perceptions' (*T* I. iv. 6. 252); again, 'They are the successive perceptions only, that constitute the mind' (*T* I. iv. 6. 253). If this is the case, it is a problem why we have 'so great a propension to ascribe an identity to these successive perceptions, and to suppose ourselves possest of an invariable and uninterrupted existence thro' the whole course of our lives'. This problem Hume deals with by saying that 'in our common way of thinking' we confound two ideas, that of an object that remains invariable and uninterrupted through a supposed variation of time (the idea of *identity*) and that of several different objects existing in succession, but closely related—this later being, 'to an accurate view' an example of *diversity*. The 'confusion and mistake' is due to the similarity in 'the feeling' induced by the activity of imagination in contemplating each. Attempts to correct this propensity can never succeed for long, and we eventually yield to it, and call interrupted and variable objects the same when they are not.

We then may seek to justify 'this absurdity' and feign some principle to override the interruption and variety, e.g. that of soul, self, or substance. Hence controversy about identity is not 'merely a dispute of words', but involves acceptance or rejection of metaphysical inventions.

Hume then says that this thesis can be justified if he can show that those objects which are variable and interrupted but 'are suppos'd to continue the same', consist of a succession of related parts (*T* I. iv. 6. 255).

He first takes us through some thought-experiments in which he tries to show that certain types of change do not prevent us from calling the object which undergoes them the same, even though such changes 'absolutely destroy' the identity of the whole. The changes are those that are very small, or are *proportionately* small, or are gradual, or are consistent with a '*sympathy* of parts to their *common end*', i.e. some principle of organization. Having illustrated this by reference to physical objects and organisms, he turns to *personal* identity; this he also characterizes as 'fictitious', and says that it too resides not in 'some real bond among . . . perceptions' but in the way the imagination unites our ideas of them. They are so united because of the resemblances between our perceptions, and the causal interactions between them, which are so common that they are related like the members of a republic or commonwealth.

B.  This analysis of Hume's argument treats it as fundamentally sceptical. I assumed that he regards the ascription of identity to changing or interrupted objects, including persons, as erroneous, and as requiring psychological explanation *because* it is erroneous. I assumed in addition that the mistake he claims to uncover and explain is one that is committed not only by those philosophers who invent justificatory principles such as the self, but also by everyone else; the *philosophical* error is that of trying to invent a real bond among our perceptions when there is none there to be found to justify the *common* mistake. On this reading, his own account of how the mistake comes about is one that begins by examining what is *really* there, viz. the succession of distinct but related perceptions, and uses the relationships between them as factors that account for our propensity to talk of them as though there is more there. In other words, his account does not provide the sort of justification that a real self would provide if it existed, but explains the genesis of the practice that his philosophical opponents vainly try to support. On this reading, the ascription of identity to persons is the most striking example of the tendency for human nature to generate beliefs that cannot be shaken by sceptical arguments, but are not open to justification by metaphysical constructions either.

Against the thesis I ascribed to Hume I suggested that the mistake he claims to uncover in our ascription of identity is not a mistake at all, since it is not a necessary truth that sameness requires invariableness or uninterruptedness. In rare instances it might in fact do so, but only when the sort of object being contemplated is one whose nature is defined in this way, most objects not being classified by terms that have this severe restriction built into them. The doctrine that sameness and change are incompatible I also attributed to an insufficiently clear distinction between numerical identity and similarity (or in his terms, numerical and specific identity). The factors which Hume lists in his thought-experiments as causes of our erroneously ascribing numerical identity are not causes of any

such error, but are rather factors which are incorporated into the
concepts of kinds of objects as typical, expected and therefore per-
missible changes. Identity is only destroyed by those changes which
are in a given instance excluded by a concept. When this is understood,
the dispute between Hume and his opponents can, I suggested, be
better understood. Both sides agree that identity excludes change, and
are mistaken in this; but since they agree on it, they are in opposition over the appropriate estimate to make of our obvious propensity to proceed conventionally as though it does not exclude it.
Hume's opponents try to justify the convention by uncovering an
unchanging core to things or persons at a deep level, and Hume is
easily able to show that there is no independent evidence for such a
hypothesis. But he himself is forced to argue that the convention
arises through an inattention to facts which we do not overlook, as
he suggests, but incorporate into our concepts. Both sides of the dispute, therefore, are attempting to explain away a paradox that does
not exist.

C.   This reading, and the criticisms that depend on it, have not gone
unchallenged. This is hardly surprising in view of the well-known
ambiguity which any reader of Hume's epistemological writings has
to face, and which I undoubtedly underrated. This is the ambiguity
in Hume's assessment of the common beliefs or conventions whose
origin in human nature he seeks to describe. These beliefs are not
generated by reason but by the 'sensitive' parts of our natures. This
is why reason cannot justify them—if it could do this, either by examination of the evidence, or by the construction of metaphysical substitutes for it, then the arguments it could produce might have had
some bearing on their initial appearance. It also explains why sceptical arguments cannot dislodge them—the factors that produce them
are more powerful than reason is. In supporting this view Hume seems
clearly to be engaging in genetic psychology, good or bad; a switch
in philosophical method which is openly proclaimed in the subtitle
of the *Treatise*. When expressed at this level of generality, Hume's
procedures do not involve any of the confusion between philosophy
and psychology of which he is sometimes accused. Indeed, they offer
good evidence for thinking that the distinction between the two is
made clearly by Hume for the first time. But *detailed* confusion
frequently arises in the most sympathetic reader of Hume when one
asks how far his account of the origin of these beliefs amounts, in

spite of everything, to some sort of justification of them? He proclaims a clear enough distinction between himself as a philosopher and himself as a man, but does he always observe it? He does not think that scepticism is demonstrably false as well as unnatural, as Descartes does. It is not demonstrably false; it is rather *vain*. But does this mean it is vain but true, incredible but correct? Or does it mean that it is false just because it is vain? Textually the answer seems to be that Hume sometimes talks one way and sometimes the other; that at some stage in the process of telling us how we have come by the beliefs which it is impossible to justify by reason but vain to doubt, he will start to talk as though the belief then under examination is true. Certainly this is what seems to happen in the case of personal identity. As he proceeds to account for the fact that our conventions are the way they are, he gradually seems to put aside the doubts about their validity that he appears to raise as the Section opens.

This ambiguity is also present in the argument of the earlier and longer Section II, 'Of Scepticism With Regard to the Senses'. As I read the two Sections, the structure of the argument in each is the same. In the earlier Section he begins quite emphatically. Scepticism is not an open option even for the philosopher who professes to hold to it. 'Nature has not left this to his choice. . . . We may well ask, *What causes induce us to believe in the existence of body?* but 'tis in vain to ask, *Whether there be body or not?* That is a point, which we must take for granted in all our reasonings' (*T* I. iv. 2. 187). He then tries to account for the origin of this belief, which he insists cannot be traced either to the senses or the reason, but to the imagination. What the imagination does, to summarize, is disguise the disjointedness and interruptedness of our successive perceptions and thus generate the 'fiction' of continued and distinct existence. This universal fiction he refers to as 'the vulgar system', and attributes it to all perceivers. Philosophers, noticing that our perceptions are *not* distinct or continuous, produce a 'palliative remedy' in the shape of a theory that will resolve the apparent conflict between the sensible realities and the fictions: they claim that although our perceptions are fragmentary and interrupted, they are due to objects which are not. This theory is devoid of independent justification, and fails to give respectability to the vulgar system in consequence. The only remedy for the conflict is 'carelessness and in-attention.'

In the Section on Personal Identity we seem to have the same pattern, but the argument is much more compressed. He *begins* this time

by attacking the philosophical theory of the self; having demolished
it, at least to his own satisfaction, he then asks what, if not the actual
existence of the inner entity philosophers have invented, causes us
to 'suppose ourselves possest of an invariable and uninterrupted existence'. He accounts for it, as I read him, by saying that we ascribe
identity (which he has defined in terms of invariableness and uninterruptedness) in cases where we do not find it, and that this ascription 'is commonly attended with a fiction', such as that of the self.
In paralleling the two Sections, I want to raise several queries about
how the Identity Section is to be read. (a) Can we take it for granted
that he thinks that a sceptical doubt about personal identity is vain
in the same way that the corresponding doubt about the existence
of bodies is vain? (b) If the answer to this is affirmative—and all
readers seem to think that it is—then does this preclude our interpreting him as saying that nevertheless the doubt is justified? Are
we able, or are we not able, to read Hume as saying, qua philosophical
analyst, that the belief in personal identity is mistaken, i.e. *false*, and
yet saying, qua social scientist, that human nature is committed to
it? (c) Lastly, though of course this is connected with the preceding,
how far is he making a sharp distinction, especially in his negative
criticisms, between the beliefs of the vulgar and the theories of the
philosophers?

I still incline to read both Sections as explicitly committing Hume
to the view that the common belief is false, feigned, or fictitious, yet
ineradicable; and that the error of the philosophers does not lie in
thinking they cannot find a basis for it, but merely in trying to invent
such a basis in metaphysical theory subsequently. I still consider this
is the most natural interpretation of these two Sections; it provides
also, for what this is worth, an explanation of the undoubted fact
that Hume's prose does not, particularly in the latter half of the
Identity Section, continue to suggest that the ascription of identity
is mistaken. This would be natural enough for someone who, in common with everybody else, found the sceptical doubts he was unable
to allay by rational methods altogether unnatural; common sense,
like cheerfulness, would keep breaking in. But this reading has been
challenged in two interesting essays on Hume's theory of Personal
Identity, one by James Noxon, and the other by Lawrence Ashley
and Michael Stack.[2] The essence of their reading is that Hume does

[2] Noxon 1969; Ashley and Stack 1974.

not regard the ascription of identity to changing things as necessarily mistaken and requiring explanation; what he regards as mistaken is the ascription to changing things of *strict* identity. It is only *strict* identity which he defines in terms of invariableness and uninterruptedness. Persons do not have strict identity, but identity of another, more permissive sort which Ashley and Stack call, using a term of Hume's, *imperfect* identity, and which Noxon less happily seems to want to equate with *specific* identity. On this view, most objects, and all persons, have imperfect identity, which has as its conditions the limited types of variation and interruptedness that I read Hume as listing as sources of the belief in a fictional strict identity. On this reading, the only *mistake* is that made by philosophers, who want to ascribe *strict* identity to persons, and are only able to manage this by inventing fictional entities such as the self. On this reading, also, Hume appears as the defender of the conventions of ordinary speech against the otiose constructs of metaphysicians.

Now there is no doubt that Hume comes out better if read this way. He comes out better because the conditions that he lists as factors persuading us to ascribe identity to changing things are indeed the conditions that are incorporated into our substantive concepts and supply our criteria of identity in the language. So Hume has got our conventions right. But I still do not think that this reading of him fits what he says, even though it is an excellent presentation of what he *ought* to have said.

In the Section 'Of Scepticism With Regard to the Senses', Hume is discussing a common ('vulgar') *belief*, which he identifies as that in distinct and continued existence, and which is clearly distinguishable from the philosophical theory of representative perception. The ambiguity of attitude is present but most of the time both opinions are described by the use of words like 'fallacy'. In the Section 'Of Personal Identity', however, the very fact that he begins by attacking the philosophical constructions makes it harder to be quite certain how far he is attacking them alone, and how far he is attacking a belief that everyone has. But it is not very hard. He does indeed say that 'we' feign the continued existence of the perceptions of our senses, and 'run into' the notions of soul, self, and substance; a sentence (*T* I. iv. 6. 254) which seems to put the vulgar system of perception on the same footing as the philosophical inventions. But these inventions are all said to be 'feigned' in order to justify an 'absurdity', viz. The assertion that 'different related objects are in

effect the same', and the fictions (to which he adds Shaftesbury's reasonings about plants and animals in a footnote) are said to serve the
purpose of connecting objects together and disguising their variation.
While the inclusion of these philosophical theories might lend some
plausibility to the suggestion that they are all that he is attacking,
the conjunction of them with the vulgar theory of perception indicates that the error the fictions are designed to conceal is a common
one.

But there seems to be no simple vulgar counterpart to the vulgar
theory of distinct and continued existence. The counterpart in the
case of personal identity is not very happily called a belief. It is rather
a *convention*: the convention of calling things the same in spite of
changes. Hume treats it as a belief, though he realises it is one embodied in our conventions. He denies that disputes about identity
are merely disputes about words on the grounds that the disputes
generate metaphysical fictions, and that these are dangerous. But he
talks of the fallacious ascription of identity as something which,
though contrary to the facts, can take place without a 'breach of
the propriety of language'.

But herein lies the difficulty of his argument. He does see, very
accurately, what our linguistic conventions are. That is to say, he
does see very accurately under what sorts of conditions we ascribe
identity through change. He also sees that philosophical fictions result
from looking for invariance where such identity is ascribed. The question is whether he also thinks that in ascribing the identity one is
necessarily ascribing the invariance or overlooking the change. It seems
to me clear that he does think this, even though all the correct things
he says about our ascription of identity can be freed from it. (i) Having
demolished the philosophical fictions, he seems then to assume it to
be puzzling that we ascribe an identity to the successive perceptions
that the philosophers attempt to unite by means of them. Why should
this be puzzling unless he assumes, with those philosophers, that there
is a prima facie contrast between numerical identity and variety?
(ii) He then goes on to give an account, reminiscent of his earlier
discussions in Section II,[3] of the idea of identity or sameness; and
he introduces it as that of an object that remains invariable and uninterrupted through time, saying it is distinct, 'and even contrary'
to the idea of several different objects existing in succession, and

---

[3] See especially *T* I. iv. 2, 200–204.

connected together by a close relation. Yet the two are 'generally confounded with each other', and this in turn generates the habits which issue in the regular ascription of identity to changing things. This is the basis of his account of our conventions, which I fully agree is a correct account; but the basis of his account is not itself presented as a point about a linguistic convention. It is presented as the account of a mis-application of two concepts, based on the felt likeness of the phenomena to which they are applied. Such an account presupposes an understanding of the concepts referred to. Consequently what Hume is offering us, though indeed an accurate account, indeed a sympathetic and even at times approving account of our linguistic conventions, is still one which accounts for these conventions as the outcome of a mis-classification of phenomena. And such an account presupposes a convention opposed in its form to the one it explains, i.e. it presupposes that it is strictly incorrect to call changing things identical, even though most men lazily do it, and only pernickety philosophers would try to restrain them. It radiates the sort of tolerance that can only make sense if there is a prior fault. And there is none. For it is the conventions he is explaining that give us the sense of the concepts.

To summarize: Hume says that the identity of a person is not something really belonging to the perceptions that make up his mental history, but something which we attribute to them because of the union of their ideas in the imagination when we reflect on them. We read it into the manifold of mental phenomena, and do not find it there. But he unfortunately represents the ascription of it as the reading into the variety of mental phenomena the kind of invariance that fits a paradigm of identity which he shares with his philosophical opponents. In this he is ascribing a strict accuracy to the sceptic which, for once at least, belongs quite straightforwardly to the ordinary language-user.

II

A.   So far I have been arguing in support of one of a pair of interpretations of Hume's text. These two interpretations share a common feature. They are both interpretations of Section VI which treat what Hume says there about personal identity as merely a specific instance of a general thesis about identity through change. The issue between the two interpretations is an issue about what this general thesis about identity is. It is therefore not an issue about the identity of *persons*, except incidentally: In this Second Part I want to turn to criticisms of Hume's Section that centre on alleged inadequacies in his theory as a theory about the identity of persons, rather than about identity in general.

(1) The question Hume asks in Section VI is a question about what induces us to ascribe identity to a succession of perceptions. Now even though he tries to answer it by means of a highly general thesis about identity, the question itself is importantly restricted. It is a question about our ascription of unity to a *succession of perceptions*; i.e. it is about what we call a *mind*, rather than what we call a person. The latter, at least in common speech, is a psychophysical entity, whereas the former consists exclusively of psychical components. It is natural, and correct, to regard this restriction as a deeply damaging one. It looks damaging in at least two ways. (a) In the first place it seems to exaggerate the problem Hume raises about the unity we ascribe to the sequence. The changes that take place in a man's body are far more gradual than those that take place in his mind; and it is only his mental life that we think is subject to interruptions. Perhaps Hume's puzzle comes from subtracting the body from the concept of a person and still expecting the mental phenomena that remain to exhibit the same stability that the body gives to the psychophysical person. I have made this criticism before, and it still seems sound enough. But although there are inevitable shifts in the text, and although the whole Section is entitled 'Of Personal Identity', it is probably most accurate to take an interpretative clue from the fact that Hume's restriction to *perceptions* is quite explicit and deliberate, and see how his Section looks as an account of whatever sort of unity *the mind of a person* exhibits, rather than an account of the sort of unity that a *person* exhibits. If we read him like this, it is a *mind* that is nothing but a bundle or collection of different perceptions; and it is the status of our alleged belief in *its* unity that Hume is examining. So although there is little doubt of Hume's tacit Cartesian identification of a person and his mind in many passages, and although the restriction this leads him into makes his problem unnecessarily difficult if the problem is supposed to be one about the unity of a person, perhaps something true and important can be salvaged from it if we read it as a problem about the supposed unity of a person's mind.

(b) Here, however, we run into another criticism, which seems dam-
agingly sharpened as soon as we restrict our consideration to the
sequence of perceptions that make up the history of a man's mind,
and ignore the rest of him. For Hume is thought now to have no
answer to the question, 'How do I distinguish between the series of
perceptions that makes up *my* mind from the series of perceptions
that makes up *your* mind?' It is at least extremely likely that the reference to the public world of separate human bodies has something
essential to do with our capacity to distinguish persons from one
another. But does not Hume make this distinction impossible by concentrating solely upon the mental constituents of a person's life? Does
he not presuppose the distinction between one mental history and
another in raising his problem about the internal unity of each series?
And how can he be in a position to do this when he leaves the body
that each series is attached to out of consideration?

Some readers think[4] that the question of how one distinguishes
one mind from another is at least a part of the question that Hume
is asking in Section VI. It seems clear that this is not so. The question he asks at least *looks* quite different: 'What is it that makes me
think I am entitled to ascribe unity to the perceptions that made up
my mental history?'[5] I shall call the question that Hume does *not*
ask, the question about Individuation; and I shall call the question
he does ask, the question about Mental Unity. The criticism that I
want to look at is this: Does not the very asking of the question
about Mental Unity presuppose that there is already an answer to
the question about Individuation?[6]

(2) A more common criticism of Hume is that however plausible
his genetic explanations of our fundamental epistemological commitments in terms of human nature are in other cases, explanations
of our belief in self-identity along these lines are bound to be self-
defeating. Many versions of this criticism can be found,[7] although
it is not as easy to express as one might like. I take the point to be

---

[4] I think A. H. Basson interprets Hume this way in his discussion of *T* I. iv. 6. See
Basson 1958, 130–33.

[5] This is of course an attempted paraphrase. His words are 'What then gives us
so great a propension to ascribe an identity to these successive perceptions, and to
suppose ourselves possest of an invariable and uninterrupted existence thro' the whole
course of our lives?'

[6] I think this criticism is involved in Strawson's criticisms of the 'no-ownership'
theory in ch. 3 of Strawson 1959. It is also found in Penelhum 1967, 100.

[7] One version of it is in Passmore 1952, 82–3.

something like this. On Hume's account, a human mind is nothing but a bundle or succession of different perceptions. Yet all of us have a propensity to believe that it is more than this, that it possesses some unity through time. In order to explain how this belief comes about, Hume has to give an account that parallels in certain respects his description of how we come to believe in the distinct and continued existence of perceived objects: and in this case as in that one, the account dwells on how it feels to perceive one sort of sequence of impressions and how it feels to perceive another. Now however much plausibility there may be in such an account of our belief in the external world, there is bound to be very much less plausibility in such an account of our belief in self-identity. For the story Hume tells can only be true if there is something that perceives various sequences of impressions and is able to notice that they feel the same, or at least is able to fail to notice that they are differ-ent. And this seems to presuppose the actual existence of the very self-identity that he suggests is a fictitious *product* of the process described. Put more crudely, I can only wonder if I am the same person I was yesterday, if I am, not if I am not. Kant may or may not have been right when he said that a similar worry about the object-ive character of my perceptions of physical phenomena is ultimately unintelligible; but he certainly seems to have a strong argument on his side when he says that any sort of comparative judgement about a sequence of perceptions that I have requires the identity of the self who has them, and cannot justify a doubt about that identity, even though one may not be able on this basis to characterize the self any further. This is the best-known and most widely-felt diffi-culty in Hume's account of self-identity. It is expressed in what MacNabb has noticed to be a hexametrical question, 'How can a series of conscious states be aware of itself as a series?'[8] I shall there-fore refer to it as the problem of MacNabb's Hexameter.

(3) The third and last criticism of Hume that I wish to consider concerns the consistency of what he says in Section VI with the use he makes of the idea of the self in his account of the Passions in Book II. The idea of the self (he even calls it an impression on occa-sion) is an important part of the associative mechanism that he makes use of in his account of the origin of the indirect passions of pride and humility: these arise, and only arise, when certain pleasing or

---

[8] MacNabb 1951, 251.

displeasing phenomena are related to this idea. In addition, the account which he offers of the principle of Sympathy, and the opposed principle of Comparison, require the idea of the self as an enlivening force or a basis of contrast. How can this be consistent with his apparent denial in Section VI of the first Book that the idea of the self even has content? He does of course make a formal distinction between 'personal identity, as it regards our thought or imagination, and as it regards our passions or the concern we take in ourselves' (*T* I. iv. 6. 253). But the *Treatise* is obviously lacking in any account of how this distinction is to be made, as opposed to the use of it. This apparent inconsistency in Hume's work has been stressed by Kemp Smith, who would interpret it as a sign of the temporal priority of Book II over Book I.[9]

B.   (1) Let us return to the criticism that Hume cannot account for my ability to distinguish between the string of perceptions that make up my biography from the string of perceptions that make up yours—the problem of Individuation. There is a certain oddity about putting the question in the way I have put it. It suggests that each of us is somehow presented with a large number of discrete perceptions, and has the task of sorting them out into parallel strings, one of them being his own mental history, and the others being the mental histories of other people. This is of course not what happens. Each of us is only presented with *his own*. While Hume does slip from time to time (as in his famous remark about supposing it possible to see clearly into the breast of another), on the whole he proceeds as though each of us is presented with a series of perceptions with which he proceeds to perform two tasks. The first task is the imaginative construction of a world of distinct and continuing objects of perception. The second is the generation of a psychologically comfortable ascription of biographical unity to the sequence of perceptions out of which this world of objects has been constructed. The question of how we generate the belief in a *community of perceivers* is not really raised, let alone dealt with. One can only suppose that Hume would deal with it as an extension of the *first* task, and would think of our awareness of the mental lives of others as an inference from our knowledge of (or belief in) the behaviour of

⁹ Smith 1941, 179–83.

their bodies taken as signs of their mental lives. I can see no reason to think he is very much further on than Berkeley in his discussion of other minds. So one reasonable response to the suggestion that Hume has no answer to the question about Individuation, since he takes it for granted that he can distinguish between one biographical string of experiences and another, is that he does not do this. All he asks is how the one string that I have is thought of by me as a unitary one, and once this question is answered it provides an account of the development of the idea of oneself that could serve, in combination with the belief in external objects, to generate the further belief in a community of perceivers. The notion of other selves will on this account be *subsequent* to the idea of one's own self, not prior to it. If one says, following Strawson, that the existence of other perceivers is presupposed in even saying that one is only presented with *one's own* perceptions no doubt this is true. But Hume does not have to admit (does he?) that each of us realizes that the only perceptions he has are his own until after he has generated the idea of himself and then that of others. Hume of all people is not going to be distressed by the fact that it is only after human nature has generated a belief that one is in a position to raise philosophical doubts about it. This is only a problem for him if he maintains that there have actually to *be* perceivers besides me before I can wonder whether there are any; he merely says, if this reading of him is correct, that I can only wonder about this if my nature is the sort that can generate *belief* in such persons.

My argument here is a modest one. It is merely that in one sense of the word 'presuppose', Hume does not presuppose an understanding of the distinction between the series of perceptions that constitute my mind and the series of perceptions that constitute your mind when he asks his question about Mental Unity. Of course there is another sense in which he does presuppose it. He knows that this distinction, or the belief in a community of perceivers that it reflects, is one of the common-sense convictions that his account of human nature has to explain; so the processes of psychological construction that he describes have to be capable of generating it, at some stage. But this is not to presuppose it in a vicious sense; it is not to make his account of human nature incoherent or circular. This is even more obvious when we reflect that he is only trying to account for our beliefs' existence, and not claiming, at least when he is careful, to justify them.

(2) So much for the question Hume does not ask, but has been said by some to be unable to answer. I turn now to the difficulty that he is commonly thought to encounter when he deals with the question that he does ask, viz. The question about Mental Unity. The difficulty is said to be that he accounts for the genesis of the belief in the mind's unity in a way that seems to appeal to, or (let us use the word again) presuppose the very unitary subject that he represents as a fictitious *product* of the mental processes he describes it as going through. How good a case can we make for him in response to this criticism?

We must begin by rejecting, with other commentators, the view that Hume is committed by his analysis to the truth of the philosophical fictions he begins Section VI by attacking. For this criticism to have force it would have to be shown that only the entities thus invented by his philosophical opponents could perform the mental functions that he describes. But it might still be true that he is committed, in his account, to the continuing existence of *something* that performs those functions, even though it is not the Pure Ego his philosophical opponents say it is.

Nelson Pike has recently offered a 'limited defence' of Hume against even this contention.[10] I understand his argument to be this. Hume is best understood as offering his bundle theory of the self as an analysis of *the idea of a mind*. It is not an attempt to analyse the idea of a 'whole person'. Nor is it an attempt to analyse the meaning of the word 'I' in sentences like 'I see a chair'; this last is something on which Hume has 'nothing directly to say'. What he offers is a theory about the proper understanding of whole sentences reporting mental events. These have to be understood as stating that the event reported *belongs to a particular series*, viz. the series that constitutes my mind. This does not mean that my mind sees the chair; *I* do. But to say I do is to say (and only to say) that the perception of the chair is one of the perceptions in the series of perceptions that constitute my mind. The relation of a mind to its perceptions is that of inclusion. If we then ask how we are to understand the statement that I mis-ascribe identity to the changing perceptions in the series, the answer is that the series that constitutes my mind includes within it a further perception, or mental act, of mis-ascription, in addition to those to which such identity is mis-ascribed. If we now

[10] Pike 1967, 159–65.

raise the question expressed in MacNabb's Hexameter, the answer to it is along the same lines: the series of perceptions that is my mind includes within it a further perception that is an awareness of the whole series.

If this is a correct reading of Hume's text, it amounts to the view that statements about a continuing mind are reducible to statements about the perceptions that constitute that mind. So minds, in Russell's immortal phrase, disappear upon analysis; perceptions remain as the only things that there ultimately are. If this is a correct reading of the text, then Hume has, if not an answer to the problem of MacNabb's Hexameter, at least a potential programme of analysis that might supply one if it could be carried through. A successful completion of such an analysis of statements about our mental lives would show that Hume is not committed to the existence of any entity, over and above perceptions, that *has* those perceptions. But I incline to think that this is an anachronistic reading of Hume's text and embodies far too radical a de-psychologizing of his philosophical objectives, however plausible an account it may give of what he ought to have said if he had been doing logical analysis instead of social science. My reasons for thinking this are these.

(i) When Hume says that each of us is nothing but a bundle or collection of different perceptions, he is not only at pains to distinguish this from the view of philosophers who suppose that these perceptions all belong to a Pure Ego, but also to distinguish it from the view of the common man that the mind has an invariable and uninterrupted existence. Now if what he is offering is an analysis of the meaning of statements about the mind's acts or contents, then such an analysis (as Pike very clearly shows) would leave no place for any mention of the Pure Ego. *This* could very well disappear upon analysis, just as it puts in no appearance upon introspection. But it is another matter when we come to the ordinary man's view that the mind possesses the sort of Unity that Hume describes as 'an invariable and uninterrupted existence'. On my reading of him, the belief that he expresses this way is one that is (a) false, and (b) embodied in the 'proprieties of language'. This can only mean that this belief is *both* part of the meaning of our ordinary statements about the mind, *and* false. Now if the Unity to which this belief commits us were to disappear upon analysis in the way Pike's interpretation of the text would require, then it could not be maintained that the analysis was a correct analysis of ordinary statements about mental acts and processes. It seems clear, in fact, that Hume is offering a theory that is intended as a corrective to common speech, not a mere translation of it. It is important to notice that Hume does not suggest that our idea of the identity of the Mind is empty, or non-existent, as he says the idea of the Pure Ego is. He treats it rather as akin to the idea of necessary connection: something that does not replicate an item discerned *among* our perceptions, but whose use involves the reading into them of something that has its origin in the operation of the mind upon them. Consequently the idea of the Unity of the Mind is not devoid of content, and statements about the mind involve the use of it; it is merely not the idea of something that is *there* among the perceptions. But if this is Hume's theory it does not demand an analysis of ordinary statements about mental acts and processes that leaves no reference to this idea. It *precludes* such an analysis.

(ii) This seems to me to be confirmed by Hume's difficult second thoughts about personal identity in the Appendix. He confesses there to a continuing perplexity about reconciling the distinctness of our perceptions and the absence of a perceived bond between them. These are only hard to reconcile because he does not feel he can ascribe unity to the series of perceptions when these 'real connections' are not discernible. But there would be no reason to expect there to be a discernible bond between the perceptions if sentences about a mind's mental acts were analysable into sentences that merely reported their inclusion in the series. For then there would be no need to think of the presence of a bond between them as something that should remain when the analysis was completed.

So I remain obstinately psychological in my interpretation of Hume. But it is possible, perhaps, to psychologize Pike's thesis, or the one he ascribes to Hume. Such a psychologization would go as follows. Perceptions are all that the mind consists of. A mind is just a series or bundle of them. Our ordinary, conventionally constructed, state-ments about our minds treat them as having a unity through time that a dispassionate scrutiny of the series does not reveal. So we have a puzzle: how does our conventional understanding of the mind arise? Since the series of disconnected perceptions is all that there is, the question becomes this: how does the series come from time to time to include within it perceptions that are misinterpretations of other perceptions in the series? No doubt in answering it we may fall into the bad habit of using the common forms of speech which embody our conviction that the series has a unity that it does not actually have. But strictly speaking we should speak of individual, atomic perceptions as the units of the mental activity that generates the fiction of Mental Unity. Further along in our account we would presumably have to explain how it was that the series comes also to include the idea of physical bodies that some of the perceptions are 'of' (an account that Hume supplies) and later still how it comes to include the idea of other contemporaneous series of perceptions or other minds.

It seems to me that this is Hume's actual programme. Perhaps it is impossible to carry out. Much twentieth-century argument about our conceptual schemes and their possible variations is designed to show this. I cannot enter into these arguments here. It does seem to me, however, that Hume has a programme which is designed to deal with the sort of difficulty about his apparently appealing to an en- during mind while denying that the belief in one is true. But the programme is psychological, not logical, even if a logical programme might furnish a more successful defence against the Problem of MacNabb's Hexameter.

If this is Hume's programme, however, it does run into one very obvious difficulty that I suppose is a logical one. The series that makes up the mind includes awarenesses of other perceptions; ultimately there will be some that are awarenesses of themselves as being mem- bers of a particular series, a particular mind. MacNabb asks how it can be that a *perception* can be aware, correctly or mistakenly, of anything. Awareness, like all mental acts, is something that *I* do or have, not something that does or has anything. Even though Hume's account is not an attempt to reduce statements about minds to statements about perceptions, it is still an account that can only be expressed if perceptions themselves can be the subjects of sentences about mental activities. I find this perplexing. At some times, when faced with such sentences (and I have used some in this paper) I think I understand them well enough. At other times I feel I do not under- stand them at all. Yet I feel a great reluctance to let anyone tell me on the basis of general arguments that I cannot possibly understand them. I simply do not know whether I can make sense of them or not. If I am not unique in this, then I suspect something of the same bewilderment faces those who have felt that Hume *must* presuppose a continuing mind when he tell us how, on his view, the illusion of one arises; they are expressing a feeling that he cannot be entitled to ascribe all these activities to perceptions. If their strictures have demonstrable force, however, and do not just depend on the fact that Hume's usage is inconsistent, then this force will have to come from general arguments about what our conceptual schemes permit us to say and not to say, or about how far we are able, or unable, to form concepts on the basis of private experiences. I make no comment on the force of such arguments. I merely suggest that Hume can only be shown to be guilty of absurdity on the basis of very general considerations like these, and not because of detailed inconsistencies in his psychological programme.[11]

(3) I turn finally to the alleged conflict between what Hume says about the self in Section VI of Book I and what he says about it in his analysis of the Passions in Book II. There is no doubt that the 'idea, or rather impression, of ourselves' assumes considerable importance in this latter analysis. There are two parts of the argument of Book II where it is especially prominent. (a) It is vital to his account of pride and humility. Pride is, roughly, the emotion that results when some pleasant fact does not merely give me pleasure, but is connected with myself. Humility (more accurately shame) is the emotion that results when some unpleasant fact does not merely seem unpleasant to me, but is connected with myself. He expresses the connection between these emotions and the self by saying that the self is the *object* of the emotion. He distinguishes between an emotion's object and its cause, the cause being the pleasant or unpleasant fact that excites me, and the object being that to which my view is directed when excited. It is very doubtful whether Hume's distinction can be equated with the one often drawn at present between an emotion's cause and its intensional object, since Hume clearly regards both the ideas of the exciting fact, and of the self, as causally related to the passions of pride and humility. For present purposes, however, it is enough to agree that the idea of the self is

---

[11] In presenting my arguments in this portion of Part II, I have proceeded as though the interpretative theses of Part I can be taken as established. Even if this is not granted, however, I would still argue that a psychological reading of Hume's programme is the more accurate, and that he is not doing logical analysis. The response to the problem of MacNabb's Hexameter would therefore have to take some form close to the one I have offered, and face the difficulty this faces, even if Pike's version of Hume would succeed in avoiding it. I am particularly indebted to Pike's essay for the realization that Hume's account of the self has internal defences against the criticisms most commonly levelled at it, but must differ in the interpretation of the theory and the identification of the available defences.

2222

an indispensable element in the associative process that provides the setting for these emotions.[12]

(b) In addition to the use of the idea of the self in the analysis of the indirect passions of pride and humility, Hume also makes critical use of it in his strange account of the principle of sympathy (*T* II. i. 11). The account is one in which Hume seeks to explain how it is that a passion that I am first aware of in idea as being undergone by another person, comes to be shared by me also. Such a sharing of it amounts to its transformation from the status of an idea to that of an impression (the two being distinguished of course, by their liveliness). What he needs to find, as he presents the problem, is some enlivening force that will effect this transformation. He claims to find it, of all places, in the idea of the self. The exact role it plays here is one that I find obscure, but it seems to consist partly in producing an awareness of my similarity to the other person, and thereby opening me to feeling the emotion he has with an intensity approaching that with which he feels it. When we look at these accounts it is clear that Hume is not guilty of the sort of inconsistency of which he is accused. The idea of the self that we do not have according to Section VI of Book I is the idea of the Pure Ego. There is nothing to suggest that that is the idea he uses in Book II. What his accounts need is obviously the idea of oneself as contrasted with others. He has to take for granted that there is some answer to the question about Individuation, so that someone can be aware of himself as distinct from other persons. This is made obvious when we turn from his account of pride and humility, to that of the origins of love and hatred (*T* II. ii. 1–3). Love is, roughly, the passion that arises when some pleasant experience is associated not with the idea of myself, but the idea of another person; hatred is the passion that results when that experience is unpleasant. Similarly, sympathy is contrasted with comparison (*T* II. ii. 8), a process whereby I come to have emotions opposite to those another person is having by contrasting his condition with my own. Here again it is clear that what Hume is using is the distinction between myself and others. His theories here seem quite consistent with the sort of account of the origin of the distinction between one person and another that I suggested his discussions in Book I would allow him to construct; and the worst he seems guilty of here is not trying to fill it in.

[12] See particularly Sections 2–5 of Part i of Book II.

We have to recognize one other implication, however. We are not only proud or ashamed of things that happen to us here and now, but of past and future happenings. For this to be possible we have to think of ourselves and others as having pasts and futures. The form this particular assumption takes is, on Hume's account, that of the erroneous ascription of Unity through time. It would seem therefore, that his theory of the emotions does not merely involve him in using the distinction between myself and others, but in ascribing Unity to them, or at least the belief in Unity. This is no doubt one place where he takes for granted the propriety and correctness of the convention whose basis he has really undermined in his analysis of the concept of identity. This is not an inconsistency between Books I and II, however; it is rather an inconsistency in the account in Book I. Whatever we say to this, the point remains unaffected: he does not deny that we have an idea of ourselves as distinct from others, nor does he deny that we have an idea of Mental Unity. And as a piece of psychology, the account of the passions merely requires him to show that we *use* both these ideas; not that they are epistemologically sound ones.

# 4

## *Self-identity and Self-regard*

IN his discussion of personal identity Hume draws a distinction to which his readers have not paid much attention. It is a distinction between 'personal identity, as it regards our thought or imagination, and as it regards our passions or the concern we take in ourselves'.[1] I want in this paper, to examine this distinction and the use Hume makes of it. Although in doing so, I will be commenting some of the time on questions of Humean exegesis, my main concern is to try to throw some light on the role that the idea of oneself plays in our thinking about some of the areas of the emotional life that Hume considers.

### I

Let us first see why Hume introduces this distinction where he does. It appears in the Section 'Of Personal Identity' (Section VI of Part IV of Book I of the *Treatise*), and he says he must make it in order to answer a question about self-identity which he says, correctly, will carry his readers 'pretty deep'. The question he wants to ask is this:

What then gives us so great a propension to ascribe an identity to these successive perceptions, and to suppose ourselves possest of an invariable and uninterrupted existence thro' the whole course of our lives? (*T* I. iv. 6. 253)

This is a question about the origin of what I shall call the belief in the Unity of a person. He raises it after dismissing the view of 'some metaphysicians' that each of us is aware of a *self* that has

---

[1] While this complaint was justified at the time this essay was first written, the situation has improved, and the importance of Hume's account of the passions within his system is more widely recognized. The most important examples are Baier 1991, McIntyre 1989 and 1995, and Ainslie 1999. Árdal 1966 remains the fundamental study.

perfect identity and simplicity, and asserting that as far as he and the rest of mankind are concerned, each of us is 'nothing but a bundle or collection of different perceptions' in which there is 'properly no simplicity . . . at any one time, nor identity in different'. I interpret his answer to it as one that denies that the invariable and uninterrupted existence he refers to is an actual feature of human life, and offers us a psychological account of how we come to suppose that it is. It is this which constitutes his account of 'personal identity, as it regards our thought or imagination'. The upshot of his account is that the life-history of a person (or mind) is merely a sequence of 'different perceptions', which has no 'identity in different', but to which such an identity is indeed ascribed by the 'thought or imagination' because of various connections and relationships between its successive members.

This is not the question of how one such biography is to be distinguished from other parallel ones—which I will dub the question about Individuation. I do not think Hume ever addresses himself to this question directly. I have argued elsewhere that a case of sorts can be built up, in the terms of Hume's own philosophical system, for denying that this question needs to be raised before the question of Unity can be (see Chapter 3). I shall not repeat this here.

But whatever the precise dimensions of the problem of the Unity of the person, readers of the *Treatise* have noticed that Hume proceeds in Book II as though the problem is safely behind him. They have sometimes felt that he is not entitled to proceed like this, and that he makes use of the idea of the self in his account of the genesis of some of the passions, and in his description of the mechanism of sympathy, in a way that is inconsistent with what he has said about it in Book I. There is little doubt that at least part of the reason for his introducing the distinction between personal identity as it concerns the thought or imagination, and personal identity as it regards our passions, in the midst of his discussion in Book I, is to forestall this criticism. He would achieve this end by making readers think that the role the idea of the self is said to play in Book II is one it might very well play whether his treatment of it in Book I is correct, or whether it is not: that the two discussions are logically independent.

Of course, if this is what Hume wishes his readers to think, he may be wrong. It might turn out on reflection that the uses he ascribes

to the idea of the self in our emotional life, or the uses that the idea
of the self actually has in the emotional life, are uses that it could
not have unless the analysis in Book I, or some part of it, were false:
or that if the analysis of Book I were true, it would expose our uses
of the idea of the self in the emotional life to a charge of confusion or
irrationality.

Before looking at this possibility, I must put aside another.
Hume clearly does not think that the idea of the self that plays a
key role in the genesis of some of the passions is the one he ascribes
to those metaphysicians that he attacks at the outset of the Section
in the first Book. He insists that he at least does not *have* such an
idea, because it is not traceable to any impression. Although some
commentators seem willing enough to accuse him of the most
blatant inconsistency at this point, there seems little need to read
him as though he holds that our emotional life depends critically
upon an idea that by his own account we do not even have. There
may be inconsistency, but it is likely to be at a deeper level than
this.

He tells us himself what idea he has in mind when he refers to
what he calls the 'object' of pride and humility as 'self, or that succession of related ideas and impressions, of which we have an intimate memory and consciousness' (*T* II. i. 2. 277). This adjectival clause
is manifestly inserted to make it clear that he is *not* referring to the
alleged idea of a metaphysical pure ego, but to that sequence of perceptions for which it was supposed to provide a principle of unity:
to what many philosophers have called the empirical self. His use
of the idea thus identified makes it clear that he takes it for granted,
in Book II, both that the problem of the ascription of Unity to that
sequence need not be raised again, and also that we do have at our
disposal, and presuppose in our emotional life, some manner of
answering the question about Individuation. With regard to the
latter question, there are countless places where his description of
the arousal of the emotions requires us to be able to distinguish other
persons from ourselves, and from one another; and it is certainly a
pity that he never offers a direct and detailed answer to the question of Individuation in order to help his readers understand how
these vital distinctions are available to us. But not offering an
answer is not the same as being in no position to offer one; and does
not of itself constitute inconsistency, open or concealed.

The case is more complex, however, when we look at his use of the idea of the self in Book II in order to compare it with his views on the question he *does* try to answer in Book I—the problem of the Unity of the person. Suppose it should emerge (as I think it does on the most cursory investigation) that his account of the emotions requires him to ascribe to us not only the use of the distinction between oneself and another, but also the presupposition of the Unity of oneself through time? It would then follow that Hume would be making use in Book II of the belief in something that he described in Book I as a fiction, as something read into a sequence of heterogeneous perceptions that does not contain it. Admittedly he holds that such a fiction is one of which we could not rid ourselves if we tried, but it is a fiction for all that. This is something that he refrains from recalling to us in Book II; for he has a well-known habit of himself adopting in one place those beliefs he has tried to show in other places to be baseless but ineradicable.

Ineradicable or not, the fictional status of the Unity of the self has an intriguing consequence, which is the reason for the exegetical comments in this essay. An emotion that is founded on a fiction is a mistaken or false emotion. Insofar as the ascription of unity to oneself is an inescapable element in the genesis of any of our emotions, then these emotions would seem to be mistaken or false mental states. To decide how far such a sweeping conclusion is justified, we would have to decide whether Hume is right in holding that the unity of the self is a fiction. I cannot undertake this here. I have argued elsewhere that Hume gives no adequate reasons for such a radical doctrine. But he does espouse it; and I think it likely that he introduces the distinction between personal identity as it concerns the thought or imagination, and personal identity as it concerns the passions, in order to prevent any difficult consequence it has from obstructing his account of the passions.

What I wish to do is to see what we can learn from him about the role we give to the idea of the self in our emotional life and in our moral criticisms of it. I wish also to ask what presuppositions have to be made for such roles to be possible. Although Hume's expository separation of the two aspects of personal identity is not enough by itself to clarify these presuppositions, let alone justify them, I shall suggest in conclusion that when the presuppositions are understood, his making the separation in the way that he does is still instructive.

## II

I turn first, then, to the functions that Hume says the idea of one-self discharges in the genesis of the passions. It must be remembered here that Hume regards every passion as a unique and simple impression. Any account that he gives of a passion, therefore, cannot be presented as an analysis of it, since what is simple is unanalysable. It must rather be an account of how such an impression arises and what its results are. An account so circumscribed is bound to be one in which what contemporary philosophers would think of as points of logic appear as psychological accounts of causes and consequences. If we treat them as points of logic (which I shall do) it must be clear that we are not following Hume's own procedure. Hume's psychologism is at all times deliberate, and to translate him into the language of conceptual analysis is to commit an anachronism.[2] So when Hume tells us the role of the idea of the self plays in the passions, he understands this to be a causal role. There are two places where it is prominent: in the genesis of the indirect passions of pride and humility and in the mechanism of sympathy.

The distinction between the direct and the indirect passions is itself a causal distinction. The indirect passions have a more complex origin than the direct ones do. They do not arise merely from 'good or evil, pain or pleasure', but also require the 'conjunction of other qualities' (*T* II. i. 1. 276–7). He lists them as 'pride, humility, love, hatred, envy, pity, malice, generosity, with their dependents'. He explains their special character another way, by saying that they do not only have a *cause* (an 'idea which excites them') but also an *object*, which he describes as 'that to which they direct their view, when excited' (*T* II. i. 2. 278). This looks a quite different way of distinguishing them, but it is not. We can see that it is not when we notice that he tells us that two passions like pride and humility have one and the same object (namely myself), but that the object cannot be 'sufficient *alone*' to excite them. So, paradoxically, both the cause and the object are causes of these passions, and neither is sufficient alone. The pattern is roughly this: that some pleasing fact can give

---

[2] There are indeed one or two places in which he explicitly rejects interpretations that would make logical connections out of what he considers to be causal ones. See e.g. his discussion of the relationships between benevolence and love, and anger and hatred, in *T* II. ii. 6.

me joy, but neither pride nor love; to generate pride or love this pleasing fact (the cause) has to be joined with the idea of myself, in which case it then generates pride, or with the idea of another person, in which case it generates love. If the fact is displeasing, it will give rise to humility if joined with the idea of myself, and hatred if joined with the idea of another. The self or the other person (or, more exactly, the ideas of them) are the objects of these emotions, but it is clear from his account that they are nevertheless to be understood as partial causes of them.

The mechanism of sympathy is one which Hume considers to lead to an imaginative, participatory awareness of the passions of other persons. The process seems to be one in which I first become aware by inference from another person's behaviour that he is experiencing a particular passion. The idea of his passion, however, becomes more lively and gives place to an impression: some sort of counterpart in me of the very passion that he has. Hume clearly thinks that we pass from a mere cognizance of his emotional state to a participation in it by some kind of imitation, a transition that his system incorporates as the enlivening of an originally faint perception into a vivid one. What does the enlivening is the idea of the self. It seems to do it through my recognition of the similarity between the other's mental life and my own. Passions are catching; and the idea of the self is one of the vehicles of the emotional infection.

In spite of the great importance that the mechanism of sympathy has in Hume's theory of the passions and in his moral philosophy, I shall not discuss it here any further. To include it would lead to unnecessary prolixity, when there is no question about the status of the idea of the self in the emotional life that arises exclusively in connection with it. For the mechanism of sympathy, as Hume outlines it, to operate, each of us has to be aware that every other person is a person like himself; but the theory does not help us to spell out the nature of that which is thought to be the same in each one.[3] I will confine my examination to the self-regarding indirect passions of pride and humility. My objective in this is not to carry the exegesis of Book II of the *Treatise* into detail, but to discover the role that the idea of oneself actually plays in these emotional states.

---

[3] Any special problems raised by the doctrine of sympathy are likely to be problems about what I have called the problem of Individuation, which is not my concern here. See Chapter 5.

Indeed, Hume's theoretical framework forces us to leave him behind if we are to avoid misleading ambiguities. I argued above that his distinction between the cause and the object of the indirect passions, is, in spite of appearances, one which he has to treat as a distinction among the causes of those passions because he thinks all passions are distinct and separate impressions. We may think that the point he makes in this way is really a logical one: that whatever we may feel, it cannot be *called* pride unless something pleasing has come into our purview, and is connected with ourselves, and cannot be *called* humility unless something displeasing has come into our purview and is connected with ourselves. Leaving this aside for the present, it is noticeable that Hume is revealingly ambivalent about the nature of the alleged causal sequence that produces pride and humility. While his arguments that the cause and the object are each causal conditions of the passion entail that both precede it, when he sets out the sequence most nearly formally, he places the idea of the self, which he has identified as the object, as an idea that comes to the fore *after* the passion of pride or humility has arisen, not before.[4] This is of course suggested by his calling the object 'that to which they direct their view, when excited'. If they are understood in this way, then pride and humility are passions that make us think about ourselves, not passions that arise in the mind after we do so. Of course, one wants to say, they are both. It is true that I cannot be proud of something unless I presuppose it has some relationship to me; and it is also true that it cannot feed my pride unless it turns my attention *from* itself *to* me. But the trouble is that a linear causal account of the relationship between the self and its qualities and the passions of pride and humility cannot do justice to this. Like all Hume's ambivalences, this one represents his awareness of the complexities of the facts even where his own theories require him to oversimplify them.

For the concepts of pride and humility are not homogeneous. One variation within the concept of pride is reflected in the shift in Hume's causal account of it. I might feel proud of some action or event because of my connection with it, or its with me, on the one hand; or on the other I might be led to reflect on my personal merits by some

---

[4] 'We must suppose, that nature has given to the organs of the human mind, a certain disposition fitted to produce a particular impression or emotion, which we call *pride*: To this emotion she has assigned a certain idea, viz. that of *self*, which it never fails to produce,' (*T* II. i. 5. 287).

pleasing fact that I am responsible for. In general terms, I can on
the one hand be proud *of* something, because of its actual or supposed connection with myself, or, on the other hand, I can have a
general tendency to self-glorification, with its attendant overestimate
of those deeds and qualities that would justify it. In the latter case
the occasion of my pride may not be that of which I am primarily
thinking when I feel it. In the case of humility, the heterogeneity of
the phenomena Hume describes is even more obvious, since, as Árdal
says,[5] one does not feel humble *of* anything; at the most one feels
humble because of it, and the humility one feels is, roughly, a generally low or negative estimate of oneself. What one feels with regard
to the fact that occasions humility here is *shame*.

We can distinguish, then, between pride as general self-satisfaction,
self-glorification, vanity, or arrogance; and pride as directed to
particular facts or events or qualities with which one is connected,
which I shall call particular pride. We can also distinguish between
humility or general self-deprecation, and *shame*, which is directed
to particular facts or events or qualities with which one is connected.[6]
Hume's language and his associative theoretical framework, do
not encourage a sufficiently clear distinction between these, and
different members of each pair seem to be under consideration at
different points in his text.[7] I do not wish to suggest that these distinctions are adequate to do justice to the many ambiguities in
these complex notions, but they are a sufficient beginning for present
purposes.

It is easy to see that they are needed. For one concept in each
pair may apply to situations that exclude the other member of the
pair. Even though it is true that a proud man (one who has a high
estimate of himself) is also someone who is likely to feel proud of
facts or events or qualities connected with himself, and to do so quite
frequently; and while it is true that a humble man (one who has a
low estimate of himself) is someone who is at least readily capable
of shame, the connection is not universal. My self-regard can be fed

[5] Árdal 1966, 33. I am indebted here to the very helpful discussions in ch. 2 of
this work.
[6] The distinction corresponds roughly to the one Ryle makes in ch. 4 of Ryle 1949
between motives and agitations.
[7] The ambiguity comes out nicely in his remark at *T* II. i. 7. 297 that 'by *pride* I
understand that agreeable impression, which arises in the mind, when the view either
of our virtue, beauty or riches or power makes us satisfy'd with ourselves: . . . by *humility* I mean the opposite impression'.

by my shame at particular facts about my actions and circumstances, and can manifest itself in such shame. The man who is too
proud to stoop readily to deceit on his tax form or to stay in a cheap
hotel is the very man who will be ashamed when he does so. My
self-deprecation is not reduced or contradicted by the fact that I am
proud of some things that are connected with me. A poor or
obscure man who is proud of his children's wealth or success is not
necessarily a single step on the road from humility to arrogance when
he feels this; indeed, his very humility may be a major source of the
pride he feels.

## III

I turn first to particular pride, and shame. Here the passion, in a
way which is familiar but hard to define, is directed at the phenomenon
which occasions the arousal of it. The occasion will be what Hume
calls the cause. He holds that the idea of the self is also in some way
indispensable to its arousal. Leaving his associationist psychology for
the more fashionable idiom of informal logic, I shall try to clarify
the role that each plays.

To begin with the occasion, Hume is wrong when he says that the
cause of pride has to give me pleasure, and the cause of shame has
to give me pain. At least, this is wrong if by 'pleasure' we mean 'enjoyment'. I can certainly be proud of very unenjoyable things, such as
paying my tax bill under difficulties, enduring physical pain, or
facing danger; I can also be proud of others doing this, if they are
connected with me, and my being proud does not entail that I find
the contemplation of their doing these things enjoyable. Similarly,
I can be ashamed of things that give me enjoyment, such as eating
food that my diet forbids, or watching movies of violence.

But although Hume is mistaken if he thinks that what occasions
pride is always enjoyable, and what occasions shame is always
disagreeable, he is nevertheless close to some important truth when
he holds that pleasure and pain are in some manner necessary for
pride or shame. In part this just means that being proud and being
ashamed are themselves agreeable or disagreeable mental states (as
when he tells us that 'the sensation of humility is uneasy, as that of
pride is agreeable' (*T* II. i. 5. 288–9)): a proposition of whose universality I am unsure, but which I have no wish to contest. He is

also right in thinking that pleasure and pain, somehow interpreted, play a necessary role in the attitude we take to that which occasions our pride or shame. But this role is not played by enjoyment or dislike. It is played, rather, by our being *pleased* or *displeased.* Those things of which I can be proud but which I do not enjoy are things at which I am still pleased. And those things of which I am ashamed but enjoy, or do not find disagreeable, are still things at which I am displeased. That these are necessary for pride or shame is a logical, and not a psychological, truth.[8] It is not that before I can experience the passion of pride or shame I must first experience the prior passion of pleasure or displeasure, as Hume's account requires: though an insistence on the logical character of the connection does not prohibit such a view either. It is merely that for it to be true that someone is proud or ashamed of something it must be true that that of which he is proud or ashamed is something which pleases or displeases him. He can be pleased or displeased without also being proud or ashamed; but he cannot be proud or ashamed without being pleased or displeased.

What sorts of things can one be pleased or displeased about, and therefore be able to take pride in or feel shame at? In non-Humean language what objects do pleasure and displeasure, and therefore, pride and shame, have? They appear to be ontologically quite heterogeneous: to include physical things, events, abstract objects, facts, qualities, processes, and many more. I can be pleased by my house, my wedding anniversary, the fact that I am a professor, the colour of my eyes, the growth of my bank balance, and innumerable other things. If one were to try for ontological economy, and seek to reduce the categories to one, the only plausible candidate here would seem to me to be that of facts. The plausibility of this choice derives from the apparent ease with which one can translate statements about the objects of one's pleasure or displeasure into statements of an overtly factual form. If I am pleased at my dog's new tricks, then I am pleased (at the fact) that he can perform them. If I am ashamed of losing my job, I am ashamed of the fact that I have lost it. But there are awkward cases, whose significance would be considerable in an ontological debate. If a child is pleased by his new balloon, into what fact or facts is 'his new balloon' to be

---

[8] On the distinction between pleasure as enjoyment and pleasure as being pleased, see Perry 1967; also Penelhum 1964.

translated? Is it the fact that he *has* a new balloon? Is it the fact that his new balloon has a funny face on it, or is red? No particular choice seems required here, even if the disjunction is finite. Fortunately ontology is not our present concern, and my other arguments will not be affected by the view I express. For presentational economy I would suggest the following: for someone to be pleased or displeased at something, either that at which he is pleased or displeased is a fact, *or* there is some fact, of which he is aware, about that which pleases or displeases him without which it would not do so.

Such a formula covers a multitude of problems. One, which can be left unresolved here, is whether one can think one is pleased or displeased by one fact when one is really pleased or displeased by another: can one, that is, misidentify the object of one's pleasure or displeasure? Another difficulty: what if the fact one is pleased or displeased about is not a fact at all, and one is therefore pleased or displeased mistakenly? Here again I ignore ontological complexities, and state that for someone to be pleased or displeased at something, either that at which he is pleased or displeased is a fact, *actual or supposed*, or there is some fact of which he is aware or thinks he is aware about that which pleases or displeases him without which it would not do so. I can ignore the problem of the ontological standing of supposed facts here, as I have ignored the problem of the ontological standing of actual ones. Perhaps actual and supposed facts can be combined into one class, for example, of propositions, so that one should then ponder *their* ontological standing, but I shall not explore this. (It is worth noting that there is at least one obvious difficulty in the way of suggesting that the category used here should be *beliefs*: even if it is true that I cannot be pleased that my horse has won unless I believe that it has, it is not true that it is my belief that it has won that is what I am pleased about.)[9]

It is very common, though probably not necessary, that the fact which pleases or displeases me is subjected by me to some sort of appraisal, for example, a moral or social or economic one. Such an appraisal would furnish the arguments I might subsequently offer if my pleasure or displeasure (or pride or shame) is criticized. It does not seem impossible, however, to feel pleased or displeased

---

[9] One can of course be pleased about one's beliefs: I am pleased that I am not a Conservative. But it is the fact that I hold non-Conservative beliefs that pleases me here, not some supposed fact that those non-Conservative beliefs assert.

at something *simpliciter*, without having appraisive *reasons*: a result of which is that if our pleasure or displeasure is challenged, the best one can do to defend it is show that the critic's contrary appraisal is unfounded, so that even though I was pleased without reason, there is no reason for me to have felt *displeased*, and vice versa. We have to face the fact that at times we seem to feel pleasure at something that we can see we ought to appraise (and therefore in a sense do appraise) negatively, such as a colleague's discomfiture, and it seems doctrinaire to insist that it *must* look good to us if we do.

So much for what it is that can occasion the pleasure and displeasure. Clearly not every case of these is a case of pride or shame. A necessary condition of one of the latter emotions occurring is the connection of that which arouses them with myself. Hume's insight here seems clearly sound; or at least a logical counterpart to it is. Let us now explore it in some detail.

For the present I will leave aside the question of what *sort* of connection with myself a fact I am proud or ashamed of has to have, and will merely illustrate varying ways in which such a connection may be required for these emotions to be possible. We can readily see that what people take pride or shame in varies widely from person to person and from culture to culture.

Let us imagine the case of a prominent member of a tribe whose wife and immediate family are very fat. Let us suppose further that obesity is highly regarded in that tribe as a sign of wealth and leisure. In that culture, then, being fat is thought pleasing—in contrast with our culture, in which slimness in every social class is the norm, so that obesity is found displeasing. This is not by itself enough to make our citizen proud. For he may not share the preferences of his own tribe and may instead share ours. In that case he cannot be proud of his family's girth, because he is not pleased by it, even though everyone else around him may be.

Even though he cannot feel pride if he does not feel pleasure, he does belong to the select group of those who are *entitled* to do so. If only he *did* feel pleased, he could feel proud. Only he, or other members of the family, or their cook, or their doctor, or their banker (if the tribe has a bank) are in the logical position to be able to feel pride as distinct from mere pleasure (what Hume calls joy) or admiration, or other disinterested emotions; and of course only members of this group can feel shame as distinct from distress or contempt. If the tribe is as sophisticated in its sins as our own society is, and if the family is socially prominent, then it might very well happen that other members of the tribe who could not feel pride or shame might say that they do, in order thereby to imply the connection with the family that such a claim would require.

Even though someone is logically in a position to feel proud or ashamed of something, and does in fact feel pleasure or distress at it, he still may not happen to feel pride or shame at it. He may just happen to be the sort of person whose emotions are too disinterested either by nature or by training. It is not true that pleasure plus connectedness entails pride, or that displeasure plus connectedness entails shame. It is only true that pride entails pleasure plus connectedness, and shame entails displeasure plus connectedness.

There are occasions when the connectedness seems to be the only source of the pleasure or the displeasure. It might be that the fat family's cook takes no pleasure in the fact of fatness *per se*, but is pleased by the family's fatness because, and only because, it is due to their enthusiasm for her cuisine. A philosopher might say that it is *really* their enthusiasm for her cuisine that pleases her in that case, and not the fatness it causes, but while one can say this, we do not always do so. Their doctor may be displeased by their fatness, not because he is distressed by such things in themselves, but because such things in his patients reflect unhappily on his ability to get them to listen to his instructions on diet. Here it seems that the fact about the family's obesity which accounts for the cook's pleasure and the doctor's displeasure is simply the fact of its connection with themselves. We can put it by saying that the cook is proud of their obesity, but would not be pleased by it if it were not for its connection with her; that the doctor is ashamed of it, but would not be displeased by it but for its connection with him. (I do not think we can say without paradox that the cook is proud but not pleased, or the doctor ashamed but not displeased; the pride entails the pleasure, the shame the displeasure.) In these cases, although the cook and the doctor have to be aware of the obesity of the family, this fact would not, alone, even generate pleasure or distress; it is the fact of its connection with themselves that produces each—though it might not produce either.

To summarize: for me to feel pride or shame, it is logically requisite that that of which I am proud or ashamed pleases me, or displeases me, and is connected with me. Both are logically necessary; neither singly is sufficient; and in some cases their combination may not be sufficient either. Hume seems mistaken in thinking that each must please or displease me independently of its connection with myself, though no doubt this is often the case. And just as I can be pleased, and therefore can be proud, or can be displeased, and therefore can be ashamed, or a supposed fact as well as an actual one, so I can be proud or ashamed in virtue of a supposed connection with myself as well as an actual one. In such cases the pride or shame can be called mistaken.

I turn now to the question of the nature of the actual or supposed connection that is necessary for pride or shame. Here there are competing temptations. On the one hand there is a strong temptation to say that the connection has to be one that established the fact which I am proud or ashamed of is a fact for which I have some responsibility. On the other hand there is a temptation to hold that any sort of connection is capable of generating these emotions. The second view is nearer the truth than the first. It is possible to hold, as a moral conviction, that one *ought* only to be proud or ashamed of that for which one is responsible, but one must not represent this conviction, even if it is true, as a logical truth. It is indeed sometimes true that looser connections that generate pride or shame carry some imputation of responsibility, as in the case of the snob who is proud that a member of his club has been knighted, and feels in his pride that some of the merit that led to the honour has somehow accrued to himself. But however common such suppositions may be, it is not clear that they are present by necessity, even though they might enable us conveniently to classify such forms of pride or shame as false. Indeed, the humble man who is proud of something connected with himself may remain convinced that the connection he has with it is not one that allows him to take any credit for it, and he may even be proud for that very reason.

So far I have written as though the fact that pleases me when I am proud, and the fact of which I am proud, are one and the same, the pride being consequent upon the connection with myself which the fact has. The last question, however, raises the possibility, which is perhaps more in accord with Hume's analysis, that they are not. Perhaps what I am proud of, in each case, is not the fact which pleases me, but the *fact of my connection* with it. Perhaps to say that Jones is proud of his children's achievements is not to say that the fact that they have these achievements makes him proud, but to say that he is proud of the fact that the people who have these achievements are his children. I do not know how to settle such an issue, given that on either reading it is the fact that they are his children that *makes* him proud. There is perhaps no point in deciding it in most cases. (There may be a point in some: the man who is proud of his ancestors' great deeds is probably proud of the fact that the people who did these great deeds are his ancestors, rather than of the deeds they did.) I shall continue for convenience to follow my previous idiom, in which what I am proud or ashamed of is a fact that generates pride because of its connection with myself, rather than the idiom in which what I am proud or ashamed of is the very fact of this connection.

It would seem, then, that pride or shame can be generated by very varied sorts of connections, Men can feel proud or ashamed that they themselves have performed certain actions, have certain qualities, or own certain possessions, and also of the fact that others related to them, acquainted with them, of their nationality, or of their political affiliation, have performed certain actions or have certain qualities or own certain possessions. This variety is a natural source of moral criticism, to which I will now turn.

Criticisms of the emotions of pride or shame can take many forms. They can be thought to be too great for what occasions them; or not great enough. They can be thought to be morally or aesthetically bad emotions in themselves, so that one ought to strive not to feel them even in situations where the necessary conditions of them are present; or one can be thought emotionally deficient for not feeling them when these conditions obtain. They can be criticized as based on a wrong appraisal of the facts that arouse them. They can be thought inappropriate because the connection with oneself that is needed to arouse them is a connection that is judged to be of a sort that ought not to do so. They can be mistaken, or false, because the supposed facts which arouse them are not facts at all. And they can be mistaken or false because the supposed connection with oneself that helps to arouse them does not exist. I shall comment here only upon the last three types of criticism.

(a) The suggestion that a particular connection with oneself ought not to lead to pride or shame, even though it exists, is a familiar source of moral disputes. Disputants here tend to operate with an implied scale on which certain types of emotional response are paired off with facts to which they are thought appropriate, each disputant seeking to persuade others to adopt his own scale. In the present case argument is likely to proceed, at its best, with the parties agreeing that a certain type of connection would justify pride or shame (such as the connection of a parent with his child, or of a teacher with his pupil) and then comparing this agreed type of connection with the controversial one to see whether the latter lacks some crucial feature. It might be argued, for example, that the affluence of my children is something of which I can be proud, but that of my neighbours is not, since the former connection entails a responsibility for that affluence which is absent from the second.

(b) I can continue being pleased at the actual or supposed fact that *p* only for as long as I continue to believe that *p*. Once the supposition ceases, so does the pleasure at that which is supposed. If pleasure continues, it is necessarily a different one. The same is true of the pride of which pleasure, in this sense, is a condition; and the same reasoning holds for displeasure and the shame that depends upon it. If I am proud because of a false report that my child was top of the class, my pride in his being top necessarily ceases when I find he was not; if I need to go on being proud, then I have to take pride in his being almost top of the class instead. It is easy enough for most of us.

(c) Of greatest importance here is criticism based on the nonexistence of the supposed connections with myself. If I cease to believe in these, then here again my pride or shame necessarily ceases also, and if I believe in them when they do not exist, my pride or shame is mistaken or false. This is also a familiar source of moral disputes and of morally reformist arguments. For example, it is possible in some theologies to hold that all genuinely good human deeds are in fact done not by ourselves as we suppose, but through an infusion of divine grace, so that our pride in our achievements is mistaken because they are not really our achievements. More modestly, it is possible to hold that some of the deeds I am ashamed of in my childhood are deeds which, though they were done by me as I suppose, were in some manner not examples of full agency because of my tender years, so that my shame depends upon a mistaken understanding of the connection they have with myself and should cease to exist after therapy. I may be proud of my supposed descent from Sir Francis Drake, only to discover that my great-grandfather took the name of Drake by deed poll. Where a connection is still thought to exist, but merely not to be the one imagined, it is of course quite possible that the pride or shame could continue, with greater, less, or identical intensity. I may, for example, continue to feel pride in my ancestry if I discover that it does derive from Drake, but does so illegitimately.

The questions of error we have just considered take on a particularly intriguing form when we ask if they can be produced by errors about the nature of the very self with which the facts that arouse pride or shame are thought to be connected. The connections, whatever they are, have to be connections with the being feeling the pride or the shame. If these connections logically require a continuity of the self through time that it in fact lacks, then the pride or shame that depends on the positing of these connections is always mistaken. This would not prove the absurd conclusion that such pride and shame never occur; only that they always depend on a false supposition of personal identity.

Read strictly, Hume is committed to this view. The sorts of connections that are required for pride and shame are either the kind that make the occasions of these emotions earlier items in the same personal biography that later includes the emotions themselves, or they are connections that in other ways require the identity of the self at the time of the emotion with the bearer of his name at some earlier stage—such as the connection between the presently proud teacher and the earlier instructor of his now brilliant student. When Hume tells us that personal identity is a fiction he tells us, strictly speaking, that the condition of such connections is never met. Of course we all believe that it is met, since we all share the conventional belief in the Unity of the person; and he tells us in Book I why he thinks we do this. Our error is what makes the self-regarding passions possible, and of course they will reinforce it once it is made. They do not produce it. Hume does not refer to them when he tells us how the error is first entrenched. It comes from the 'thought or imagination'. But once it is entrenched, the many emotional states it makes possible help to make it even less likely than ever that we will heed the sceptic when he points the error out to us.

The sceptic is in fact wrong, and the conventional ascription of self-identity is not shown to be fictitious by the sorts of consideration Hume advances for this; but this is not the place to argue this. Hume himself talks in Book II as though the problem of the Unity of the person has been solved, and such Unity has been established, not merely as though the fiction of it has been explained. Unless we are prepared to accept the falsity of *all* pride and shame we have to follow him in thinking that the problem has a solution, whatever that solution is.

Whatever it is, we must also follow him in thinking it has to come from the thought or imagination, and not from the passions themselves; for they require it, and so cannot produce it. At least, it cannot come from the consideration of those passions whose freedom from falsity depends on what the answer is. The fact that I feel proud or ashamed of something that I believe I did, and which someone did do, does not show that I did it. The pride or shame does not show its own freedom from falsity; it only guarantees the fact of my belief. And the fact that I feel indifference rather than pride or shame does not show the lack of a connection either. Indifference can also be mistaken: both in the sense that some other attitude may be more appropriate, and in the sense that it may depend on a false belief about what occurred, or about its connection, or lack of connection, with myself.

The appropriateness of the emotion depends on what the facts are and what their connections with the self are believed to be. The correctness or falsity of the emotion depends on the truth or falsity of these beliefs. We cannot justify one emotion, or discredit its alternatives, without independently establishing what the facts are, and what their connections with the self are. For the latter to be possible there have to be independent criteria of personal identity which determine the self's temporal boundaries. Even in the subjectivity of the emotions, this much psychological objectivity is necessary.

Nothing in the above proves that the self's boundaries have to be drawn where we conventionally draw them (wherever this is). It could be that some things that are conventionally classified as part of my past might not have been, or might in the future not be—conventions are not immutable. It might even be that an argument for changing them could be mounted on the very bases I have outlined. It would go somewhat as follows: it is indeed true that I cannot, in logic, be proud or ashamed of what has no connection with me. It is also true that the closer the connection some fact has with me, the more nearly universal is the agreement that it is something that it is morally appropriate, or is reasonable, to be proud or ashamed of. Hence something that, for instance, my immediate ancestor did is something it is more generally agreed I can be proud of, or ashamed of, than is something done by a remote ancestor. Now by convention something done in my youth has a closer connection with me, even in middle age or old age, than something done by even my most recent ancestor; for it was, after all, done by *me*, not by someone else. Hence, pride or shame at it is as appropriate here as it will ever be. But let us now reflect that pride in my past actions can readily lead to moral rigidity and self-righteousness, and shame at my past actions can readily lead to pathological guilt. Both of these are notoriously undesirable. So although the pride or the shame are prima facie appropriate, they are not appropriate *all things considered*. A person is best able to make his contribution to a changing society if he is not emotionally burdened by his past. Here then, we have excellent moral grounds for changing the temporal boundaries of the self. If we drew these boundaries more narrowly we could generate a convention in which a middle-aged man's youthful actions were classified roughly as the actions of his immediate ancestor are now classified: as the deeds of an earlier self. This would loosen the conventional connections by making it less appropriate to be proud or ashamed of those actions: a man would be as free of reflected glory or disgrace from what is now thought of as his own past as he now is free of reflected glory or disgrace from the past doings of his progenitors.

It is tempting to say that this argument is incoherent. For if it is the case that we judge such emotional involvements with past actions as undesirable or inappropriate, and that is the reason for changing the conventions, does it not follow from this that the undesirability of such involvement is discernible on the basis of our *present* conventions? And if someone takes the opposite moral view, and thinks that emotional involvement with such past performances is a good thing, can he not enforce *his* moral preferences on the proposed conventions as well as on the present ones, by insisting that one ought to feel just as proud or ashamed of the doings of an ancestor self who inhabited one's present body as one feels of the recent doings of the present self that inhabits it? Does the proposal not shift the weight of a moral decision onto a conventional one?

I think these criticisms would indeed be sound, but I do not see that they would show the proposed conventional change to be incoherent. They merely show it to be at best morally pointless, and at worst morally undesirable. I shall now, however, change the proposal in order to produce one that is more philosophically sophisticated, and more tempting, but which I want to argue *is* incoherent.[10]

We can produce it by making use of some of the arguments that Hume offers in Book I. There Hume does not only say that our conviction of self-identity is erroneous, but gives an account of what generates the supposed error. The causes he lists do not include emotional causes, but we can generate our imaginary proposal if we extend his account to include these. He stresses that the bundle or collection of different perceptions that is a person's life history is one that reveals on examination a large number of interrelationships between the perceptions within it. It is these interrelationships that help to disguise the diversity of the contents of the mind from us, and reinforce our belief in its fictional identity. It is their existence to which he draws our attention when he compares the self to a republic or commonwealth. One such interrelationship, on his view, is memory, in which a later perception is a derivative copy of an earlier one. Now it is clear that he might very well say (though in Book I he does not) that some later perceptions are emotional responses to earlier ones. Let us say this for him; and let us now add the suggestion that these relationships are themselves reasons for ascribing identity to the series that includes them. If we think of the relationships as grounds for ascribing identity, it is plausible, though of course not necessary, to add that their absence might be a reason for withholding such an ascription. The analogy with memory is very seductive here, at least for anyone who is prepared to hold that some memory connections with one's own past are necessary and not merely sufficient grounds for calling it one's own. We now have an argument for the view that the emotional concern I show for events in my past is one of the factors that make them a part of it; and that an emotional or emotionless, detachment from it, or in more fashionable parlance an alienation from it, is a ground for not so regarding it. So if I do not feel either proud or ashamed of the deeds of my youth, this is itself a reason for not calling them mine but merely calling them the doings of an ancestral self that used to occupy the body that I now have.

---

[10] My arguments at this stage in the essay run parallel to some criticisms I made of Parfit's famous essay 1971*b* (in Penelhum 1971*a*; see also Parfit's response 1971*a*). Since Parfit's views have since found much fuller expression in Parfit 1984, it is important to stress that in this essay my target was, and remains, a strawperson of my own invention, whose views are at most suggested to me by Parfit's.

Such a view would have strong appeal to someone who disapproves of emotional absorption in one's past doings. It differs critically from the position I outlined earlier that was also intended to reflect that sort of disapproval. In addition to the major premise that states the undesirability of such absorption, it offers a minor premise to the effect that the later pride and humility help to constitute the identity of the person feeling them with the person who performed those deeds. Consequently the freedom from emotional involvement with one's past that previously appeared as a desirable consequence of the proposed conventional change cannot appear now as a consequence of it at all, but as a condition of the proposed convention having application. So the sense of remoteness and emotional distance that we sometimes experience when we recall our past may be sufficient to constitute a severance from it. And the emotional closeness that pride or shame in it involve may be what keeps it attached to us, like a shell.

There is much in our talk of moral rebirth, conversion, self-estrangement, and even (in its nonphilosophical sense) self-identity, which can, if carelessly interpreted, give such a proposal plausibility. Such talk, however, abounds in metaphor, and to serve its present function, metaphor it must remain. For such language is the language of moral criticism and reformation; and this is a language in which men who vary greatly in their degree and type of emotional concern with their pasts, are judged and compared according to a critic's standards. To apply standards to a group it is requisite that its members be comparable in relevant respects. And men would not be comparable in respect of their estimates and evaluations of their pasts if the nature of those responses themselves determined whether they were their pasts or not. Nor would indifference be an attitude that could be weighed against pride or shame as it has to be if it severed the identity of the agent and they created it. An emotion cannot be well or ill grounded if it creates the grounds on which it is to be judged. It is one thing to say that our concern for our pasts is a burden from which we should be freed, but another thing altogether to say that to eliminate the concern is to eliminate one of its occasions. It is true, of course, that we can be proud or ashamed both of what we regard as part of our own past and of what we regard as connected with ourselves in looser ways. But this does nothing to show that the presence or absence of these emotions, or their strength or weakness, can be a criterion of which type of connection an event or action has.

Perhaps it ought not to be thought important, in judging an emotion, whether what it is a response to is part of the history of the man who has it. This is a moral and not a conceptual thesis. Perhaps it is more important that something leads to certain emotional responses in a man than that it is connected to him by the chain of identity. This too is a moral and not a conceptual thesis. Neither thesis is assisted by the suggestion that the character of the emotional response, or its absence, determines whether it is part of his past or not. On the contrary, both are hindered, for they can only be discussed if there is common agreement on what the criteria are for deciding which things belong to a man's past and which do not.

## IV

I turn now, more briefly, to the much vaster subject of pride and humility as self-glorification and self-deprecation. These are not naturally spoken of as passions at all, and it is not to Hume that one turns in the first instance for an analysis of them.[11] What follows here will consequently be much more loosely connected with Hume's text than what has gone before.

While particular pride and shame are emotional states of moderate duration, and what one is particularly proud or ashamed of is something connected with oneself, pride and humility are normally of longer duration, and are not episodes in their own right at all. One cannot be suffused with them or overcome by them as one can be with their particular counterparts. One cannot be humble of anything, and the idiom 'proud of . . .' is one whose use indicates particular pride, except in the case of the expression 'proud of himself' which may be ambiguous. For to be proud or humble is to estimate oneself very highly or very modestly. It is clear that this estimate has as its object the very subject who makes it, not mere facts connected with him. These facts serve rather as the grounds on which the high or low estimate could be justified. (In this role, incidentally, their ontological heterogeneity, or the appearance of it, vanishes; for

---

[11] I must admit some temptation to agree with Robert Payne's judgement that 'When Hume writes of pride in *A Treatise of Human Nature*, he is like a man scrambling for shellfish among the rocks' (Payne 1960, 142). A Humean concern for detail, however, might have saved Payne from going on to say that Hume's 'dullness' shows us that 'the English (*sic*) have failed to understand pride through most of their history'.

things and processes and events only serve in the creation of grounds for anything as constituents of the facts that constitute such grounds.) It is likely that the proud man will feel proud of his own past actions, or his connections, and the humble man feel ashamed of his; but exceptions to this are readily intelligible in specific cases.

The relationship of pride and humility to pleasure and pain is difficult. I have suggested that particular pride and shame entail, if they are not even species of, being pleased and displeased. It is noticeable that there are contexts in which being pleased and displeased are not properly describable as emotional states. Sometimes each seems merely to consist of a favourable or unfavourable appraisal, rather than the emotional condition resulting from it. When the committee says it is pleased to note that the budget is balanced, it is expressing a favourable appraisal of this fact, not recording some emotional state into which its members have been thrown by it. In this context pleasure and displeasure seem to become acts of judgement, not passive emotional conditions that happen to someone. It is in this way that one could say that pleasure and pride, and displeasure and humility, are related: that if I am proud, then I am pleased with myself in that I rate myself favourably, and if I am humble then I am displeased with myself in that I rate myself unfavourably. The pride and the humility are the favourable and unfavourable estimate. The fact that I estimate myself highly causes me to enjoy what I do more, and the fact that I estimate myself poorly causes me to enjoy what I do less, so the proud life is in this distinct sense pleasanter, more enjoyable, than the humble one.

Complexities and ambiguities abound with both notions. Pride is often discussed in theological contexts as though it included all forms of inordinate self-concern or self-absorption, not only those that involve a high estimate of oneself. One very common form of such self-absorption is obsession with one's own inadequacies, so that one can find oneself speaking of some apparent forms of humility as examples of pride in this sense! It is this very extended understanding of pride as self-centredness that makes it plausible to argue that concupiscence or sensuality are derivatives of it, in the sense that losing oneself in the concerns of the world and the flesh is a means of hiding one's limitations from one's own sight.[12]

---

[12] This very broad extension of the idea of pride is present, for example, in Niebuhr 1949, vol. 1, chs. 7 and 8.

Similarly with humility, though the ambiguities here are less serious. In theological contexts, again, the concept is sometimes widened to cover all cases of the absence of self-absorption, and it is in this wide sense that it is held to be requisite for love or faith. But since such states are also, in such contexts, said to be the fruits of grace rather than the products of unaided human nature, it is also common to hear that humility in the narrower sense of holding oneself in low esteem, is a necessary concomitant of their appearance. I have to leave these matters aside, and I turn instead to some of the possible criticisms to which pride and humility are subject.

(1) They can be the target of general moral or theological objections. It can be held, for example, that all high estimates of oneself are morally evil, or all low estimates are morally debilitating. Or it can be held that some degree of such estimation is in order, but that marked degrees of the one or the other are never appropriate. Such criticisms, however, are likely to be supported by alleged facts about the nature of human beings which men are said to overlook, for example, that they are finite, or created, or have a will to power which is conventionally suppressed.

(2) There can be specific criticisms of the factual presuppositions of the high or low estimate: that the man's achievements are less than imagined, or his motives mixed, or his motivation not charity but fear. Such criticisms imply that if the facts were as they are imagined by the estimator to be, the pride or the humility would be morally acceptable.

(3) There can be criticisms based on the view that some of the facts that serve to support the pride or humility are not of a kind that should do so—again, this type of argument would take the form, as a rule, of a concentration on the differences between these facts and others that the critic accepts as justifying the high or low appraisal. Here pride because of one's wealth (as opposed to particular pride *in* one's wealth) might be criticized by contrast with pride based on political achievements.

(4) Most importantly for our present purposes, there can be criticisms that concentrate on the relation of the facts that support the estimate to the person who is making it.

These can take three forms: (a) The critic can say that the facts that would justify the high or low appraisal of myself are not facts about *me*—that I did not perform these deeds, but other people, or that the ancestry or association I lay claim to is spurious. (b) He may say that even though the connections with myself are as I believe them to be, they are not the sort of connections with myself that justify my self-estimate: that pride or humility is perhaps justifiable if I have certain achievements or character, but not if based on my ancestor's or fellow members' achievements, even though these may be related to me in the way I say. (c) He may base his attack on an analysis of the self which precludes the identity of the proud or humble man and the bearers of the merits and defects that he claims to be his.

Taken strictly, Hume's analysis of the self in Book I would provide the basis for an attack of the last sort. For if it is correct, the unity ascribed to the person through time is fictitious, and anything done by, or connected with, an earlier stage of a person cannot in consequence, be ascribed to, or said to have the same connection with, a later stage. This would not preclude pride and humility from occurring, but it would make them ineluctably groundless, for they would presuppose that the object of the high or low estimate the subject made incorporated stretches of personal history that it could not incorporate. All other criticisms of pride and humility would be ruled out if this were true, and since Hume recognizes that our self-estimates all proceed as if it were false, he too assumes the truth of his own alleged fiction in his account of pride and humility.

There is an interesting historical contrast to Hume's procedure, one which would have surprised Hume if he had been aware of it, and which has been noticed since. I refer to the doctrines of the Buddha.[13] Buddha is said to have argued that the Hindu view of the self as identical with the cosmic soul is false, somewhat as Hume rejects substantial analyses of the self. And just as Hume infers from the absence of a pure ego that the Unity of the individual which pure ego theories are designed to supply is mythical, so Buddha is said to have gone beyond the denial of the identity of the eternal *atman* to the denial of the conventional belief in the persisting identity of the individual. Such conventional belief is an example of *avidya*, or ignorance, and is a major source of the compulsive craving that is the source of human misery. For only if the self has some degree of

---

[13] The likeness between the Humean and Buddhist doctrines of the self has certainly been noticed before. It is discussed at length in Jacobson 1966. Parfit 1984 claims affinities with the Buddhist tradition (on which see Haksar 1991). For a detailed study of the *anatta* doctrine, see Collins 1982.

permanence does the grasping of things to it hold any intelligible promise of satisfaction. The realization (not of course merely an intellectual matter) that the permanence is not there, that instead there is, as it were, only a hole in the middle, is part of the progress to enlightenment which ultimately releases the soul from craving and the misery attendant upon the service of it. This doctrine parallels strikingly the Augustinian derivation of sensuality from pride as the primal sin.

Hume's response to a similar metaphysical predicament is quite opposite. He finds the supposed falsity of the belief in the unity of the person a source of bewilderment and anxiety, and the only cure for the malaise that a sceptical concentration upon it produces is the careless acceptance of the fiction with which we disguise its falsity from ourselves, and the immersion in the life of passion and social intercourse which the acceptance of this fiction makes possible. Instead of nirvana, there is backgammon. So in Book II, the bewilderments of Book I are left behind.

If we take the view, as I would, that Hume's perplexity is groundless, and that he has not demonstrated the falsity of our belief in the unity of a person, this does not of itself free us from the need to consider philosophical attempts to question our right to draw the boundaries of the history of individual persons in the ways that we actually draw them, whatever these may be. When this is recognized, we are open once more to the suggestion that our moral and emotional lives would benefit from their being drawn differently. So we can now imagine a parallel to the forms of conceptual revisionism that I imagined earlier when discussing the relationship between particular pride and shame and self-identity. It could be said that our self-estimates might change if they were made in a different context, in which a person was thought to have a past in which those actions or characteristics now included within it were not included, or in which other such actions or characteristics were included which are not included now. I would say here, as before, that a recommendation for conventional change based on this possibility is not incoherent, but is either undesirable or pointless. It could be said, second, that the very presence of such self-estimates now ought to be construed as reasons for including those actions and characteristics offered as grounds for them, and their absence construed as a reason for not including them. I would say here, as before, that such a suggestion makes the character of such judgements one of the conditions of the propriety of their having that character, and thus removes them from the sphere of detached criticism.

In conclusion: Hume may have distinguished between personal identity as it concerns the thought or imagination, and personal identity as it concerns our passions, merely in order to prevent the sceptical perplexities of Book I from obtruding themselves in Book II. But if we are free of those perplexities we can see that his distinction was a wise one for more than tactical reasons. For whatever the span of the self is taken to be, our emotional life, or that part of it which we have scrutinized here, requires for its logical structure that the span of the self is given. And criticism of the emotional life requires this also. What I take to be myself determines what I can be proud or ashamed of, and not the reverse. The personal identity that concerns the passions has to be one and the same as the personal identity that concerns the thought or imagination. But it is the thought or imagination, and not the passions, that have to determine its boundaries.

# 5

# The Self of Book I and
# the Selves of Book II

ONE of the more familiar problems of interpretation in Hume's *Treatise* is that of reducing the sense of shock that arises from the apparent differences between what he says about the self in Book I and what he says about it in Book II. One way in which scholars have attempted to reduce it is to take him very seriously when he distinguishes, in the Book I discussion, 'betwixt personal identity, as it regards our thought or imagination, and as it regards our passions or the concern we take in ourselves' (*T* I. iv. 6. 253). If one does this, it becomes possible to see that what might seem to be inconsistent positions are compatible, and merely represent complementary aspects of an extended account of how human beings represent their natures and identities to themselves in thought and feeling and choice.

This, at least, is now widely believed. The belief has led to very illuminating accounts of Hume's analysis of the emotional life and its relationship to his more famous theories in epistemology.[1] In spite of these, I think there is an egregious gap in Hume's psychology which we should not be tempted to suppose he has filled. Unless I have misread them, two recent authors have yielded to this very temptation.

## I

Since I have said Hume's psychology has an important gap in it, I should begin by making clear what the gap is, and emphasize that

---

[1] There is now a good deal of literature that demonstrates the value of taking Hume's distinction seriously. I think, for example, of McIntyre 1989, Baier 1991, ch. 6, Chazan 1992, and Ainslie 1999. This essay is intended only to suggest that the insights these scholars find in Hume do not fill the gap in his system to which I wish to draw attention.

I do not think I have uncovered an *inconsistency* in Hume's theories of the self. He has, of course, been accused of such inconsistencies.[2] His account in Book I has itself been said to be inconsistent because he ascribes to the self there a tendency to confuse invariance and succession in telling us how we come to generate the fiction of continuing identity; such a story seems to ascribe a continuing reality to the mind in the very process of showing how the belief in it can come to exist when there are only successive perceptions to constitute it. This is a special application of a wider charge sometimes levelled against him, that although his associationism appears to reduce all explanation to relationships between perceptions, he is bound to depart from this restriction in ascribing tendencies and mistakes to the mind. Given the nature of the belief he is explaining when he discusses self-identity, the special application is troubling.[3] He has also been accused of inconsistency in assuming at the outset of his discussion of the indirect passions in Book II that we have an idea, or even an impression, of the self, when in Book I he has appeared to deny this.

Many have argued (and I have been among them) that Hume can be acquitted of these charges. Mercer, for example, has made short work of the last one (Mercer 1972: 27–30). When Hume introduces the self in Book II he says clearly that he is referring to 'self, or that succession of related ideas and impressions, of which we have an intimate memory and consciousness' (*T* II. i. 2. 277), not to the idea of the pure ego constructed by rationalist philosophers. The charge of confusion in the argument of *T* I. iv. 6 has been rebutted by several writers, beginning with Nelson Pike (Pike 1967, McIntyre 1979). In the briefest summary: since the mind is nothing but a series of perceptions, Hume's question in Book I is not a question about how it is that a mind he tacitly assumes to be more than this comes to think it *is* more than this, but a question about how the series that the mind actually is, comes to include within it from time to time perceptions *of* the series that represent it as having an identity that it (strictly) lacks. The actual relationship of the mind to its perceptions is one of inclusion, and Hume's puzzle is how certain perceptions *of* the mind come to be *in* the mind. This reading of Hume may well leave him with some unattractive problems, but it does not convict him of contradicting himself.

[2] See, for example, Passmore 1952, 82–3, and MacNabb 1951, 251.
[3] On this wider question, see Wolff 1966 and Wilson 1979.

If something like this is accepted, we can see Hume in Book I as combining scepticism about philosophical defences of a natural belief with the assumption of an obligation to give an account of how our nature generates the belief. The belief is one which he, as a human being, holds himself, and one which he regards it as a 'vain' philosophical exercise to question. He can therefore consistently leave it unquestioned throughout, and perhaps must do so. Instead of a neo-Cartesian attempt at justification, Hume offers us here, as he does in the case of our belief in outer objects and in natural necessities, an account of the belief's origin that gives it what we may call psychological intelligibility.

But the shock of transition from Book I to Books II and III does not go away when these considerations are recognized. In the latter two books, Hume deals with the whole range of human motives and feelings, and with the basic requirements of social life and morality. To do this, he has to draw on a far wider range of beliefs than those he considers in Book I. By the time we reach Book III, we find a Hume who is no longer examining how individuals confined to their perceptions[4] form the view of a world of causally-related objects and a unified mind in spite of this limitation, but a Hume who is examining the effects on individual conduct and choice of social convention, property rights, and promise-making. We have moved, as Nicholas Capaldi puts it, from someone who starts from an 'I think' (or Cartesian) perspective to someone who holds a 'We do' (or social constructivist) perspective (Capaldi 1989). Many problems of Hume interpretation come from the fact that Hume has both of these perspectives; the link between them is Hume's science of man, which shows us how instinct saves us from the immobility that the 'I think' perspective would impose on us if we were primarily rational beings as Descartes and his followers maintained. Instinct supplies us with the beliefs we have to have in order to think and act as members of society.

The science of man, to provide this link, has to begin as individual psychology, and can only develop gradually into the more clearly social science that we find in Book III and again in the second *Enquiry*. It is natural to suppose, ever since Kemp Smith and Árdal, that the place to look for the key linkages that hold the whole system

---

[4] Note particularly *T* I. ii. 6, 67–8.

together is Book II (Smith 1941, Árdal 1966, Baier 1991). Indeed it is. But I want to suggest we need to be careful not to overestimate what we can find there.

## II

I referred earlier to the distinction Hume makes in *T* I. iv. 6 between personal identity 'as it regards our thought and imagination' and personal identity 'as it regards our passions or the concern we take in ourselves'. The context of this remark makes it clear that he is only to concern himself with the former ('The first is our present subject'), and that what he says later about the self and the passions will at most contribute incidentally to the understanding of how we come to attribute identity to the mind. He does mention it once more in Section VI, when he tells us that 'our identity with regard to the passions serves to corroborate that with regard to the imagination, by the making our distant perceptions influence each other, and by giving us a present concern for our past or future pains or pleasures' (*T* I. iv. 6. 261): that is, the life of the passions creates relationships among the perceptions that compose our inner life that reinforce our tendency to view them as part of one life.[5] But the key word in this sentence is 'corroborate'. The psychological work of establishing the belief in self-identity is primarily the work of the understanding and imagination, and the life of the passions only reinforces it.

In earlier work I have argued that although Hume offers us an account of how we come to believe in the unity of the self, he does not ever seem to address the question of how we come to believe in the reality of the distinction between oneself and others—what I referred to as the problem of individuation, as distinct from that of unity.[6] Hence, although Hume can be acquitted of inconsistency in his psychological account of how we come to believe in the unity of the self, there is still a large gap in his system: he tells us nothing about how we come to have the essential distinction between the self whose unity (or rather the belief in whose unity) he does explain, and the existence of other selves with whom we have to do. This,

---

[5] On this theme see McIntyre 1989.
[6] See Chapters 3 and 4, and Penelhum 1976.

again, does not show any inconsistency between Books I and II, but it does leave without explanation the acquisition of a fundamental distinction that is required for the emotional life he tells us about in the latter. I suggested one might speculatively construct some such account by combining what he says about our belief in external objects with what he says about the self's unity; but this would indeed be speculative construction, and it is not done for us by Hume himself.

I still think this is true. But a contrary view appears to be suggested by some comments of Capaldi, and Robert S. Henderson has explicitly claimed that Hume answers the problem of other selves in his account of the indirect passions.[7] I would like to look at how Hume does in fact make use of the idea of the self there, to see if perhaps there is any case for thinking that his earlier remark about distinguishing the two aspects of the idea of the self should be read in a way different from that I have accorded it here. Is there a case for thinking that Hume believes that the mechanisms that generate the passions explain how we come to recognize that we belong to a community of perceivers and agents?

### III

Hume says a great deal about the role played by the idea of the self in the mechanism that generates pride, humility, love and hatred. Self is said to be the *object* of the first two of these passions. Hume distinguishes carefully between the object of a passion and its cause. The cause, he says (*T* II. i. 2. 278) is that which excites the passion, and the object is that to which the passions direct their view, when excited. He introduces this by saying that the self cannot be their cause 'or be sufficient *alone* to excite them' (my italics). I think his phrasing here shows it to be a mistake to think that the idea of the self is not itself a condition (or cause) of pride or humility; it merely shows it cannot be the only condition, and that something else (what we may call the exciting cause) is needed also. But if we pursue the cause-object distinction in the text, it seems to suggest more.

For example: 'The first idea, that is presented to the mind is that of the cause or productive principle. This excites the passion connected with it; and that passion, when excited, turns our view to

---

[7] Henderson 1990, 42. On Capaldi, see n. 13 below.

another idea, which is that of self. Here then is a passion plac'd betwixt two ideas, of which the one produces it, and the other is produc'd by it. The first idea, therefore, represents the *cause*, the second the *object*, of the passion' (*T* II. i. 2. 278). This seems to say something strange: that the idea of the self is the *product* of the passion. (And it seems to do so in language that implies that the idea of another would be the product of the passion of love or hatred.)

Again, in *T* II. i. 5, where Hume gives us the mechanics of pride in some detail, he describes the following sequence: (i) a perceived quality of a thing or person, or the thought of it, (ii) a pleasant sensation, (iii) the similarly agreeable impression of pride (via the association of impressions), (iv) the idea of oneself, as the object of pride. This also seems to say clearly that the object of pride is something the passion produces.

But let us now look at another passage, at *T* II. i. 6. 292, where Hume explains the difference between pride and joy: 'In order to excite pride, there are always two objects we must contemplate, viz. the *cause*, or that object which produces pleasure; and self, which is the real object of the passion. But joy has only one object (*sic*) necessary to its production, viz. that which gives pleasure . . .' This suggests a different relationship between the idea of the self and the passion, a relationship in which the contemplation of the self is something that helps to produce pride, and is not produced by it. How could we need to 'contemplate' the self in order to feel pride if the idea of the self is something the pride produces?

There is an obvious reply to this difficulty. Both Hume's statements are true. When I feel proud, the emotion does indeed turn my thoughts to myself. And it does that because I am aware that what has made me feel proud is some quality or object that is connected with myself. I feel proud when I am struck by the beauty of *my* house, or am pleased by the charm or success of *my* daughter.

Yes. But the problem is that the two facts, both obvious, have to be accommodated into one sequential account, couched in the language of Hume's associationism. Perhaps this could have been done better if Hume had said something which he clearly implies and which looks true, namely that the object of pride is, after all, also one of its causes, and insert the appearance of the idea of the self *both* before *and* after that of the impression of pride. But the complexity and artificiality of this would have been very great, and it is not surprising that Hume has not done it.

Hume has to presuppose that someone who feels pride already knows that the phenomenon that generates it is something related to him or her self, as well as that he or she is turned toward a contemplation of the self by the stimulus of that phenomenon. As the statement at *T* II. i. 6. 292 indicates, he is fully aware of this, even though he does not insert the fact as an item in the sequence (between (i) and (ii)?). But this shows that we have to read the account he does give in a way that makes it clear that although the idea of the self is 'produced' by pride in the sense that it is *called up* by it, it has in every instance to be an idea that we have and use already. It needs to be *in our repertoire*. There is no way in which the mechanism of pride and humility could be the *origin* of our consciousness of the distinction between ourselves and others; for it requires us already to have that consciousness.

## IV

I do not think that Hume makes any suggestion that he is accounting in these passages for the fact that we have the self–other distinction. He does, certainly, say (at *T* II. i. 3. 280 and again at *T* II. i. 5. 286) that the connection between pride and humility and the self is natural and original, but he seems merely to be telling us in these places that it is an ultimate fact that pride and humility direct our attention to the self (a fact that many would now be inclined to explain as a logical truth). He is not, as far as I can tell, saying that the presence of the idea of the self and others in our repertoire, is an ultimate fact in the same way; and given his views about the origin of ideas in Book I, we might expect him to entertain some theory about this, since he is so forthcoming about other aspects of the idea of the self there. So I think that he merely holds it to be natural and original that pride calls up the idea of the self, not that the associative mechanism of pride is the origin of that idea's existence in our minds.

Whether or not Hume's treatment of the self in Book two is compatible with what he says about it in Book I (and I think it is), I see no reason for supposing that what he says about its role in the mechanism of the indirect passions is, or is intended to be, an explanation of how we *get* the idea of the self as distinct from others—of how we individuate. We have to be able to do this in order to feel pride or humility or love or hatred. These passions do not, either in fact or in Hume's theory, create this capacity retroactively.[8]

I have not shown some hitherto unnoticed weakness in the argument of Book II. I have merely sought to show that that argument does not have a recently suggested strength. There are indeed many respects in which it does build vital bridges between the epistemological quandaries of Book I and the social theories of Book III. But it does not contain any answer to the psychological question of how we come to recognize that our own perceptions are indeed our own only, and that there are a large number of other selves too. It presupposes, from the outset, that we already know (or believe) this, and can make our discriminations accordingly.

In the course of his difficult but important discussion of the idea of the self in the *Treatise*, Capaldi makes the point that the idea of the self is not a simple idea but a complex one, because it represents a succession of related ideas and impressions, and is therefore not one which Hume denies we have when denying the reality of the idea of the pure ego. He then says there are two questions to consider with regard to the real-but-complex idea of the self, viz. how is the idea acquired? and what are the relationships among the impressions and ideas that compose the self? This is followed by the statement that 'the answer to the first question is that the complex idea of the self emerges originally in action as the object of the indirect passions of pride and humility'. In a note he adds, 'It is through others that we come to learn about ourselves' (Capaldi 1989: 170 and 347 n). I do not deny either of these claims, or their importance. But although the idea of the self may *emerge* when Capaldi says it does, and although the ways we think of ourselves and take concern for ourselves are indeed largely formed through our interaction with others and our sympathetic resonance with their emotional lives, it does not seem to me that, even if we confine ourselves strictly to Hume's own account of these matters, we can see, in either of these important facts, an explanation of how we come to discriminate between ourselves and others. Hume has given us no direct account of this, and therefore has not answered Capaldi's first question.

---

[8] I take it to be self-evident that the passions of pride and humility require not merely the idea of the self itself, but the idea of the self as distinct from others. Hume of course asumes this when he tells us how, in sympathy, our pride is augmented by the attitudes others have towards us.

V

There are other important aspects of Hume's comments on the nature of the self in Books II and III that I must emphasize I am not denying, or even criticizing. Annette Baier rightly stresses the importance of his remark at *T* II. ii. 5. 365 that our minds are 'mirrors to one another', and makes clear in her comments on it how many profound dimensions there are to Hume's conviction that only social life can cure the solipsistic sceptical melancholy of Book I (Baier 1991: 136). I would like to acknowledge and use this interpretative insight.

The mechanism of sympathy is commonly treated by commentators as a way of accounting for my concern for others. This of course is true; but when Hume first introduces it in *T* II. i. 11, he uses it as a 'secondary' cause of the self-regarding passions of pride and humility. They emerge in part through the opinions of others. *I* share, through sympathy, in the admiration of *me* expressed by others. My pride in my own achievements is, at least secondarily, the doing of others (if 'doing' is the word) as well as my own.[9] So the story of pride and humility, thus augmented by the sympathetic mechanism, is an account of how our *concern* for ourselves is fed by our awareness of others and their passions. This story is naturally embellished when one attends to the fact that one is loved (that is, in Hume, admired and praised) *for* those qualities that Hume calls the causes of the passions others direct toward me as their object: I will ascribe to myself those qualities for which others admire (or despise) me.[10] Hence they create, partly or even wholly, aspects of the self that is the object of my concern. They are the sources of my own self-image. The self ('as it concerns the passions') is a social construction.

The self thus constructed will be physical and visible, as Baier points out.[11] It will often not come to have pride or humility in its qualities, until after others claim to perceive them and praise them or condemn their absence. It may not even *possess* them before then. I may, for example, simulate and cultivate a quality that others would praise

---

[9] This seems clearly to imply that phenomenologically love and pride are the same, differing only in their objects.

[10] See Chazan 1992 for a reconstruction of the processes that Hume's theory postulates.

[11] Baier 1990, 139 f. See *T* II. i. 8. 302 for an example.

in order to preclude their blaming me for not having it; I may, that is, internalize a social demand that reaches me through the praise and censure of other people. This is one account Hume gives of the origin of our sense of duty (at *T* III. ii. 1. 479), thereby making conscience an artificial social product, and bringing the psychology of Book II to the service of the ethics of Book III. So the concern we take in ourselves will affect the self's nature, and be the source of beliefs we have about it.[12]

## VI

Hume's arguments on the self have been severely criticized, and it is important, when considering the limited questions of interpretation I have raised here, that many of the criticisms raised against him be put aside. It may well be, for example, that the question about the unity of the mind which he raises in Book I cannot be answered satisfactorily if one does not simultaneously answer the question of how it is that we can distinguish one person from another.[13] It may well be, further, that even though Hume is not inconsistent in his account of how a self that consists only of perceptions comes to think it is more, his account is radically defective in some other way—for example in his explicit assumption that it is intelligible to suppose there could be perceptions that no one has.[14] A critic of Hume's philosophy may wonder whether his accounts of the origins of the natural beliefs, and of the function of our instinctual nature in the emotional life, provide adequately for our need to criticize and

---

[12] When we recognize this, questions present themselves that the text will not readily answer for us. For example, does the fact that the constructed self must be ascribed physical qualities to occasion pride or love imply that in Hume's view the passions are the source of our belief that we have physical bodies at all? Such a suggestion would surely stretch the evidence.

[13] I have said this myself. The classic statement of this view in our day is ch. 3 of P. F. Strawson 1959.

[14] 'All these (perceptions) are different, and distinguishable, and separable from each other, and may be separately consider'd, and may exist separately, and have no need of any thing to support their existence' (*T* I. iv. 6. 252). And earlier, 'Now as every perception is distinguishable from another, and may consider'd as separately existent; it evidently follows, that there is no absurdity in separating any particular perception from the mind; that is, in breaking off all its relations, with that connected mass of perceptions, which constitute a thinking being' (*T* I. iv. 2. 207).

evaluate beliefs and emotions.[15] These are questions on which I have
not touched here. I have been trying to discern what limits there are
to the enterprise of mining Hume's theory of the passions to recon-
struct what his theory of the self is. And it seems clear to me that
at some level that very theory depends repeatedly and fundamentally upon the subject's recognizing himself or herself as one subject
among others, each of whom has a private mental life too; and that
although, given that recognition, the theory of the passions tells us
many profound things about how each of us comes to form a self-
image through interaction with others, it cannot itself be the source
of that recognition. And Hume has not included, in his account of
human nature, any other explanation of where that recognition comes
from.

It may be an easy matter to write this story, though I suspect there
will be a number of versions of it if we try. It seems certain, however,
that they will all be sympathetic reconstructions; for Hume himself
has not supplied it.

---

[15] I have wondered this in Chapter 4. See Chazan 1992 for a suggestion of how
Hume's analysis of pride might permit such criticism.

# 6

## *Hume, Identity and Selfhood*

HUME was not given to philosophical retractions; but he did express
open dissatisfaction with his views on personal identity. It is therefore a great source of scholarly frustration that he did not make
it very clear what he thought was wrong with them. Many have
tried to decide what it was. I incline to the view that a recent contribution to this debate by Donald Ainslie comes close to the truth
on this matter, although the vagueness of Hume's text in the
Appendix to the *Treatise* makes it impossible to be certain.[1] Even
if this view is right, however, I doubt that it indicates a clear awareness on Hume's part of what is really wrong with his philosophy of
mind on this issue, or that it helps us solve any of the puzzles I have
been concerned with in Chapters 2 to 5. But in arguing this, I can
at least take the opportunity of delving a little deeper into some of
them.

I attempt, first, to identify the purposes behind the negative
opening passages of Section 6 of Part iv of Book I of the *Treatise*.
I then comment briefly on the criticisms Hume makes there of the
philosophical theories with which his own is contrasted, and follow
this with a paraphrase of what I take his account of the origins
of our belief in self-identity to be. My objective is to augment,
rather than to repeat, my previous arguments on these themes. I then
turn to the vexed question of the nature of the anxiety Hume
expresses in the Appendix to the *Treatise* about his own arguments
in *T* I. iv. 6; and I conclude with brief comments on the self and
the passions.

---

[1] My arguments here, especially those of Parts I and IV, are greatly indebted to
Ainslie. I think he has at last managed to crack the code, both of Hume's brusque
arguments in the first paragraphs of *T* I. iv. 6 and of the Appendix. He should not
be credited with any of the mistakes I make.

I

I had best begin by noting that there is indeed some difficulty in the
very terminology of 'the self'. Antony Flew drew our attention to
this fact years ago (Flew 1950), and has had occasion more recently
to rebuke me for not heeding it (Flew 1986: 94). He is of course right
that philosophical talk of 'the self' is indeed technical in a commonly
unacknowledged way.[2] In Chapter 2 I attempted to take due note
of this, by echoing Hume's derision for a particular philosophical
theory that he regards as a technicality he judges unintelligible. But
it is clear that he does not think his own later uses of the phrase in
Book II are technical ones. He uses it there as the name of an idea
that he says is always present to us and is constitutive of the setting
of the indirect passions of pride and humility. This is an obvious
indicator that he does not think that the idea he refers to by it is
the same idea he has attacked as nonsensical (or nonexistent) in
*T* I. iv. 6.

Let us return, however, to the Section 'Of Personal Identity' in
Book I. He begins that Section with an attack on a philosophical
theory that is used by those who hold it to explain a conviction that
they, and he, think we all have, and whose origin he feels he has to
account for in another way. Several exegetical questions arise. Who
held the theory Hume attacks? What is the conviction that they, and
he, think we have? What is Hume's reason for rejecting the theory
they offer? What account of the conviction does Hume himself present as an alternative to theirs? This last question has at least two
components. There is the problem of Hume's view of the epistemic
status of the conviction: does Hume think it true, or false? And there
is the problem of what factors in our nature generate it. All these
questions should be considered in advance of any consideration of
the doctrines of the self in Book II, since Hume himself puts them
first and obviously thinks they are behind him when he gets there.
There is, also, no hint in the Appendix that he thinks the anxieties
he expresses there are relevant to the doctrines of the second Book.

His targets are not identified by name. But identifying them
may have some bearing on the question of what Hume considers

---

[2] For a contemporary response to Flew's original essay, see J. R. Jones 1950. See
also Kenny 1992, ch. 6.

himself to have established (and is later anxious about) in his criticisms of them. He describes them and their opinions as follows:

There are some philosophers, who imagine we are every moment intimately conscious of what we call our SELF; that we feel its existence and continuance in existence; and are certain, beyond the evidence of a demonstration, both of its perfect identity and simplicity. The strongest sensation, the most violent passion, say they, instead of distracting us from this view, only fix it the more intensely, and make us consider their influence on *self* either by their pain or pleasure. To attempt a farther proof of this were to weaken its evidence; since no proof can be deriv'd from any fact, of which we are so intimately conscious; nor is there any thing, of which we can be certain, if we doubt of this. (*T* I. iv. 6. 251)

Further down the same page, he further characterizes the theory as maintaining that 'self or person is not any one impression, but that to which our several impressions and ideas are suppos'd to have a reference'. The major part of this view, then, is that the self has perfect identity and simplicity, is in some sense the subject or point of reference of all our perceptions, and is known by us in an intimate and certain way—let us say intuitively. (As described in this passage, the self is not said to be a *substrate*, whatever that technical notion might mean, but it is said to be a point of 'reference' of our experiences, one might say to *own* them.)

Hume does not even say that those who held this theory are the same ones whose belief in the immateriality of the soul he has attacked in the previous Section; but it would at least be harder to find candidates if we rule them out. The doctrine that the soul is simple, or 'indiscerptible' (that is, not composed of parts) has been traced by Mijuskovic through the seventeenth- and eighteenth-century debates about immortality, and was held by the Cambridge Platonists, by Leibniz, by Samuel Clarke and by Berkeley.[3] It was thought to be a key premiss in arguments for immortality; the soul was thought to be immortal by nature because, in contrast to material

---

[3] Mijuskovic 1974: a most valuable monograph, to which I am indebted in what follows. The theological importance of the doctrine of the soul's simplicity (a reason, of course, for Hume to reject it) is that it was thought to show that the soul's immortality followed from its indissoluble nature, and therefore was demonstrable by natural reason. Hence Clarke's dispute with Dodwell, who maintained that immortality was a miraculous divine gift known to us only through revelation (Clarke 1978, vol. 3). Berkeley espouses the argument from simplicity in Principle 141 of the *Principles of Human Knowledge*.

things, it was not subject to dissolution by the separation of parts. Thus far, any of these thinkers could be a target in the opening passage of Section 6. The doctrine that the self is the point of 'reference' of our experiences raises further questions about Hume's intent in Section 6. What is referred to here by Hume, however obliquely, is the doctrine that the self provides for the unity of consciousness, without which our mental (at least our intellectual) life would be no more than a sequence of discrete thoughts that could never add up to a judgement, or a sequence of discrete sensations that could never add up to a coherent perception of objects. For there to be judgements or perceptions, the ideas or sensations need to be had and to be combined by one and the same subject, not to be separate. The unity that the self provides here was thought by rationalist philosophers to derive from its simplicity, and to entail it. This claim about the self is to be found, as Mijuskovic makes clear, in Smith, Cudworth, Clarke, Leibniz and Berkeley. In view of the centrality of the doctrine of the unity of consciousness in Kant's epistemology, there is a tendency for all of us to think of it as Kantian in origin, when Kant is rather concerned to distinguish what is true in it from what is false.

This should help us to see that a great deal more is at issue for Hume in this opening passage of the Section than the dismissal of a piece of otiose metaphysics. What is at issue is his whole procedure in pursuing the science of man. To make this clearer, I begin with a quotation from Norman Kemp Smith, which is used by Mijuskovic. Smith is indicating the way in which, in his judgement, Kant's claims about the unity of consciousness undermine the Humean doctrine of association:

To attempt to explain the unity of consciousness through the mechanism of association is to explain an agency in terms of certain of its own effects. It is to explain the fundamental in terms of the derivative, the conditions in terms of what they have themselves made possible . . . Ideas do not become associated merely by coexisting. They must occur together in a unitary consciousness; and among the conditions necessary to the possibility of association are therefore the conditions of the possibility of experience. Association is transcendentally grounded.[4]

Kant is of course not our concern here. If he were, it would be essential to disentangle the precise relationship between his commitment

4 Smith 1918, 254.

to the doctrine of the necessary unity of consciousness and his rejection of rationalist psychology.[5] For Hume, those who most emphasized the former were the protagonists of the latter, and he had to reject all they stood for in order to pursue his naturalist agenda. This meant that he had to reject the doctrine of the unity of consciousness as it reached him in their writings. He has to deny that mental activities like reasoning or sense-perception require a subject's holding together impressions or ideas in some sort of conscious unity; he has rather to hold that any such mental activity can be accounted for in terms of his own teachings about the associations of ideas and impressions.

He could not pursue his science of man, however, without assuming something that his rationalist opponents also believed in: that the mind has the ability to scrutinize and chronicle the progress of its own perceptions, and (by implication) that at least on some level prior to that of the careful introspection on which this science relies, the mind's contents are 'perfectly known' (*T* II. ii. 6. 366). This assumption he certainly inherits from Descartes, though his use of it is utterly different. Roughly, he holds, and must hold, that our conscious mental life must be known to us, but rejects the Cartesian claim that in knowing the contents of consciousness we are also aware of a self that owns them. The former finds its most unambiguous expression in *EU* VII. 66, where he tells us that 'consciousness never deceives'. The latter is made clear at the outset of Section 6. Because of the latter, Donald Ainslie holds that the primary target of the opening passage is Descartes. Clearly he must indeed be one of those intended; and since the thinkers attacked in this passage are not said to espouse doctrines of substance, Locke will also be a key target of Hume's criticisms. But I see no reason to think they are the only targets.[6]

I suggest, therefore, that far from its being the case that Hume does not see what Kant later makes clear (which many of us who admire Kant's insights are inclined to suppose) Hume is in this Section attempting to defend his own procedures against the threat of the earlier, rationalist versions of the doctrine of the unity of consciousness that Kant is sometimes supposed to have invented.

[5] Ameriks 1982. See also Paton 1951.
[6] Mijuskovic 1974, ch. 2. Mijuskovic also makes a case for the view that Descartes' commitment to the argument for the soul's simplicity is less than total.

For Hume the sequences of association on which his psychology depends have to be seen as ultimate—not in the sense that there *are* no deeper facts behind them, but in the sense that they are as far as our knowledge of ourselves reaches. The rationalists are wrong in thinking that they have some intuitive access to the deeper facts on which these sequences depend.

When Hume tells us at *T* I. iv. 2. 207 that there is no absurdity in separating off a perception from the mind to which it belongs, and tells us, there and again at *T* I. iv. 6. 252 that we are nothing but bundles or collections of perceptions, he is not only offering, as a discovery of his science of man, that the mind has no real identity through time, but he is also insisting that the mind is not simple or indiscerptible but is indeed composed of separable parts. And when he says that the mind is 'suppos'd, tho' falsely, to be endow'd with a perfect simplicity and identity' (*T* I. iv. 2. 207) there is no good reason to suppose that he thinks this false supposition is confined to the rationalist thinkers he attacks at the outset of *T* I. iv. 6; there is reason to suppose he thinks we are all prone to the error. What his philosophical opponents do is compound it by offering an empty metaphysical postulate to justify it. In exchange for this, he has a naturalistic account of its origin.

In a recent essay on 'Personal Identity and Objective Reality' Geoffrey Madell argues that the awareness that the experiences I am having at any time are all *mine* is an underivative and unanalysable fact about them.[7] I suggest that Hume is insisting that his science of man can show, through introspection, that such a view is false. He thinks the 'no-ownership' thesis is demonstrable experimentally. With this in mind, we can turn to his brusque attack on his rationalist opponents at the outset of *T* I. iv. 6.

## II

Given the fundamentals of his science of man, their teachings have to collapse at once on the basis of an appeal to introspection. To them, of course, such an appeal is merely question-begging, since to them the self is necessarily not reducible to any one of the impressions or ideas that it has, and would therefore be beyond the reach

---

[7] Madell 1994. See also the fuller arguments of Madell 1981.

of any procedure designed to identify one or other of them alone. In addition, it is clear that the language Hume uses to express his criticisms is language that anyone inclined to the rationalist view will say he has no right to use. Hume, after all, says (*T* I. iv. 6. 252) 'For *my* part, when *I* enter most intimately into what I call *myself*, *I* always stumble on some particular perception or other, of heat or cold, light or shade, love or hatred, pain or pleasure. *I* never can catch *myself* at any time without a perception, and never can observe any thing but the perception.' Hume's text italicizes 'myself', but I have also italicized the three occurrences of 'I' and the one occurrence of 'my' to emphasize that Hume himself uses the language which his rationalist opponents would feel that they, but not he, can explain and justify. What, they would surely ask, is the 'I' that stumbles on this or that perception and fails to find anything further, and why would Hume suppose that a method designed to scrutinize impressions and ideas is a method suitable for determining whether or not it is present? And how can he deny it is present while continuing to refer to it?[8] The reply to this is that Hume knows our use of I-language needs an explanation and intends, very shortly, to offer one; and that given the commitment Hume has to the conceivability of the independent existence of perceptions, it will be an explanation that makes their belonging to me a contingent fact about the way they happen to be grouped together.

But Hume's attack invites another criticism. While apparently an appeal to introspection, it can hardly be that in any simple way. To look for something and be confident you have failed to find it, you would seem to have to know what success in such a search would be like. Yet Hume interprets his failure to find the self as defined to be a demonstration that there is no idea corresponding to the term, from which it would follow that we do not know what we are searching for.[9] I think there is a Humean answer to this: that Hume does not presuppose that the doctrine he attacks is a clear one, but infers from what the rationalists say about the self that if it were a reality it would be accessible to us; on the assumption, fundamental to *his* science, that what is accessible to us would be discernible by introspection, he invites us to look, and infers from his and our failure

---

[8] The clearest expression of this criticism in recent literature is in ch. 1 of Chisholm 1976, 37–41.

[9] See, most recently, Shoemaker 1996, 3–4.

to find it not only that it is not there, but that we did not really know (and his opponents did not really know) what it was that he and we were searching for. So the meaninglessness of the doctrine is a conclusion that on Humean principles can be shown indirectly from the outcome of the introspective process.

A quite different sort of criticism goes as follows. Not everyone agrees that the introspective process, appropriately carried out, yields the results Hume says. While most would assume that introspection is the scrutiny of the mind's *contents*, there are mystical thinkers who hold that meditative techniques yield an ultimate awareness of the self that *has* the experience of those contents, as distinct from the experiences it has. Hence W. T. Stace:

> Our normal everyday consciousness always has objects . . . Suppose then that we obliterate from consciousness all objects physical or mental. When the self is not engaged in apprehending objects it becomes aware of itself. The self itself emerges. The self, however, when stripped of all psychological contents or objects, is not another thing, or substance, distinct from its contents. It is the bare unity of the manifold of consciousness from which the manifold itself has been obliterated . . . The empirical ego is the stream of consciousness. The pure ego is the unity which holds the manifold of the stream together. *This undifferentiated unity is the essence of the introvertive mystical experience.* (Stace 1960: 86–7; italics original)

In assessing this criticism, it is important to note that there is deep disagreement among the mystical schools about what it is that meditative techniques of self-emptying reveal: whether it is a universal self (Advaita), one of many individual selves (Samkhya-Yoga) or an Emptiness that belongs to no self at all (Buddha).[10] Of course these techniques are not to be simply identified with the introspection that Hume appeals to when he tells us nothing is within. These authorities seem to converge with Hume's verdict, however, when they all agree that the reality that is revealed by self-emptying methods is not one of the mind's *contents*.

Many of Hume's readers have been satisfied with his verdict to this same extent, and have happily followed him in seeing the failure of introspection to show us the self as a refutation of the rationalist theories he is attacking. I was so minded in Chapter 2; and although a later interest in the doctrines I have just referred to makes

[10] See Smart 1964 for a reliable guide to this huge field.

me now very doubtful of the adequacy of his methods for determining the limits of spiritual realities, I shall confine myself here to other matters, and assume for the purposes of argument that he is so far successful. He summarizes the result of his argument in two famous assertions: that, other than a few metaphysicians, mankind are 'nothing but a bundle or collection of different perceptions', and that the mind is a kind of theatre where perceptions successively make their appearance, although there is, properly speaking, only the perceptions and no place that they are 'in'. 'There is properly no *simplicity* in it at one time, nor *identity* in different; whatever natural propension we may have to imagine that simplicity and identity.'

This last sentence makes three things clear. First, the propensity to imagine both identity and simplicity is a natural one, and is not confined to philosophers. Second, simplicity (or indiscerptibility) is a supposed feature of the mind at one time; it is a special form of synchronic identity. This is important to notice, since simplicity seems to vanish from consideration in the remainder of the Section until the penultimate paragraph, and the detailed account of the factors leading to our belief in identity seems otherwise confined to an account of the genesis of the belief in the mind's identity through time— its supposed diachronic identity. Third, it is clear that this sentence summarizes the results of the careful application of the experimental method on which the science of man depends, when this science concerns itself with the nature of the mind itself; and the result is the revelation of the absence of those characteristics that common sense ascribes to it and that the rationalist tries to justify. This is a key illustration of the fact that Hume thinks his mental science and his scepticism are not merely compatible, but that the former supports the latter.

So, once more, Hume does not fail to realize the supposed fact of the unity of consciousness that Kant was later to make clear to us, as Kemp Smith claims. He rather goes out of his way to deny it. He then asks what factors, in its absence, make us ascribe it to the bundle of perceptions that he thinks he has shown to be without it. So he proceeds at once to the question; 'What then gives us so great a propension to ascribe an identity to these successive perceptions, and to suppose ourselves possest of an invariable and uninterrupted existence thro' the whole course of our lives?' He is careful to precede his answer by drawing the distinction between personal identity as it regards the thought or imagination, and personal identity as it regards the passions, and to tell us that it is only the former that now concerns him. The question is clearly designed to introduce an account of a common belief or practice (the 'propension' to ascribe identity) that the rationalists have tried, unsuccessfully, to justify. In a way that is reminiscent of his treatment in *T* I. iv. 2 of our belief in the continued and independent existence of perceived objects, he is about to offer an alternative account of this propension, but one that is not offered as a justification.

Two points, however, before turning to his story. First, Hume immediately directs our attention to two *ideas*, and to how we can distinguish them if we try but commonly do not. His story, then, will be one about the *ideas* we have of the successive perceptions that form our mental life: about how we respond to the survey of the recollections we have of our past experiences. This is clear independently from the importance that memory has in the positive part of the story. So, once more, he is about to tell us about the formation of our belief in the *diachronic* identity of the mind, rather than its synchronic identity—about its supposed unity *over* time, rather than *at* a time. (Simplicity reappears as an afterthought in the Section's penultimate paragraph.) Now if the unity of the members of a heterogeneous bundle of perceptions needs explanation, both aspects need it. We shall have to return to this.

Second, if we confine ourselves as he does to the problem of the diachronic identity of the mind, the question he poses is 'How is it that when I survey my past experiences in all their variety and changingness, I think of them as forming a unit?'. This is all that he seems to extract from the question that many would think he *ought* to have asked, viz. 'What makes me think of all these past perceptions as *mine*?' Now in Chapters 2, 3, 4, and 5 I have complained, as others have, about the fact that Hume does not seem to ask how each of us differentiates between his or her perceptions and other peoples'. I do not propose to add to my earlier comments on that theme here. I merely note that for him the only meaning the question he asks seems to have is 'What makes me think of all these perceptions as mine *rather than no-one's*?' He does clearly think (indeed he emphasizes) that perceptions may quite conceivably exist unowned (*T* I. iv. 2. 207). And he identifies the question of why we think we own the ones we have with the question of what makes us ascribe a unity to them in the face of their variation through time, insisting that this question is best treated in the same way as questions about our ascription of identity to plants and animals, thereby showing that his science of man has, as one of its key objectives, the denial of the rationalist contrast between the structure of the mind and that of material things.

At this point I can only reiterate that the puzzles Hume addresses are framed on the assumption that once introspection has revealed that nothing is present to the mind but its impressions and ideas, it follows that the mind has no real identity; and that this entails a misunderstanding of this concept.

### III

I come, finally, to the question of what his genetic story is. I have earlier represented it as a story that ascribes error to the ordinary consciousness, and represents his rationalist opponents as thinkers engaged in a vain attempt to justify the errors of the vulgar by the invention of metaphysical fictions. I do not wish to repeat earlier arguments, but will here add a few points of detail.

In broad outline, I see Hume's story as the following. (1) We commonly confuse the two distinct ('and even contrary') ideas of identity and diversity. We do this because it feels much the same to 'consider' (or survey in the imagination) a succession of closely related 'objects' as it does to consider an object that continues without interruption or change over a stretch of time. This similarity of feeling 'is the cause of the confusion and mistake, and makes us substitute the notion of identity, instead of that of related objects'. No arguments I have read encourage me to think Hume does not mean it when he calls this a mistake. He describes it in the next sentence as that of ascribing to the related succession 'a perfect identity'. The mistake is one that we are so prone to make that even if we incessantly correct ourselves and return to a 'more accurate method of thinking' (that is, the sort of thinking that Hume has pressed on us when telling us that we are nothing but bundles of perceptions) we cannot 'sustain our philosophy' and we yield to the error and say that successions of related objects are 'in effect the same'. (2) This supposed error is one that Hume describes in terms that embrace everyone, not only his rationalist opponents. But he depicts their theories as arising naturally from this universal error. We (everyone) often try to 'justify this absurdity' by feigning 'some new and unintelligible principle' that disguises the interruption or variation that we are denying. His examples are familiar: the continued existence of our sense-perceptions, the soul, the self, substance, or some other imagined feature that connects the items in the related series. These he calls *fictions*. They introduce an element of seriousness into disputes of identity, which would otherwise be merely verbal. (3) He proposes to prove his hypothesis by showing that those variable and interrupted objects which are supposed to continue the same consist of a succession of parts connected by the three associative principles of resemblance, contiguity or causation.[11] He then tells a progressive story: we must attribute 'a perfect identity' to any mass of matter if its parts continue uninterruptedly and invariably the same; but if a small or inconsiderable part is added or subtracted we overlook it, even though the identity of the whole is, 'strictly speaking', destroyed by it. Even though the change in a considerable part destroys the identity of the whole, this too is overlooked when the change is small in proportion to that whole. Further, when even major change comes about gradually and insensibly, the 'easy passage' of the mind makes us overlook the fact that its identity is in fact destroyed. When changes, however gradual, are finally noted, we may persist in the ascription of identity if the parts continue to 'conspire' to a common end—as in the case of a ship that has undergone repairs. This tendency is reinforced if the parts that serve the common end are also causally interrelated in their operations; this leads us, in the case of plants and animals, to continue to ascribe identity in the face of an entire replacement of their parts over time. Finally, Hume gives us two examples of difference being ignored in the ascription of identity: the confusion of numerical and specific identity (as in the repetition of what we choose to call the same noise), and the decision to view even the most rapid and radical change with acceptance, if it is characteristic of the sort of object to which it takes place— as in the Heraclitean example of a flowing river. (4) If we turn to *personal* identity, the same principles must be operative, since 'the identity, which we ascribe to the mind of man, is only a fictitious

---

[11] 'For as such a succession answers evidently to our notion of diversity, it can only be by a mistake we ascribe to it an identity; and as the relation of parts, which leads us into this mistake, is really nothing but a quality, which produces an association of ideas, and an easy transition of the imagination from one to another, it can only be from the resemblance, which this act of the mind bears to that, by which we contemplate one continu'd object, that the error arises' (*T* I. iv. 6. 255).

one, and of a like kind with that which we ascribe to vegetable and
animal bodies'. He begins by repeating his judgement that the
perceptions of the mind do not reveal any real connections among
themselves, so that the unity we attribute to them must be due to
the 'uninterrupted progress of the thought along a train of connected
ideas'. Since this progress must be due to the associative principles,
he turns to these, and immediately rejects contiguity as irrelevant.
Resemblance comes into play because of the way the memory
produces images that resemble past perceptions. Causation is the
paramount factor, since it relates our multifarious perceptions to one
another, much as social interaction unites the members of a republic or commonwealth. (5) He concludes his story by stressing the
centrality of memory in the production of our belief in self-identity.
Memory serves to make us aware of the causal relations between
our perceptions; and once we have become aware of this, we can
postulate the prior reality of perceptions that we are no longer able
to recall. Hence memory, though crucial to our belief in identity,
does not produce it but discover it. His point here, intended obviously as a rejection of Locke, seems to be that although memory is
the source of our awareness of the causal interactions among our
perceptions that make us ascribe identity to them, the judgements
of identity that it makes possible apply to many parts of our history to which memory does not give us access now. (6) Hume then
draws the moral that many of the disputes about personal identity
that exercise philosophers are merely verbal or grammatical ones that
can be ignored unless some 'fiction or imaginary principle of union'
is introduced to support one side or the other—as in the case of the
theories he attacked at the outset of the Section.

Some brief comments now upon each of these stages. (1) I have
seen no arguments that convince me Hume does not mean what he
repeatedly says when he says we are *mistaken* to ascribe identity to
successions of related objects. He indeed says we all do it, and indeed
thinks that we are unable to avoid doing it, and that we incorporate such ascriptions into the 'proprieties of language'. But he still
says it is a mistake to do it, and that careful introspective attention
to the associations of our ideas will reveal this, as well as explaining how it comes about. I still reject the suggestion of Ashley and
Stack (1974) that Hume thinks we can distinguish between a strict
and a less strict *sense* of identity, and believes that self-identity in
the less strict sense is a fact. That sort of suggestion would ascribe

to Hume a view like that of Butler and Chisholm.[12] Butler distinguishes between a 'strict and philosophical' sense, and a 'loose and popular sense' of identity, ascribing the former to persons and the latter to biological organisms, on the ground that the former does not admit of change of parts and the latter does. Chisholm, interpreting this view, shows how it leads to the further thesis that those things that have identity only in a loose and popular sense are logical constructions out of those that have it in a strict sense. Hume does indeed write of the identity of those things that we describe as identical after changes that are small in proportion to the whole as an 'imperfect identity' (*T* I. iv. 6. 256), and Ashley and Stack (1974) therefore interpret him as holding that persons are logical constructions out of the perceptions that constitute their histories. I would rather argue, in the light of his own analogy (*T* I. iv. 6. 259–60) between the ascription of identity to minds and the ascription of necessity to causal sequences, that the associative mechanism makes us *add* something to the mind's survey of the sequence of our perceptions that is not in the objects surveyed but has the mind's survey of them as its source. I think this precludes the view that Hume holds the mind to be a logical construction out of the perceptions it includes, even though Pike (1967) is wholly right to stress that Hume maintains with stark clarity the thesis that the mind is *in reality* nothing more than those perceptions. To ascribe the logical construction theory of minds to Hume would be mistaken in the way in which it would be mistaken to suggest that he thinks statements about causes can be translated without remainder into statements about the regular sequences that generate our belief in causal necessity. To hold that xs are logical constructions out of ys is to hold that statements about xs can be translated into statements about ys without change in truth-value; Hume holds, on the contrary, that the experimental understanding of our perceptions undermines the statements we make when we talk of minds.

I think my opinion here is confirmed by noting that at *T* I. i. 5. 14 he introduces identity as a *philosophical* relation ('apply'd in its strict sense to constant and unchangeable objects'), postponing 'the nature and foundation of personal identity'; when he does turn to the latter in *T* I. iv. 6, he clearly analyses it as a *natural* relation.

---

[12] Butler, Dissertation 'Of Personal Identity' appended to the *Analogy of Religion*. Butler 1900, vol. 2; Chisholm 1976, ch. 3.

His analysis of how we come to believe in it has the purpose of explaining away our tendency to think (as Butler and those whom he follows thought) that persons have identity in the strict sense, by showing that they are in the same boat as far as the ascription of identity is concerned, as the plants and animals with which Hume's opponents contrasted them.[13] We think the mind has strict identity, when in reality it does not have identity at all; so the mind of common sense belief cannot be a logical construction out of its perceptions, since if it were, such a false judgement could not emerge as the result of translation from the language of perceptions to that of common sense.

The upshot of these considerations is that I should amend the claim in Chapter 3 that the belief in personal identity is not really a belief but a convention. I should rather say that the conventional ascription of identity to changing and complex objects is the expression of a belief that they somehow satisfy the conditions for ascribing strict identity to them, in spite of the fact, which the science of man makes clear to us, that they do not.

(2) This brings us naturally to the status Hume accords to those *fictions* which he thinks we invent to disguise the variations that should strictly destroy the identity we ascribe to changing objects. Annette Baier has claimed (Baier 1991: 103 f.) that when Hume describes some beliefs as fictions, he is not claiming that they are false, but only that they are unverifiable; they are 'plausible stories we tell ourselves to organize our experience'.[14] The real identity of our own mind is not the only such fiction: another important one is the belief in the independent existence of the objects of sense-perception; but I confine myself here to the fictions referred to by Hume in *T* I. iv. 6. It is certainly clear that Hume believes the fictions generated about identity are unverifiable. That is the way he attacks his rationalist opponents, but it is hard not to read him as thinking their fictions to be false. It is true, however, that on his own principles he cannot insist that we *know* metaphysical speculations like these to be false; we can only show them to be baseless.

I am not quite able to leave the matter here, however. If we engage in the introspective investigation of our perceptions as the science

---

[13] It would seem unlikely that Hume had read Butler's *Analogy* at the time he wrote Book I of the *Treatise*; but the views he counters are in this respect like those of Butler.

[14] Baier 1991, 103 f. The disagreement here is with Penelhum 1975.

of man enjoins us to do, we will find nothing, Hume tells us, to correspond with the uniting principles that the rationalists believe in. Thus far, we might be able to hold that such principles are merely beyond verification, but could still, as a matter of fact, be true (rather as some have held that Hume privately believes that there are secret connections underlying our ascription of necessity to causal sequences, even though he and they agree that such connections are inaccessible). But Hume does go on to say that we are nothing but bundles of perceptions, and that the theatre is not a real place; and he is talking here about the nature of the mind itself, not about possible theories of the nature of the world beyond the mind. And he does, if I am right, tell us that the judgements the fictions are intended to justify are false, even if we cannot know this about the fictions themselves. So I still incline to take him literally when he tells us that '(t)he identity, which we ascribe to the mind of man, is only a fictitious one' (*T* I. iv. 6. 259), and not read him as saying merely that this identity is *fac*titious. He may not be entitled on his own principles to deny the existence of the bonds of which he denies the reality of the evidence; he may even, as a naturalist, welcome this fact; but I think he does intend us to conclude that these particular fictions are untrue.

There remains the question of the relative status of the sophisticated fictions of the philosophers and the mundane ones of which everyone is guilty. When he introduces fictions into his account of how we disguise variations for ourselves, he lists both common-sense beliefs and philosophical ones: the continued existence of our perceptions, the soul, self, and substance. This suggests that he thinks we are all prone to fictionalize our experience, and raises the question of where common-sense fictionalizing ends and philosophical fictionalizing begins. This is an issue of importance, since common-sense fictions must be a part of our natural beliefs, and the philosophical fictions cannot be. I have little to say here except that the ineradicability of a fiction would have to become a criterion for its not being a philosophers' fancy. On this criterion the fiction of continued existence of perceptions would qualify as natural, but the soul, the self and substance would fail. Most fictions, then, are the consequence of philosophers' attempts to justify opinions that the vulgar hold, but that the science of man exposes as baseless. The fictionalizing tendency, however, would seem to be a universal trait, just as the formation of baseless opinions is.

(3) and (4). I shall not repeat here my earlier arguments to the effect that Hume's paradigms of identity and diversity are erroneous, and that in consequence the alleged mistakes he thinks our conventions disguise are not mistakes in fact. If these arguments were sound, it follows that what Hume represents as psychological reinforcements of a set of universal errors are instead merely factors that we incorporate into the formation of our criteria for the identity of changing objects, persons included.

## IV

There have been a number of ingenious attempts to decide what feature of his arguments in Section 6 Hume found unsatisfactory when he wrote the Appendix to the *Treatise*.[15] What Hume says is notoriously obscure. But it does seem clear that it is only his treatment of the self in Book I that bothers him; and I agree with discussants who stress that in interpreting his dissatisfactions we have to confine ourseves to matters that could have occurred to *him*, rather than seek to show he is exercised about defects in his views that have subsequently exercised *us*. This last consideration rules out, for example, Hume's being concerned that he has not explained how we come to distinguish one person from another. I am not optimistic that I can explain what most commentators find mysterious, but I will offer a few comments that seem apposite in the light of the preceding.

Hume begins with a lucid rehearsal of the main line of argument in Section 6. There is no distinct impression of self; all perceptions are distinct and therefore separable; so it must be the 'composition' of our perceptions that forms the self, and there is no absurdity in supposing the perceptions that compose it to exist without it. 'So far I seem to be attended with sufficient evidence.' But when he comes to explain how we attribute identity to the perceptions thus 'loosen'd', he now finds his account very defective.

What does he find defective about it? Since no connections are discovered among our perceptions, the attribution of identity to them must be a matter of our thought connecting them together when we reflect on 'the train of *past* perceptions' (my italics). This ought not

---

[15] I would single out for particular mention Fogelin 1985, ch. 8; Garrett 1997, ch. 8; Humber 1995; and Ainslie, forthcoming.

to surprise us, he says, when we reflect that some philosophers think personal identity arises from consciousness. (Locke is clearly meant here.) But Hume's hopes vanish, he says, when he comes to 'explain the principles that unite our successive perceptions in our thought or consciousness'.

I think that Ainslie's suggestion is the one that makes the most natural sense of this last sentence. Hume has repeated, with apparent approval, his previous account of how we attribute identity to our perceptions by looking back over them in memory (i.e. surveying the ideas we now have of them). But he now says he is baffled how to account for how this comes about. He seems to think there is some problem about how the perceptions to which we attribute identity are held in consciousness for us to do this to them. What seems to be at issue is the coherence at one time of those perceptions that make up the process of judging all the past ones to form a unit. The perceptions that are the subject of this judgement are (were) successive, but what seems to bother Hume now is how they can all be united or held together *now* for us to judge (or misjudge) them to have formed one mind together with the present reflection upon them. It is a problem of the *synchronic* identity requisite for the attribution of *diachronic* identity to the past perceptions of the person now looking back upon them. (When speaking of synchronic identity I refer to the unity of the mind during the (short) time in which it surveys its past and ascribes identity to it. I do not suggest that we are here considering the unity of the mind at one timeless instant. The fact that poses the challenge to the synchronic unity of the mind is the simultaneous presence of a number of distinguishable, and therefore separable, perceptions during an act of contemplation.)

If this should be what Hume intends, it would provide a passable explanation of why he goes on, ostensibly in mere summation, to say that he cannot reconcile two principles that are clearly compatible, viz. that all perceptions are distinct existences and that the mind never perceives any real connection among distinct existences. The first would be intended, on this reading, as an account of why there is nothing to be found among our past perceptions that justifies attributing identity to them; and the second as a reason for finding it mysterious that our present consciousness can hold the ideas of those past perceptions together in a manner that enables this attribution to be made now.

I think this suggestion makes reasonable sense of the Appendix passage; but of course it raises many questions, even within Hume's system. Before attending to these, it is worth remarking that at the close of Section 6 Hume takes a short paragraph to tell us that what he has offered as an explanation for our belief in the identity of the self can also serve to account for the belief in its simplicity. 'An object whose different co-existent parts are bound together by a close relation, operates upon the imagination after much the same manner as one perfectly simple and indivisible, and requires not a much greater stretch of thought in order to its conception. From this similarity of operation we attribute a simplicity to it . . .' (*T* i. iv. 6. 263). The notion of the soul's simplicity is normally explained by pointing out that simultaneous thoughts and sensations and feelings are not intelligibly thought of as separable parts of a composite. Hume is committed to denying this, and to be explaining our belief in its truth on the same principles that he has offered to explain how we believe in the self's diachronic identity.

I am therefore inclined to accept Ainslie's view that it is the synchronic identity of the mind that ascribes diachronic identity to its own past that is the subject of Hume's worry in the Appendix. This view fulfils the requirement that the concern he expresses must be one that he could have felt about the argument of *T* i. iv. 6, but does not embrace other facets of his treatment of the self in the *Treatise*. And it seems to fit the course of the text of the Appendix, which reiterates his earlier account of the belief in diachronic identity and ends with an apparent concern about our belief in synchronic identity.

Unfortunately I do not feel convinced, however, that on his own principles Hume *ought* to be worried in the way that he is. I say this without having any inclination to embrace those principles.

On Hume's account, when the mind attributes diachronic unity to its past perceptions, those past perceptions are not present to the mind now; what is present now are the ideas, that is the memories, of them. Why should the unity of these with his present perceptions be a special difficulty? If my argument in Chapter 3 is sound, he should be able to accommodate the experience he has when making a judgement of identity into the mental science he uses to explain such judgements away.

His account ought to go somewhat as follows. When I ascribe identity over time to all my past perceptions, what really occurs is that the latest in the series of perceptions that constitutes my mind is a complex group of simultaneous perceptions that includes the ideas of the past ones I have had and the impressions and ideas I am currently having, and the idea of their all forming one unitary mind. Hume may not have helped himself by dismissing the relevance of contiguity to the account of identity-ascriptions, but the group of simultaneous impressions and ideas that the self judging its own identity has at the time it makes this judgement will no doubt have sufficient close relations within it to encourage the tendency to make this judgement. I would not suggest that such an account is plausible; but it would certainly seem to be a possible way, within Hume's system, of explaining the belief in the self's synchronic identity at those times when it makes judgements of diachronic identity. If his second thoughts signify that he does not think it adequate to resort to such an account, when he can resort to it well enough to explain the belief in diachronic identity, what is it about such a position that seems unsatisfactory *to him*? I must admit that none of the answers to this question that I can think of is very satisfying.

It is clear that the judgement that the perceptions composing my mind as I look back over my past constitute *one* mind is a judgement that, on Hume's account of our ascription of diachronic identity, cannot be made *at the time* the diachronic ascription is made. At that time, the present bundle of perceptions is indeed 'loosen'd'. I think, and most philosophers since Kant would think, that this ought to be a problem for Hume, since a judgement of identity across the present is a necessary component of any adequate understanding of how our consciousness functions. But what *we* think here is not the present issue. The present issue is what *Hume* should find troublesome. Hume, after all, is rejecting the Lockean notion that consciousness constitutes personal identity, and is doing so in the interests of a science of the mind that makes the basic units of all mental activity to be the impressions and ideas that make up the bundle that is all the mind is. If the doctrine of the mind's simplicity is the doctrine that it has no parts, Hume's view of the mind is that it is indeed an assemblage of parts—parts that include ideas that are, erroneously, ideas *of* the real unity of the bundle. We may find this vision of the mind implausible; but it is not just something that Hume places before us *here*. It is essential to his notion of psychological explanation that the units of such explanation are the mind's *contents*, not the mind itself that owns them. This is essential for his theory of the passions, and for his doctrine of freedom. (See Chapters 7 and 8.) If this is true, it is important for him to insist that the identity of the mind can be understood in the same way as that of plants and animals and is not of a different order as the rationalist tradition insisted. I do not see that a philosopher with this vision of mental explanation would have a special problem with the mind's simplicity, however obvious *we* find such a problem to be.

There would therefore seem to be at least one obvious way Hume could respond to the problem he sees. It would be to say that the ascription of diachronic identity is to be understood as the product of the interaction of roughly contemporaneous perceptions that form no more of a unity than the past perceptions did in reality, and that the synchronic identity we now think they have is also retroactively ascribed. The fact that such an account would mean that there is always some mental activity left over unjoined to the bundle it belongs to is just a fact about the mind's self-understanding and is not a problem for observers.[16]

If such a thesis seems implausible, its implausibility would come from the acceptance of the doctrine that a judgement of the mind's synchronic identity is an essential component in the sort of conscious mental activity of which the judgement of the mind's past diachronic identity is merely one example—from the acceptance of what Kant later told us when he wrote of the 'I think' that accompanies all our judgements. Do Hume's worries in the Appendix show that *he* came to suppose that such an acceptance is essential for his own account of how the mind comes to see itself as a unit?

If the understanding of the text of the Appendix that I have followed Ainslie in accepting is true, it seems that perhaps they do. But if so, the absence of concern for this problem elsewhere in his writings suggests that he mistakenly thought it was a difficulty confined to the matters he raises at the close of *T* I. iv. 6, and did not threaten his whole theory of mental activity. But since that theory is one that is intended to dispense with such doctrines, and the argument of *T* I. iv. 6 is designed to reinforce its foundations, I suspect that if his second thoughts had been followed by third ones, they would have been along the obvious reductionist lines that his bundle theory naturally dictated.

---

[16] It is merely one manifestation of what Ryle calls the self's 'systematic elusiveness'. See Ryle 1949, ch. 6.

## V

The importance of the theory of the passions for Hume's moral thought has been recognized since Árdal's work in 1966. It is clear that the notion of the self is an essential component of this theory, since the distinction between the direct and the indirect passions cannot be made without it. The manner in which Hume introduces it to the reader of the *Treatise*, however, tends to maximize a difficulty that has agitated commentators: that of integrating the discussion of the self in *T* I. iv. 6 and the role of the idea of the self in Book II.

Chapters 4 and 5 deal with two aspects of this problem. In Chapter 4 I argued that Hume's analysis of pride and humility requires that the boundaries of the individual personality be understood independently of the operation of the processes that generate these passions, at least if conventional forms of moral criticism of our emotional life are to remain in place. In Chapter 5 I argued that the basic distinction between oneself and others is taken as given in Book II, and that although Hume has given us an account of how we construct our belief in external physical objects, there is no trace of an account of the genesis of our belief in other persons. In spite of the increasingly rich understanding of the perceptiveness of Hume's theory of the passions in the work of Baier, McIntyre, Ainslie and others, I do not see reason to retract these arguments.

Hume introduces the self in *T* II. i. 2. 277. Pride and humility have the self as their object. The object of these passions is 'that to which they direct their view, when excited' (*T* II. i. 2. 278). Hume seems anxious to make it clear that he is not here writing of an idea that is a philosophical technicality, as he talks of 'our idea of ourself'. The self as it regards the passions is supposedly a familiar idea, quite different in this respect from the self of the philosophers that he has attacked at the outset of *T* I. iv. 6. He describes it as 'that succession of related ideas and impressions, of which we have an intimate memory and consciousness'. He is later (at *T* II. ii. 1. 329) to say that the object of love and hatred is 'some other person, *of whose thoughts, actions, and sensations we are not conscious*' (my italics). There seems to be no contradiction here with *T* I. iv. 6. But there is the open use of the common-sense assumption that there are many persons, each to be understood as having, even as being constituted by, the series of perceptions of which each one is 'conscious'. The puzzle about identity that Hume addresses, then, in his famous question at *T* I. iv. 6. 253 is a puzzle about how each of us comes to think of that series of perceptions that he or she has (or is) as a unit, as being all *his* or *hers*, rather than as separate and free-floating. He quietly takes for granted, both in Book I and in Book II, that the distinction between oneself and others is already understood.

Although Hume tells us the self is the object rather than the cause, of pride and humility, it is clear that it also plays a key role in their causation, since it is only when the exciting cause of them is seen as a phenomenon related to me that it can lead to pride. In many cases (though not all) this is a matter of the exciting cause being a quality of myself as its subject. (See, for example, *T* II. i. 2. 279: 'Beauty, consider'd merely as such, unless plac'd upon something related to us, never produces any pride or vanity.') It is perhaps this additional feature of the role of the idea of the self that has led to the popularity of the suggestion that Hume explains the origin of the idea of the self by means of the mechanism of the genesis of pride. But it seems to me, on the contrary, to make it more obvious that that mechanism requires the *prior* existence of that idea, and indeed of the idea of the self as distinct from, and over against, others.

The same judgement is in order when we look at the other important place in Book II where Hume makes use of the idea of the self—the introduction of the principle of sympathy (at *T* II. i. 11). Hume invokes the idea to account for the transformation of the idea of another's passion, generated in us by the observation of his or her demeanour, into an impression—that is, into a parallel passion in ourselves. It is enlivened by the idea of oneself. This idea cannot be invoked for such a purpose unless it is itself lively, hence Hume tells us that

'Tis evident, that the idea, or rather impression of ourselves is always intimately present with us, and that our consciousness gives us so lively a conception of our own person, that 'tis not possible to imagine, that any thing can in this particular go beyond it. (*T* II. i. 11. 317)

The phenomenon that Hume would seem to be describing here in order to explain the technical notion of sympathy, is that of the enlivening of a mere intellectual awareness that another person is feeling some emotional experience such as elation or distress into the stronger fellow-feeling that one has by imagining how it would be to have that very experience oneself. It is not the mere intensifying of the conception of *the other's* emotion, but the recognition of what it would be like if *I* felt it—as a result of which I *do*, to a degree, come to feel it. A key factor in this phenomenon is my own sense of my own inner life, of myself as the bearer of comparable experiences. It is here set against the idea of the other as the bearer of his or her distinct but presumably similar life-experiences.

The shock of transition to all this after Book I is considerable. It is only partially lessened by the fact that Hume takes pains to identify the self as the succession of related impressions and ideas of which we are intimately conscious. That distinguishes it from any metaphysical self with real identity and simplicity; but it seems to introduce, or more accurately re-introduce, another puzzle. In *T* I. iv. 6 Hume attacks the metaphysical self as something of which we are alleged to be 'intimately conscious', and to which our 'several impressions and ideas are 'suppos'd to have a reference'. He seems to proceed there to explain why we, and his rationalist opponents following us, are inclined to ascribe these features to this fictional construct. Yet these very features seem now to be introduced into the stories of the mechanisms of pride and sympathy. In the absence of the metaphysical self, how are we to understand the liveliness of our own self-consciousness, and the self-reference involved in the causes and the object of pride?

It might not seem that the problem is insurmountable in the former case, since Hume makes it clear that his science of man depends on the fact that our perceptions are known to us intimately by consciousness and that we can avoid error about them through careful reflection, even though our innate carelessness allows us to misread them if it suits us.[17] It might also seem, and has to some, that Hume's account of the mechanism of pride offers an aetiology of the notion of oneself as the player of the social roles on which society and morality depend. Both of these are truths. But they are only partial truths. The special access I have to my own perceptions has to be augmented by some sense that these are not merely known by me to be what they are, but are indeed mine and not others', for me to be proud because of them or to be able to see others' experiences as comparable to mine. And although it is importantly true that personal identity as it regards the passions is

---

[17] The key texts here are *T* I. iv. 2. 190 and *EU* VI. 66. On the latter, see Bricke 1980, ch. 7.

the sort of selfhood that defines someone as the player of the distinctive role that defines him or her in society, this can only be understood in terms of the indirect passions if these are generated by a being who already *has* a sense of himself or herself as the specific doer of the deeds, or possessor of the qualities, that generate the pride, and as the individual self to which the pride directs attention. And however illuminating Hume's accounts of the ways in which this sense of oneself functions may be, they do not tell us how we come by it.

Ainslie acknowledges this gap in Hume's system, but suggests it is to be explained by an unwillingness on Hume's part to engage in speculative developmental psychology.[18] Hume does not offer hypotheses about how infants come to be able to practise particular forms of thinking, and confines himself to describing the workings of the adult mind. No doubt this is true. But he is not unwilling to give accounts of those factors that induce the adult mind to ascribe necessity to causal sequences, to believe that its perceptions have distinct and continued existence, and to ascribe unity to the bundles of perceptions that constitute its history. It is an intriguing question how far Hume's accounts of these processes, which are in each case seen by him as fundamentally constitutive of the adult mind's experience of its world, is a psychological account in any sense that would be recognizable to twentieth-century psychologists, and what prior abilities and commitments Hume presupposes the mind to have in each of these cases before the process begins. But whatever the answer to these questions, the absence of any parallel account of how each of us comes to have the self–other distinction is striking. And I think it is this absence that creates the cultural shock that one experiences when passing from Book I to Book II.

## VI

A summary in conclusion. I have argued that Hume's purpose at the outset of *T* I. iv. 6 is to reject all accounts of the identity of the mind that judge it to be of a different order from that of organisms and physical objects. Such accounts deny the mind has parts, and maintain that its operations cannot be reduced, as Hume maintains

---

[18] Ainslie 1999.

they can be reduced, to the interactions of the perceptions that are the only units his 'Newtonian' science of man recognizes. The theories of the self that he attacks attempt a metaphysical explanation of the alleged unity of consciousness that he rejects. He believes that the introspective method of his science of man shows that the mind is an ownerless bundle of discrete impressions and ideas.

Since we all believe otherwise, Hume's next task is to tell us why we do. He insists that this story is one that parallels that of the origins of our belief in the identity of things and organisms. A foundation of this story is the claim that identity and change are incompatible, a claim that is embodied in his paradigms of identity and diversity. His account of how identity is ascribed through change is therefore an account of how this alleged incompatibility is overlooked.

When this account is applied to the human mind, Hume presents it as an account of how an observer (that is, each one of us reflecting on his or her own mental past) comes to ascribe a fictitious identity to it. I have argued that this account is free of formal inconsistency, since it can be supposed to be a tale of how a few later perceptions are added to the bundle to which this fictitious diachronic identity is ascribed. Hume adds, as an afterthought, that this account can also suffice to explain our belief in the simplicity, or synchronic identity, of the mind, since this belief is also the result of the relatedness of the parts (the concurrent perceptions) that are grouped together when such identity is ascribed to them.

In the Appendix to the *Treatise*, Hume expresses discomfort about this account. I am persuaded by Ainslie's arguments that the most likely explanation of his discomfort is an anxiety on Hume's part about how far the process of making identity-judgements can itself be subsumed under the sort of explanation he has offered. Hume seems inclined to doubt whether his explanation can extend to the manner in which the mind holds together the ideas it surveys and the ideas that constitute its survey and appropriation of them, during the moments in which it makes its judgements of identity about those perceptions that have formed its own past. He seems, that is, to be having second thoughts about his original throwaway confidence in the capacity of his account of the genesis of our belief in identity to accommodate equally our belief in synchronic identity, or simplicity.

If this is indeed what troubles Hume in the Appendix, it seems to imply that he feels his account needs to include some independent judgement of identity across the synchronous components of the mind's survey of its past, in addition to the judgement it makes about that past itself. Those of us who consider these issues in the light of Kant's treatment of them will find such a view of the facts very plausible; but it is not clear why Hume does. I do not see that his account requires the ascription of identity by the mind itself (as distinct from the ascription of identity that might be made by an external observer looking into one's breast) to be *complete*—that is, to include the present activity of judgement as well as the past perceptions that are the objects of that judgement. I fail to see why Hume could not say that ascriptions of identity to one's own mental history are always ineluctably incomplete because they are always retroactive. I would not offer such a claim as an attractive account of our self-knowledge, since I think there are significant differences between our judgements of our synchronic and diachronic identity.[19] But it does seem to me that Hume's system has formal resources to respond to the anxiety that he feels, and that he shows no independent signs of supposing that other features of his 'bundle' theory need correction.

If we look at other aspects of this theory, as it is employed in his account of the passions, he does not seem similarly troubled by any of the considerations that critics have raised about the differences between Books I and II. He confines his enquiry in Book I to the question of how one ascribes unity to one's own mental history, and never seems to consider the sources of the capacity to distinguish between one's own and those of others; and he takes this ability for granted when analysing the indirect passions. There is indeed a clear sense in which the mechanism of those passions can be said to create the self. This is the sense in which what I am proud or ashamed of, and what I admire or despise in others, make me the particular social entity that I am. Humean society is a community of conformists who mirror one another's emotions, internalize each other's moral preferences, and admire in themselves what others find lovable. This world contrasts with the solitary sceptic's world of Book I, whose author would be a 'strange uncouth monster' in it. But this world has, at its conceptual base, and as an ineradicable component of its emotional repertoire, the consciousness of the distinction between

[19] It seems, particularly, that one cannot be in error about the ownership of experiences one is currently having, though one is not immune from such error in regard to experiences one recalls having had. See my interchange with Madell in MacIntosh and Meynell 1994.

oneself and others. For although it is the direct passions, and particularly the desires and volitions, that induce actions, it is the indirect passions, especially pride and humility, that determine what I judge myself to be and to need, and therefore what desires I should seek to satisfy.[20] In this manner, therefore, the passions create the self that lives in the Humean world. But the self they create could not evolve if its owner did not make use of the deeper distinction between individuals who are distinct from each other and have each their own spatial and temporal boundaries.

[20] See McIntyre 1989, 1990, 1996; and again, Ainslie 1999.

# 7

## *Hume's Moral Psychology*

IN 1927, A. E. Taylor concluded his Leslie Stephen Lecture on 'David Hume and the Miraculous' with a judgement of Hume's attitude to his philosophical work that has been held by many other readers of Hume:

What kind of response one makes to life will, no doubt, for better or worse, depend on the sort of man one is for good or bad . . . But we can all make it our purpose that our philosophy, if we have one, shall be no mere affair of surface opinions, but the genuine expression of a whole personality. Because I can never feel that Hume's own philosophy was that, I have to own to a haunting uncertainty whether Hume was really a great philosopher, or only a 'very clever man'.[1]

Taylor is here expressing an attitude to Hume that many of us have felt: that his philosophy does not deserve to be taken too much to heart, because for all his intellectual vitality and the disturbing character of much that he says, there is a streak of frivolity in him that leads him to follow arguments to outrageous conclusions without serious consideration of the effect such conclusions may have on those who are driven to them; and that the love of literary reputation that he openly expressed, was of far greater personal importance to him than philosophical truth.

This estimate of Hume is a deeply mistaken one, and it involves a misconstruction of elements in his writings and his personality that have a very different explanation.

## I

There is no doubt that Hume writes with a lightness of touch, an ironic humour, and a degree of self-deprecation that are rare among

[1] Taylor 1927, 53–4.

great philosophers. He is not hard enough to read for a judgement of greatness to come readily to our minds, in fact. He is also able to deal with the issue immediately before him without labouring its connections with those other parts of his system not presently being considered; and this, too, to readers in an era when system-building is unfashionable, makes it harder to suppose he is trying to construct one in the way great philosophers do. And no thinker who is so frequently successful in the art of philosophical criticism can escape seeming to care first and foremost about scoring points. Such features are most easily explained as the result of a temperamental immunity to philosophical anxieties.

But the evidence is clearly against this, and another explanation is called for. The lightness is deliberately assumed for philosophical reasons by someone who is not immune to philosophical anxieties, but knows very well, and says, what it is like to be their victim. There are two well-known places where he tells us about this. One, not originally destined for our eyes, is the letter he wrote to an unnamed physician in 1734, did not (it seems) send, but preserved (*LDH* 1. 12–18). In this he outlines, with remarkable acuity, the symptoms of breakdown that he had suffered as a result of his philosophical exertions in the period prior to the composition of the *Treatise*—symptoms such as 'scurvy spots on the fingers', 'wateriness in the mouth' and a compulsive appetite, which he interpreted as signs of the 'disease of the learned'. The other is the famous concluding Section of Book I of the *Treatise* itself, where he tells us of the effects that his researches have upon him (*T* I. iv. 7. 263–74). He fancies himself to be 'some strange uncouth monster', to be 'in the most deplorable condition imaginable, inviron'd with the deepest darkness, and utterly deprived of the use of every member and faculty'. On both occasions he seeks release from these anxieties, which are the dark underside of the intellectual exhilaration that so frequently bursts through in the text of the *Treatise*; and this release is something he thinks to be available to him only if he makes himself balance the excesses of his philosophical reflections with deliberate absorption in business or social activities. These allow the resources of his nature to overcome the debilitating effects of over-indulgence in philosophical reasoning.

This clear evidence shows us that Hume was not someone for whom philosophy was an activity of minor consequence, but someone who saw himself as likely to be thrown off balance by his predilection for it. So the affable and corpulent gentlemanly loiterer (to use a phrase from Taylor[2]) whom some see as the historical Hume is, at most, a deliberately assumed *persona*, beneath which a much more complex and serious reality is at work. The *persona* is not the duplicate of the reality, but a product of experience and theory: experience of what philosophy leads to when practised in a way that does violence to our nature, and a theory that puts philosophy in its proper place.

What sort of theory is it? Any theory that suggests limits be placed on philosophy itself has an appearance of inconsistency if it is itself a philosophical theory; and the fact that Hume belongs somewhere in the Sceptical tradition might seem to accentuate this risk. To a large extent Hume's theory of human nature is not, in our terms, philosophical, but psychological, even though one of its key purposes is to determine the proper limits of philosophical thought. He certainly thinks that philosophical activity, properly pursued, sustains personal equilibrium and can keep threats to it in check—as when it protects us from the far more dangerous risks that arise from superstition (*T* I. iv. 7. 271–72). But to know when to pursue philosophy and when not, one has to understand human needs and weaknesses, and make philosophy take account of them. Hume does not *confuse* philosophy and psychology, as some suppose; but he does mix them, in a special blend of his own.

Hume, then, is a Socratic thinker. He believes that in order to avoid being plagued by anxiety we must achieve self-knowledge. The philosopher stands in need of it as much as his fellows do. Socrates would have agreed; but he did appear to think that self-knowledge was to come through the pursuit of the dialectical questioning in which the philosopher is expert, and Hume does not think this. Hume thinks that he has available a scientific mode of understanding that illuminates our nature for us, and that the philosopher must turn to this to save himself. Our nature is intelligible; and once we have learned its key features, we can avoid those influences in philosophy (and in religion) that would lead us to do violence to it. The understanding of human nature that Hume urges upon us is very different indeed from that deriving from Socrates, at least as Plato presents him to us.

## II

Hume proclaims the importance of his theory of human nature very confidently in the introduction to the *Treatise*:

[2] Taylor 1927, 53.

Here then is the only expedient, from which we can hope for success in our philosophical researches, to leave the tedious lingring method, which we have hitherto followed, and instead of taking now and then a castle or village on the frontier, to march up directly to the capital or centre of these sciences, to human nature itself . . . There is no question of importance, whose decision is not compriz'd in the science of man; and there is none, which can be decided with any certainty, before we become acquainted with that science. In pretending therefore to explain the principles of human nature, we in effect propose a compleat system of the sciences, built on a foundation almost entirely new, and the only one upon which they can stand with any security. (*T* Int. xx)

This is very ambitious language, fully comparable to the claims Descartes had made in the previous century to be rebuilding all knowledge afresh. But the bases the two thinkers offer for this rebuilding are very different. The differences help us to understand why Hume has always had the reputation of being a spoiler rather than a builder, in spite of the positive thrust of this programmatic proclamation.

In Descartes' reconstruction of human knowledge, the metaphysical separation of the mental and the physical dictates limits to science: science gets the autonomy it deserves (and which the church had denied it in condemning Galileo) because it is confined in its subject-matter to the physical world; the soul is exempted from its scrutiny because of its simplicity, its freedom and its self-consciousness. The essence of Hume's reconstruction is to be found in the insistence that there can indeed be a science of mind, and that it is 'experimental', or observational. The scientific ideal Hume has is often described as Newtonian, and the evidence for this is his proclamation of the theory of the association of ideas. This seems to duplicate Newtonian explanation in the physical realm. It does this by identifying, first, the ultimate corpuscular units that our observation of mental life reveals to us; Hume calls these perceptions, and divides them into impressions and ideas. It then provides a principle roughly corresponding to that of gravitation to account for the constant inner movement and change that characterizes the mental life we are able to introspect. This analogue to gravitation is association, which determines one perception to call up, or lead on to, another. In spite of a wise and cautionary statement that 'we are only to regard it as a gentle force, which commonly prevails' (*T* I. i. 4. 10), the gravitational analogy is offered with pride, along with a similarly Newtonian reticence about what may lie beneath that gentle force:

Here is a kind of ATTRACTION, which in the mental world will be found to have as extraordinary effects as in the natural, and to shew itself in as many and as various forms. Its effects are every where conspicuous; but as to its causes, they are mostly unknown, and must be resolv'd into *original* qualities of human nature, which I pretend not to explain. (*T* I. i. 4. 12–13)

In the *Abstract*, his own anonymous puff for the *Treatise*, he says that if anything justifies calling 'the author' an inventor, it is the use he makes of the principle of association.

Peter Jones has argued, persuasively, that the influence of Newton on Hume has been overrated, and that Hume's direct acquaintance with Newton's writings was probably limited.[3] In spite of this, however, and in spite of the fact that the doctrine of association is less prominent in his later writings than it is in the *Treatise*, and that the *Treatise* itself, as we shall see, leans heavily on psychological theories that do not combine with it without difficulty, I think that the impact of something like a Newtonian picture of the science of mind lingered in Hume's system long after the details of associationism ceased to interest him. There are two places where this can be seen most clearly. One is in his view of the self. The other is in his famous claim that reason is the slave of the passions. In both these places we find ourselves at the heart of his moral psychology.

To say there can be a science of the mental, as Hume sees the matter, is to say that what we think, feel, or will can be explained as the effect of a cause and the instance of a natural law. Human minds are not strangers in nature, but inextricably parts of it. Hume tries to demonstrate this in detail in the *Treatise* by showing how our beliefs and our emotive and conative commitments arise. The accounts are intended to treat thoughts and feelings and volitions (all perceptions, in his vocabulary) as the units of explanation, and to show how they give rise to one another. This form of explanation, at least nominally, gives the mind *itself* no role to play. If the never-ending changes in the physical world are all to be explained in terms of the attraction of material particles to one another, there is no room for the suggestion that the world itself, which merely *contains* them, exerts a force of its own. It is just the place where the events being described occur. Similarly, if the course of my mental history is determined by the associative attraction of my perceptions, so that they

---

[3] Jones 1982, 11–19.

cause one another to arise, there seems no place, perhaps even no clear sense, to the suggestion that *I*, the mind or soul that *has* them, can exert any influence over their course. All it does is *include* them. The self, or ego, as he says (*T* I. iv. 6. 253) is just 'a kind of theatre, where several perceptions successively make their appearance'. The denial of an independent real self is not an awkward consequence of Hume's theory of knowledge, which requires us to say that it is not there because we cannot find it when we look for it (although this is true); it is a cornerstone of his system, required by the supposed fact of a science of man conceived in quasi-Newtonian terms. This science is deterministic, since mental events occur as a result of laws that supposedly govern the sequences of such events alone; and if they mention minds or agents themselves, these are construed to be mere bundles, collections, or sequences of such events. 'They are the successive perceptions only, that constitute the mind; nor have we the most distant notion of the place,where these scenes are represented, or of the materials, of which it is compos'd' (*T* I. iv. 6. 253).

This understanding of human nature stands in sharp contrast to another, which for convenience I shall call the rationalist model. This derives, historically, from Plato's 'Phaedo', in which Socrates is presented as teaching that the human soul is not part of nature, but is alien to it. It can choose how far it allies itself with the alien forces of its present environment, and how far it asserts its independence from them. These alien forces make inroads upon it through the passions and desires, to which the soul can say yes or no. The implication of this is that some of the elements of our inner life, namely the passions and desires, are not truly parts of ourselves at all; what is to be identified with the true self is the reason which says yes or no to them.

This Platonic view of the soul has taken deep root in our culture in many popular, and sophisticated, doctrines that are not overtly ascribed to him. There is the common contrast between reason and the passions, a contrast that yields the assumption that when one acts from passion one acts *in passivity*, so that what one does is not fully an act at all, or that one is not fully oneself in doing it. There is the correlative assumption, philosophically expressed in modern times in the Cartesian tradition, that the self is to be equated with the rational faculty, and that one is fully oneself when it dictates what one believes and what one chooses. Descartes indeed carried this to the extent of holding that one has full freedom whether to say yes or no, not only to the passions, but to the presentations of sense, so that we can always suspend judgement when grounds are inconclusive.[4] This theory is the epistemological aspect of the general view that the unique dignity of the human soul consists in its possession of a special kind of freedom to assent to, or to reject, the promptings of the senses, the emotions, and the instincts. We can readily wonder whether all the elements in this view of ourselves are necessarily connected, and even whether they are consistent, but they are all powerfully present in popular culture and rationalist philosophical theory.

Hume's understanding of human nature is at odds with this rationalist picture of it at every important point, and he sees all its main contentions as inconsistent with the very possibility of a science of man. So he assaults it in every possible way, and in assaulting it ensures that he acquires a destructive reputation among philosophers who feel the dignity of human nature and the dignity of their own profession are both linked to the truth of the rationalist picture. One way Hume assaults that picture is by making statements of high shock-value for those imbued with it. The most famous is his dictum that 'Reason is, and ought only to be the slave of the passions, and can never pretend to any other office than to serve and obey them' (*T* II. iii. 3. 415). This is fundamentally an insistence that there can be a science of human nature in a way the rationalist picture would (in Hume's opinion) make impossible. It is of course more than this: it is also a claim that when we look and see, we shall find that human beings are creatures of instinct and feeling whose rational powers cannot, or at least should not, be used in any way at odds with this.

Kemp Smith[5] and others have made clear that Hume's theory of knowledge is itself an application of this claim about human nature. He sees our most fundamental beliefs as products of instinct; and he thinks we are lucky that they are. The rational queries of the philosophical sceptic would have the effect, if the rationalist view of the mind were true, of reducing us to a condition of chronic anxiety and indecision through our inability to justify the claims of our senses or the expectation of regularity in nature or the identity of the self. The sceptic is quite right about what we cannot rationally justify,

---

[4] See his Fourth Meditation, e.g. in Descartes 1966 edn., 92–100.
[5] Smith 1905 and 1941.

but he is also, fortunately, quite wrong about what we are able to disbelieve. His doubts are intellectually correct, but are *vain* or impotent doubts. Hume is himself a sceptic in his estimate of the soundness of sceptical arguments, but sides with the most truculent of the Common Sense thinkers in denying that these arguments can disturb us for more than brief periods.[6] These brief periods, however, are anxious ones, to be avoided by distraction, social or intellectual. Hume rejects the contention of the Sceptics of antiquity that the recognition of reason's inability to support the commitments of Common Sense leads of itself to inner peace. On the contrary, as he makes very clear in the concluding Section 7 of Book I of the *Treatise*, such recognition would lead to despair if not overcome by the resources of instinct.

Hume does see our nature as creative: in generating our fundamental beliefs, it invests our perceptions with meaning. But it is instinct and not reason that does this.

Why is it that our instincts manage to invest our perceptions with meanings that are so useful and adaptive? Hume does not profess to know, and contents himself with an ironical suggestion that there must be a pre-established harmony at work (*EU* v. 54). He never says the lifeworld our instincts create for us is one we know to be the true one.[7] His view of our beliefs is essentially a Darwinian view.

I turn now to a more detailed account of the way Hume's view of human nature underlies his account of our conduct and our morality, leaving aside his epistemology with the comment that, as Kemp Smith made clear to us, Hume's views on the interrelation between reason and passion run parallel in the two areas.

## III

Epistemology has never had much of a place in popular culture. But the rationalist understanding of human nature has a strong hold on the common understanding of our choices. We pride ourselves on the supposed fact that we are able sometimes to choose courses of action that override our passions and desires in the light of a greater

---

[6] See Chapter 9.

[7] This is what separates him so clearly from the commonsense school. See Norton 1982, ch. 5.

good. We pride ourselves on the supposed fact that when we do this, we exercise the power to be free from the influences and temptations that would otherwise condemn us to what Kant called heteronomy. And we particularly pride ourselves on the supposed fact that we are able to pursue the austere demands of duty and so function as pillars of society by putting inclination aside.

Hume denies none of the experiences on which these popular self-estimates depend. We can, and do, choose the good over the attractive, and resist many of the passions that agitate us. We are indeed entitled to talk of ourselves as acting freely on many such occasions— and equally on those when we yield to passions, and choose the attractive rather than the good. And we do, indeed, choose many actions because they are our duty, even though they do not appeal to us, and our society depends for its health on the fact that we do this. But none of these familiar experiences is to be interpreted in the way rationalists interpret them. I shall take each of these three popular views in order, and try to show how Hume offers an alternative account of the relevant phenomena. I begin with those occasions when we pursue our good in the face of inclination.

The rationalist holds that when I do this, reason triumphs over passion. Hume's alternative account of this familiar experience depends upon his analysis of the passions, which he develops at length in the largely neglected second Book of the *Treatise*.[8]

The two technical classifications that are essential for understanding Hume's analysis of conflict and choice are his distinctions between direct and indirect passions, and between calm and violent passions. Both distinctions are introduced in the first section of Book II (*T* II. i. 1. 276–7). Every passion is a unique, simple secondary impression. What makes it the passion it is, rather than some other, is therefore the felt quality it has; and questions about how it arises and how it leads to other experiences or to actions, are construed by Hume as causal questions to be dealt with within his Newtonian mental science. In calling them secondary impressions, Hume seeks to distinguish them from the sensory impressions, which he calls

---

[8] What follows here is not an attempt at the impossible feat of summarizing Book II in a few paragraphs, but an attempt to indicate the most important parts of its argument for the assessment of Hume's alternative to rationalism in moral psychology. I give a somewhat more detailed treatment in ch. 5 of Penelhum 1975*a*. Important accounts of Book II are to be found in Árdal 1966; Capaldi 1989, ch. 5; Baier 1991, chs. 6 and 7.

'original'—a term indicating (here at least) that they do not occur in us in consequence of prior perceptions, as the secondary ones do. Passions, then, always arise in us from mental causes: sensory impressions, ideas, or other passions. When they arise from other passions, they do so by association. There is, therefore, an association of impressions (based on resemblance) as well as an association of ideas.

The distinction between direct and indirect passions is a distinction between two ways in which passions may arise. Direct passions 'arise immediately from good or evil, from pain or pleasure' (*T* II. i. 1. 276), which seems to mean that they arise when something has given us pleasure or pain, or is believed to offer us the prospect of them. This at least is what he says at the outset of Book II; but when he discusses the direct passions in more detail in Section 9 of Part iii, he adds that some of them 'frequently arise from a natural impulse or instinct which is perfectly unaccountable' (*T* II. iii. 9. 439): a remark that comes close to making them original after all.[9] The indirect passions 'proceed from the same principles, but by the conjunction of other qualities' (*T* II. i. 1. 276). This 'conjunction' is described in much detail in Parts i and ii of Book II; but the key element in it is the fact that the indirect passions require a distinction between their *causes* and their *objects*:[10] roughly the qualities that occasion them and the *persons* (that is oneself or another or others) who have them. The fundamental indirect passions are those of pride and humility (that is, shame), where the object is oneself, and love and hatred, where the object is another person or persons; in each case the passion only arises when we are conscious not only of the quality that causes it, but of the fact that it is possessed by, or due to, the self or another—the 'object, to which it is directed' (*T* II. i. 3. 280).

The direct passions are a very mixed group indeed; but the critical fact about them for present purposes is that they do not only include such reactive emotions as joy or grief or despair, but some of the most fundamental determinants of human conduct, namely the *desires*. He does not only include desires for perceived objects

[9] This remark is probably intended to avoid the appearance of psychological hedonism that could be left by the earlier classification. Kemp Smith and Árdal have said that the passions Hume refers to here should be classified separately as 'primary' rather than as direct, but I cannot examine the merits of this suggestion here.

[10] This should not be equated too readily with what analytical philosophers in our time have meant by these terms. See Penelhum 1975, ch. 5.

like clothes, or for bodily satisfactions like food or sex, but mentions 'the desire of punishment to our enemies, and of happiness to our friends' (*T* II. iii. 9. 439) and even 'the general appetite to good, and aversion to evil, consider'd merely as such' (*T* II. iii. 3. 417). It does not seem very natural to write of desires as passions, unless they are very agitating and overwhelming ones, but Hume's psychology depends on his being able to counter our resistance to his doing this. He attempts to counter it through his very important distinction between calm and violent passions. When introducing it, Hume says that it is common for us to distinguish between gentle and intense emotions, and to use the word 'passion' only of the latter, but he calls this a 'vulgar and specious division' (*T* II. i. 1. 276). One and the same passion can be both mild and intense, though a given passion will usually be one or the other. It is critically important that when a passion has become 'the predominant inclination of the soul, it commonly produces no longer any sensible agitation' (*T* II. iii. 4. 419). We must therefore distinguish between the violence of a passion, which is a matter of its felt intensity, and its strength, which is a matter of its degree of influence on our choices and conduct. A passion can be strong but calm; and such a passion may overcome a more violent or agitating one. This is presumably what happens when we choose the good over the alluring—so that the aching longing for the dessert loses out to the wish to stay slim, which agitates not at all. So those occasions when we think our reason has won out over passion are actually cases where a calm passion has shown more strength than a violent one.[11]

The doctrine of calm passions is Hume's main card in the game against rationalist psychology. Its main internal difficulty is the fact that it requires him to say that passions can be 'in a manner, imperceptible' (*T* II. i. 1. 276), while classing them as impressions; when he has earlier distinguished impressions from ideas on the basis of their force and vivacity, even using the very word 'violence' in doing so (*T* I. i. 1. 1).

He supports his positive analysis of choice by some famous negative arguments against rationalism. They are to be found in Section 3 of Part iii of Book II, entitled 'Of the influencing motives of the will'. They are intended to show that 'reason alone can never

---

[11] We owe the clear understanding of Hume's distinction between calm and violent passions to Árdal 1966, 95 ff.

be a motive to any action of the will' and that 'it can never oppose passion in the direction of the will' (*T* II. iii. 3. 413). Hume argues for the first contention in two ways: he says that reason has two functions only, namely the discovery of relations of ideas, as in mathematics, and the description of matters of fact, as in the empirical sciences and common life.[12] Reason in the former function has practical import only when calculation plays a role in empirical investigation; and in its empirical function reason can affect practice only by showing us the causes or effects of objects that we already desire or shun. In other words, it is our desires that prompt us to pursue or flee from the objects of our choice. Reason merely shows us what leads to, or away from, that in which our desires make us take interest. It is never itself the source of such interest.

If reason is thus shown to be incapable of originating our choices and inclinations, then on those occasions when we make choices in opposition to a passion, it cannot be reason that moves us : it cannot provide the necessary contrary 'impulse' itself. At most it can serve some desire or aversion that is the real counter-force to the passion that loses the contest.

Hume tries to clinch these arguments by drawing on a fundamental feature of his theory of the passions: that they are secondary impressions, and not ideas. Only ideas have 'reference to any other object', because they are copies, whereas passions, as impressions, do not have any such 'representative quality'. They cannot, therefore, be 'contradictory to truth and reason', since such contradiction entails a defect in that very representative quality. This self-containedness, or lack of reference, that supposedly characterizes all passions is a feature of them even when they are desires. Hume gives the example of anger, which on his view is a desire for harm to another (what we would call hostility). When I am angry, he says, 'I am actually possest with the passion, and in that emotion have no more a reference to any other object, than when I am thirsty, or sick, or more than five foot high' (*T* II. iii. 3. 415).

As a consequence of this wildly implausible denial of the intentionality of passions and desires, Hume maintains that they cannot properly be called unreasonable. This term, though often applied to them, should, he says, be applied only to the judgements that

---

[12] I am here using the terminology Hume introduced later in *EU* IV. It is clear that the same distinction is intended in *T* II. iii. 3.

*accompany* them. 'In short, a passion must be accompany'd with some false judgement, in order to its being unreasonable; and even then 'tis not the passion, properly speaking, which is unreasonable, but the judgement' (*T* II. iii. 3. 416). Hence there is no unreasonableness in preferring 'the destruction of the whole world to the scratching of my finger' or in choosing 'my total ruin, to prevent the least uneasiness of an *Indian* or person wholly unknown to me', or to prefer my lesser good to my greater. None of these preferences require any false judgements, and could only be unreasonable if they did.

If we put aside the attention-drawing rhetoric, we can see that Hume does not deny reason an essential role in human conduct. It shows us how to satisfy our desires, and in enabling us to recognize that which we then come to want, it can even prompt them, although he does not concede this explicitly. What reason cannot do is to motivate us of itself. It is the *slave* of the passions. But there are many things that we can do with the help of a slave that we could not do if we did not have him, and for all the air of paradox with which Hume pronounces his theories, he does not deny this.[13]

IV

Hume believes that if there is to be a science of human nature, our actions and choices must show the same sorts of regularity that we find in the physical world. In tracing our choices to the workings of the passions, that arise in us through the mechanisms of association, he has tried to show that these regularities do indeed govern them. Such a programme seems to imply a denial of the freedom that we think distinguishes us from other beings, and that is associated in rationalist theory with the assertion of the supposed authority of reason. Hume seeks to show that his human science can accommodate our freedom without exempting human choice from the regularity and predictability that he finds in our natures. Hence his philosophical system contains the best-known classical statement of what is now known as Compatibilism.[14]

---

[13] For important further discussion of these very complicated questions, see Norton 1982, ch. 3; Baier 1991, ch. 7, and Bricke 1996, especially ch. 1. An older but very shrewd examination is to be found in Kydd 1946.

[14] He was anticipated by Hobbes in ch. 21 of *Leviathan*.

Compatibilism is the thesis that there is no inconsistency in holding that human actions are caused and yet are free. This is a logical thesis, normally combined with the substantive claim that our actions always *are* caused, and that they are sometimes free as well. I shall use the title to comprise the combination of all three propositions. I shall use the common term Libertarianism to name the view that it is indeed inconsistent to hold human actions can be free yet always caused; that some of them are indeed free; and that some are therefore, in some manner, exempt from causation.

Hume's position is presented most clearly in Section VIII of the first *Enquiry*, though most of what he says there is anticipated in Sections 1 and 2 of Part iii of Book II of the *Treatise*. The *Treatise* version is more aggressive, and in the *Enquiry* he describes his argument as a 'reconciling project'. This phrase might suggest that he thinks his position is fully in accord with common sense, but it clearly is not, and Hume does not seriously pretend it is. What he thinks he is reconciling are the needs of a human science and the needs of our ordinary moral discourse, and he argues that common opinion is in error about those needs. Popular opinion holds that we need one sort of freedom, that we do not have, instead of another, that we do have.

In the *Treatise* he uses scholastic terminology to name these two kinds of freedom: he distinguishes between 'liberty of spontaneity' and 'liberty of indifference'. Liberty of spontaneity consists in the absence of hindrances to the execution of one's decision. He describes it in the *Enquiry* thus: 'a power of acting, or not acting, according to the determinations of the will; that is, if we choose to remain at rest, we may; if we choose to move, we may' (*EU* viii. 95). He immediately adds that it is possessed by 'everyone who is not a prisoner and in chains'. He thinks, correctly, that this last claim is not controversial. He is also correct in thinking that liberty of spontaneity, so defined, is compatible with universal causation; for it is merely the absence of interference with the exercise of one's choices, not the absence of causal determination in the making of those choices.

Where he is controversial is in what he says about the other sort of freedom that we think we have, but in his view do not have. We think that sometimes, when we choose one way, we could equally have chosen another way. In Hume's language, we believe that sometimes, when we choose to remain at rest, we might (even though we do not) choose instead to move; and that if we choose to move, we might (even though we do not) choose instead to remain at rest. We believe in the reality of unexercised powers of choice, and see this reality as essential to our freedom as agents. Hume calls this sort of freedom 'liberty of indifference', interprets it as a denial of the universality of causation in human affairs, and insists we neither have it nor need it. Indeed, he believes the requirements of our moral thinking and decision-making are inconsistent with its existence.

He attacks liberty of indifference in three ways. First, he asserts the universality of causation, and the unreality of chance, and emphasizes that human affairs do not differ in these respects from the natural world. For example:

It is universally allowed that nothing exists without a cause of its existence, and that chance, when strictly examined, is a mere negative word, and means not any real power which has anywhere a being in nature. (*EU* VIII. 95)

To this dogmatic metaphysical argument, he adds that we can infer and predict human actions from the motives and characters of human agents in a way that is fully comparable to our ability to explain and predict natural phenomena; and when people seem to act in bizarre or unpredictable ways, we can postulate, and discover, hidden causes that account for this—again, as we are able to do for surprising physical events. So we must acknowledge 'necessity' in human affairs as well as in physical nature—this term being understood, as he stresses, in the same way as he has interpreted it in his earlier analysis of causal inferences. (It is important to recall that when he outlines what he calls some 'corollaries' of that analysis in the *Treatise* he remarks, with astonishing casualness, that 'the distinction, which we often make betwixt *power* and the *exercise* of it, is . . . without foundation' (*T* I. iii. 14. 171). One of the ways in which we 'often make' this distinction is, of course, in the popular ascription to agents of the unexercised power of choice.)

Hume's second line of attack on liberty of indifference is the more practical one that we need predictability in human affairs in order to make our decisions. He gives the melancholy example of the prisoner condemned to the scaffold, who recognizes he will get no help in escaping from his gaoler or his guards by observing their characters, and decides he would be better employed in trying to weaken the bars of his cell than in trying to change their resolution (*T* II. iii. 1. 406). The multitude of examples that human experience offers us of regular connections between character and action would not be open to us if liberty of indifference were a reality.

Hume's third argument against liberty of indifference consists in refutations of the natural, but in his view misguided, suggestion that we can introspect its reality (*T* II. iii. 1. 408). What he says here parallels the many important things he says in opposition to the claim that we can detect within ourselves the experience of the power that we ascribe to natural causes. (See, for example, *EU* VII. 64–9.) Hume does not deny there are volitions, as some have;[15] he sees them as a readily detectable component in the mechanism of human choice.[16] But he denies that we can ever detect they are themselves 'subject to nothing'.

Liberty of indifference, then, is a myth; but we have never had any need of it, and in fact presuppose its absence in practical reflection. Its reality would be inconsistent with the possibility of a science of man, as Hume conceives that. It is impossible here to explore the question of the relationship between human science and determinism, which is raised by Hume's stance. Instead, I mention an important implication of his view for his moral psychology.

If Hume is right, we are often in a position to enact the choices we make, and also to enact the alternative choices that we do not make. But we are never in a position to choose in a way other than the way we do choose. He believes in the reality of unexploited opportunities; but not in the reality of unexercised powers of choice. This entails, however, that moral praise or blame can never be applied on the ground that someone has chosen a course of action that he or she *need not have chosen*. Common opinion follows rationalism in thinking that this is in fact the basis of much praise or blame; and Hume must deny it.

He does in fact deny it, and offers an account of moral virtue that connects it with the very predictability that he insists we can find in human affairs, not with the liberty of indifference that he says does not exist.

## V

We have seen that Hume traces all choice to the passions, and rejects the rationalist understanding of human freedom. But this merely leads

---

[15] The best-known case is Ryle 1949, ch. 3.
[16] See Penelhum 1975, 111–17 and Bricke 1984.

us to what he seems to see as the major problem of his moral philosophy. Rationalists might concede the main features of his account of prudential choice, but still say that when I choose what I think is good for me instead of what I am now inclined to, I remain the servant of my desires. I do not cease to serve them when I merely postpone their satisfaction to the future. We do, however, sometimes manage to act in the face of *all* our desires, short-term or long-term. We do this when we act from duty. When we do this, reason does indeed triumph over passion.

The best-known version of this view from Hume's time is that of Joseph Butler, who insists on the supremacy of conscience in human nature.[17] He accords it supremacy over all other springs of action, including self-love, benevolence, and particular desires. Hume's account of our regard for duty is one that concedes its reality, but still derives it from our emotional natures as his science of man depicts them.

His account depends on a principle he enunciates as an 'undoubted maxim': 'that no action can be virtuous, or morally good, unless there be in human nature some motive to produce it, distinct from the sense of its morality' (*T* ii. ii. 1. 479). He recognizes that this claim has to contend with the fact that we do sometimes act from a sense of duty alone; and his attempt to accommodate this fact is at the heart of his account of justice, and is the most extensive and important of his three forms of attack on the rationalist view of human nature.

We must begin with his account of the role of the passions, or sentiments, of approval and disapproval, since he views the sense of duty as a derivative of these. Hume holds that moral judgements, in which we describe behaviour as virtuous or vicious, express these sentiments. Like all other passions, they are unique secondary impressions, and cannot therefore be analysed; but we can say how they arise and what their effects are. The story is complex; but we can see at the outset that if indeed the sense of duty is a product of the sentiments of approval and disapproval, it is a product of sentiments that arise when we pass judgement on human behaviour that must already be produced by something other than the approval and disapproval to which it gives rise. I draw in what follows on

---

[17] Butler avoids commitment on whether conscience is a rational power or a moral sense. See Butler 1900, vol. 2, 287. But the role he ascribes to it is one to which Hume must find an alternative within his own science of human nature.

Sections 1, 2, and 3 of Part iii of Book III of the *Treatise*, and Sections
V to VIII of the second *Enquiry*.

Hume maintains that moral approval and disapproval have
human characters, rather than individual actions, as their objects.
It is significant that he takes the terms 'virtuous' and 'vicious' as
the paradigms of moral language, thus making it easier to persuade
us that evaluations are directed toward persons rather than their deeds.
'If any *action* be either virtuous or vicious, 'tis only as a sign of some
quality or character' (*T* III. iii. 1. 575). He says that actions that do
not reflect settled states of character in their agents 'are never consider'd in morality'. Reason assists in the generation of approval and
disapproval by showing us the effects that certain states of character have. If, by a disinterested examination (an examination conducted
'without reference to our particular interest' (*T* III. i. 2. 472)), we find
that a particular character-trait is agreeable or useful, or disagreeable or harmful, to the agent who has it, or to others, then the mechanism that generates approval or disapproval can commence.

The mechanism is complex, and involves the workings of the
principle of *sympathy*. This principle is not to be confused with the
sentiment of compassion, which is merely one of its products. The
principle is the one that enables us to participate in the emotional
life, and the pleasures and pains, of others. Hume introduces it in
Section 11 of Part i of Book II of the *Treatise*.[18] According to his
account of it there, I become aware of the passion of another by
observing its manifestations in his or her behaviour; I have, therefore, an *idea* of it. So far, however, I am not moved by the other's
passion. For this to happen, my idea has to be enlivened: then it
will turn into an impression, and I shall *have* the very passion I have
inferred in the other person. Hume says, to the regular surprise of
the readers who encounter this so early in Book II, with their memories of Section 6 of Part iv of Book I in their minds, that what
enlivens the idea I have of the other's passion is the 'idea, or rather
impression' of myself (*T* II. i. 11. 317). He cannot here refer to the
impression of the pure ego that he was so emphatic in Book I that
he did not have, but must refer to 'that succession of related ideas

---

[18] Sympathy seems to drop out of sight in the second *Enquiry*, and it has been a
matter of considerable controversy whether this shows Hume to have abandoned it
or not. For the negative view, see the appendix to Stewart 1963; for the positive, see
Capaldi 1989, ch. 7.

and impressions, of which we have an intimate memory and consciousness' (*T* II. i. 2. 277). This is so lively and vivid that its liveliness is communicated to the idea of the other's passion, which I then come to have myself. It can then lead on to other emotions, through the principle of association.

The sympathetic mechanism enables me to share in the pleasures and pains that are the effects, in the agent or others, of those character-traits I am disinterestedly surveying. The association of impressions causes me then to experience approval (when these effects are pleasant) or disapproval (when they are painful). I *express* these sentiments in my moral judgements, and I call the character-traits I have assessed in this way virtues or vices respectively. (Their virtuousness or viciousness consists in their capacity to arouse these sentiments in observers; but these sentiments have not, of course, caused these character-traits to be present in the observed agents in the first place.)

Hume describes approval and disapproval as calm forms of the indirect passions of love and hatred (*T* III. iii. 5. 614). Love and hatred are caused by the qualities or actions of persons, but have the persons themselves as their objects. Approval and disapproval are aroused by the qualities agents display, but are directed toward the agents themselves as the bearers of the characters they manifest.

We have yet to account for the sense of duty, however. The account comes in two parts. The first is Hume's explanation of how it is that we sometimes perform acts from a sense of duty that others perform from (say) benevolence. He says that someone may be conscious of the fact that he lacks a character-trait (such as kindness to children) that causes us to approve of those who have it. He may then come to 'hate himself on that account', and may perform the action 'from a certain sense of duty, in order to acquire, by practice, that virtuous principle . . .' (*T* III. ii. 1. 479). On this view, the sense of duty is a conscious substitute for more natural motives, and is a product of self-hatred. To feel it is to feel the disapproval of your own lack of a virtuous inclination.

These phenomena occur, though we may well doubt whether they are the key to the *origin* of the sense of duty. But even if they are, they do not include a much larger range of cases: those occasions when we seem willing to act from duty even when there is no prior natural motive. These are the cases when we act from *justice*. There is no natural inclination (such as benevolence) to explain our willingness to pay our taxes or return money borrowed from bankers. Yet justice is esteemed as a virtue, and its denial is judged vicious.

The latter is the more important for the psychology of duty. The wider story of the nature and origins of justice cannot be told here. But in Hume's system justice is not a natural virtue but an artificial one: that is, it is not a settled state of character that is due to innate causes within us, but is a condition we acquire because of the influence on us of social institutions. We do have some socially unifying motives in our natural benevolence and love of family; but these motives are too restrictive to sustain large social groupings. We are able, however, to see the value of conventions that would safeguard such things as property rights, and we adopt them through an implicit recognition of common interests. Both in the *Treatise* and in the second *Enquiry* Hume uses the analogy of oarsmen who row together without any explicit mutual undertaking to do so. Such conventions often entail inconvenience for us, but we sustain them through self-interest.

Once they are established, it is easy to understand how they acquire the extra status given them through the operation of approval and disapproval. Each of us is able, through sympathy, to be conscious of the unpleasant results of unjust actions for those who suffer from them. We may suffer from them ourselves. We express our displeasure at these effects by saying that just actions are our duty, and avoid inner discomfort by doing our duty ourselves. Hence justice becomes virtuous without being attractive. Hume's most succinct summary of his account of the genesis of the sense of duty is perhaps this:

All morality depends upon our sentiments; and when any action, or quality of the mind, pleases us *after a certain manner*, we say it is virtuous; and when the neglect, or non-performance of it, displeases us *after a like manner*, we say that we lie under an obligation to perform it. (*T* III. ii. 5. 517)

## VI

For all his willingness to express himself paradoxically, Hume's moral psychology is designed to accommodate the phenomena of our daily moral experience, and only to reject a rationalist interpretation of them. He does not seek to overturn the moral conventions of common sense but, on the contrary, seeks to support them anew on foundations of experiment and observation, free of misleading and disruptive theory.[19] It is therefore important, in assessing his successes and failures, to determine how far his opinions conform to common opinion, and how far not.

I begin with a comment on his theory of obligation. For many readers its very ingenuity presents an immediate difficulty. Is it so obvious that the sense of duty is derivative? Hume is free of the wordly-wise cynicism of psychological egoism. In the second appendix to the last edition of the second *Enquiry* he argues against it, much in the manner of Joseph Butler, and maintains that those who hold it (like Hobbes) are forcing a theory on the observable facts of conduct. But why not follow Butler further and say that the observable facts also show we have a natural tendency to feel and act on a sense of obligation?[20] The reason is probably to be found not only in the determination to undermine ethical rationalism, but also in the equally strong determination, in Hume, to avoid any theory that might seem to require, or invite, theological underpinnings, and to offer instead a purely secular account of all the phenomena he explains. But in seeking to offer an explanation of conscience at all, instead of taking the fact of it as a datum as he takes benevolence to be, he is forced to interpret it as a product of the institutions of social justice, when the latter are probably regarded by most as deriving some of their hold on us from the power of our sense of obligation, not the other way about. The fact that many other philosophers try to explain them as deriving from self-interest, much as Hume does, puts them at odds with common opinion also.

There is another place where his account of moral virtue puts him at odds with common sense, and where he himself shows signs of greater discomfort at the fact. In his story of the ways we come to feel moral approval, he tells us that it is directed toward established character-traits in our natures, and arises when we disinterestedly recognize that these character-traits are useful or agreeable to ourselves or others : that they have utility, in the language of the second *Enquiry*. This account prompts a question: there are many human characteristics that have utility in this way that we delight in,

[19] In this respect, I am in agreement with the position in Norton 1982.
[20] For Butler's arguments, see the first, second, and third Sermons in Butler 1900, i. 25–57.

but are not objects of moral approval. Similarly, many human traits that are harmful or disagreeable do not elicit moral disapproval. We praise charm, wit, or eloquence, but not *in the manner* of benevolence, industry, or temperance. Why not? Hume addresses this potentially vexing question in Section 4 of Part iii of Book III of the *Treatise*, and the fourth appendix to the second *Enquiry*. He tries to dismiss it as not 'very material' and in entitling the *Enquiry* Appendix 'Of Some Verbal Disputes' evinces a lamentable and atypical inclination to dismiss a serious conceptual issue as what misguided theorists today sometimes call a 'mere' question of semantics.

But it *is* a problem; and he shows a degree of recognition of the sort of problem that it is by trying to fend off one possible explanation of the distinction we do indeed make between virtues on the one hand and talents on the other. This is the suggestion that virtues are voluntarily acquired and talents are not. He says, perhaps correctly, that there is no ground for maintaining this, and suggests instead that the relevant consideration is that virtues (and vices) can be changed by laws and by education, whereas talents can not. This is interesting, but seems wrong: one thinks of the work of remedial language instructors, long-suffering piano teachers, or physiotherapists, who all seem to be in the thankless but not-wholly-ineffectual business of modifying our talents by training.

What, then, is the ground of our distinction? We can approach it by noticing that in order to assimilate talents to virtues, Hume has to assume that the talents are used well or wisely. A virtue cannot (necessarily cannot) be used badly by its possessor, but a talent can.[21] A virtue is, in part, the predictable tendency to use some talent well, rather than badly. But using a talent well involves using it at the right times and not using it at the wrong times. We praise someone who can be predicted to do this (by calling him virtuous), because that person *chooses* to use it when it is good to, and not to use it when it would be bad to. He or she is praiseworthy because they use it in good ways when they *could* use it in bad ways instead. We praise the predictability of virtuous action precisely because we think it could be done otherwise. On Hume's view of freedom this is what we can never say about anyone's choices.

---

[21] One recalls here the definition of a virtue in Aquinas: 'a good disposition of the mind, by which we live righteously, and of which no one can make bad use'. *Summa Theologiae* 1a2ae55, 4.

Hume's science of human nature, then, seems to have the unattractive consequence that we accord moral approval and disapproval to patterns of choice that could not be other than what they are. A good character is just a piece of good fortune. While popular ethical thinking is frequently forced to give ear to this view, it is still seen as paradoxical. Good character is, for the most part, still regarded as the regular tendency to make free choices that are good, not merely to perform pleasing acts habitually.

This brings us to the bedrock of Hume's understanding of what a science of human nature has to be like. I have suggested that the common distinction between virtues and talents, which he finds a source of difficulty, exists because the popular ascription of virtue to someone involves ascribing some degree of what Hume calls liberty of indifference to that person. But Hume would respond that this entails the denial of the very predictability of human conduct that our ethical thinking requires, and is inconsistent with the scientific status of the study of mankind. Critics of a libertarian turn of mind would say that Hume's difficulties merely show we must jettison the Newtonian model of the human sciences. We must, they would say, accept that the social sciences are able to predict human behaviour (such as voting-patterns) as well as they do because, in fact, most people do choose in roughly the same ways in similar situations, even though they could, *if* they chose, not do so. But some people do, now and then, surprise us (when they could have chosen not to!) and we have to be content with statistical predictions in consequence.

So far we have found aspects of Hume's moral psychology that are at odds with common opinion in ways that seem inevitable consequences of his understanding of the science of human nature. There is another well-known claim that he makes that is indeed at odds with common opinion, but in a way he could have avoided. This is his claim that erroneous or bizarre emotions are not contrary to reason.

He recognizes that the understanding can give rise to passion by producing opinions that give rise to such states as grief or joy or resentment, or by prompting desires or volitions when we see that some course of action will lead to what we already want or think good. But he insists that this does not ever entitle us to call the passions or desires unreasonable, or to hold that 'reason and passion can ever oppose each other, or dispute for the government of the will and actions', (*T* II. iii. 3. 416). What Hume has done here is emphasize the importance of passion and/or desire in the genesis of choice and conduct, while continuing to accept, indeed to stress, the rationalist insistence on the sharp separation of reason and emotion. Hume teaches the *a*-rationality of passion where the rationalist teaches the *ir*-rationality of passion. Both, in fact, misinterpret common moral opinion, which is committed to neither view, but accepts that emotion, as well as opinion, can be both reasonable and unreasonable.

Hume seems to think that the only cases where the moral evaluations of common sense require the ascription of irrationality to the passions are cases where these are deemed to be the result of false judgements. But this is not so. On the contrary: if I pursue an objective that is harmful to me, because I mistakenly think it will be good for me, then my desire for it may be judged to be erroneous, since my judgement is; but it is not thereby judged to be unreasonable. If common sense agrees that the course I am following will lead to the objective I am pursuing, but holds me to be mistaken in thinking it will be good for me; or if it holds me to be right in thinking it would be good for me but wrong in thinking the course I am following will help me attain it, it is still likely to call my choice a *reasonable* one. The falsity of my judgement is the very thing that makes my action reasonable in cases of this sort. If I grieve at the supposed loss of a loved one who is in fact alive and well, my grief is mistaken, but not unreasonable. We apply the term 'unreasonable' to an emotion or to a desire where that emotion or desire are thought to be in some way *inappropriate* to the situation that the agent considers himself, or herself, to be in: when it is the wrong way to respond, emotionally or conatively, to a situation of that sort. If the situation is not of that sort, the response is mistaken as well. But it can be quite free of error, and still be either reasonable or unreasonable: by being moderate or excessive, helpful or unhelpful, sane or silly. These are all dimensions of rationality that can be manifested *by the passions themselves*. Hume has perceived the importance of the passions for all our choice and conduct, but has mistakenly felt obliged to deny their rationality in order to accommodate it. In this respect he shares an estimate of them with the rationalists whose theories he contests. The estimate is one from which common sense is already free.

## VII

We have seen that Hume's conception of a science of human nature reduces mental life to the interplay of impressions and ideas, and treats the mind itself as the theatre where this interplay occurs, not as a participant in it. The scholarly literature contains many criticisms and reappraisals of what Hume says about the self, almost all directed to his treatment of it in Book I of the *Treatise*. Two of the criticisms prominent in this literature are of particular importance.

The first criticism is that in spite of the Newtonianism of perceptions that Hume proclaims at the outset of the *Treatise*, and again in the first *Enquiry*, his accounts of the origins of our beliefs lean heavily on the ascription to us of propensities, tendencies, or habits. This leads some to suggest that he is committed to a crypto-Kantian psychology in which the subject of explanations is the mind and its dispositions, rather than the perceptions it contains.[22] The second criticism is that the ascription of a propensity (in this case the propensity to confuse one sort of succession with another) is essential to Hume's account of the genesis of the belief in the unity of the mind itself—thus opening him to the objection that he cannot explain how we come to have the belief he criticizes without first assuming its truth.

It is possible to respond on Hume's behalf to the first criticism by suggesting that talk of the mind's propensities should be construed as popular shorthand for a genuinely Newtonian account that speaks instead of how impressions and ideas give rise to one another *in* the mind. It is possible to respond similarly to the second by saying that the perceptions the mind has can well include perceptions *of* the series that constitute it, without there having also to be any supervenient subject beyond the series' successive members. Such responses seem to save him from charges of formal inconsistency.[23]

But the transition to the passages about the self in Book II is still a surprising one for the reader of Book I. Hume has tried to prepare us for it by telling us to distinguish 'betwixt personal identity, as it regards our thought or imagination, and as it regards our pas-

---

[22] The two fundamental essays on this theme are Wolff 1960 and Wilson 1979.
[23] See Pike 1967 and Chapter 3 in this volume.

sions or the concern we take in ourselves' (*T* I. iv. 6. 253). He also
tries to ease the transition by clarifying his use of the term 'self'
in its first introduction in Book II as the name of the object of the
indirect passion of pride: 'This object is self, or that succession
of related ideas and impressions, of which we have an intimate
memory and consciousness' (*T* II. i. 2. 277). This makes it clear that
he is not reverting to the pure owner-self whose existence he rejects
so brusquely in Book I. But this does not prepare us for the claim
that 'the idea, or rather impression of ourselves is always intimately
present with us, and that our consciousness gives us so lively a
conception of our own person, that 'tis not possible to imagine, that
any thing can in this particular go beyond it' (*T* II. i. 11. 317). More
serious, perhaps, is the fact that the account of the aetiology of the
indirect passions requires the use of the idea of the self *as distinct
from others*; and the account of the origins of our belief in self-
identity in Book I is confined to our belief in the self's own inner
unity over time, and tells us nothing of how we come to be aware of
the existence of other minds. This is a serious gap in his system, but
perhaps not a manifest inconsistency. Let us turn instead to the role
he ascribes to this lively notion of ourself in our emotional life.

Whatever this role is, he does not think it undermines his
Newtonian mental science. There is no place in his system for the
suggestion that choices are the product of anything other than the
series of passions and cognitions that lead to them. His denial of
liberty of indifference permits no consideration of what has been called
agent-causation: the theory that in free action it is the agent, rather
than the agent's desires or volitions, that is the *locus* of causality.[24]
This denial is coupled with great stress on the claim that our understanding and evaluation of human agency depends on our recognition of settled states of character. This raises, in the sphere of
action, a perplexity parallel to that raised by his critics in the sphere
of epistemology: that his view seems to require a continuing self that
*has* the character-traits he feels necessary for prediction and evaluation. We can perhaps offer a similar answer: that talk of an agent's
character is shorthand for talk of that agent's emotions and desires.

However we respond to these difficulties of interpretation, there
is a vital dimension to Hume's theory of the self in Book II that
is only lately beginning to be recognized as central to his moral

---

[24] For a classic treatment of this notion, see Chisholm 1966.

psychology.[25] It permeates his whole vision of the human condition. We find its clearest expression in the introduction of the principle of sympathy, in Section 11 of Part i of Book II. Scholars have interpreted sympathy as a mechanism to explain my concern for others, which emerges through my having myself the very feelings I discern in them. This is correct, but incomplete. The principle is introduced by Hume as a 'secondary' source of the *self*-regarding indirect passions of pride and humility. Pride does not merely come about through my taking pleasure in qualities that I recognize to belong to me; it also comes about through my sympathetically sharing the admiration (that is, in Hume's view, the love) that others have towards me when they, too, discern these pleasing qualities. So my own pride is in part the product of the mentality of others, not only of my own. And since I am loved, or admired, for qualities I have or objects I possess, my emotional life is such that I shall pride myself on those qualities or objects for which others admire me, and be ashamed of those qualities or objects for which they hate (or despise) me. They are the co-creators of my self-image, and to understand the character of my self-concern it is necessary to take the measure of the society of which I am a member.

As Baier points out, many of the features others thus make part of my self-image will be physical ones, so the self of the passions is a physicalized construct, and not the quasi-solipsist monster of Book I.[26] Once this is recognized, it is also evident that I sometimes come to have pride or humility in some characteristic I ascribe to myself only after others admire or despise it: their evaluation of it and of me may not only augment my own, but actually engender it. And I may, of course, come to simulate, or actually develop, some character-trait they would praise in order to prevent their blaming me (and hence my blaming myself) for its absence: this, as we have already seen, is part of Hume's account of the origin of the sense of duty (see again *T* III. ii. 1. 479); an account that seeks to turn the rationalist's key ethical endowment into an internalized social product.

The sort of story this tells us about the self as social construction is one we have heard since from Freud, Marx, and the existentialists, always with ideological accretions wholly foreign to Hume's naturalism. His own summary statement is as follows:

[25] It is given its due place in Baier 1991; see especially ch. 7.
[26] Baier 1991, 136.

In general we may remark, that the minds of men are mirrors to one another, not only because they reflect each others emotions, but also because those rays of passions, sentiments and opinions may be often reverberated, and may decay away by insensible degrees. (*T* II. ii. 5. 365)

It is easy to see from this insistence that the self is not discernible within but largely ascribed by transference from without, why Hume has such deep hostility to all systems that view persons as alien to the social world they inhabit. His negativity toward rationalism and its craving for autonomy is the result of its being a theoretical force that can only encourage self-distancing from the sources of emotional nourishment that make us what we are. And his intemperate rejection of the religious austerities of the 'monkish virtues' can be seen as having the same theoretical source.[27] Each is life-denying, and in a quite literal sense self-destructive. Human nature does not need to be mastered, nor does it need to be redeemed. It needs social nurture. Both reason and 'true' religion are the *slaves* of the passions.


# VIII


I have argued that Hume is a neo-Hellenistic thinker, who follows the Stoics and Epicureans and Sceptics in maintaining that we should avoid anxiety by following nature. This prescription is notorious among philosophers for combining descriptive and normative elements. Hume is not, in any general way, confused between descriptive and normative claims: there is nothing in principle confused about seeing an understanding of our nature as a guide to one's way of life, or even to the proper practice of philosophy. There is more than one way of getting and using such guidance. Hume thinks a philosopher must, first and foremost, learn to accept his or her nature for what it is. This means recognizing that it is so programmed that our instincts furnish us with beliefs that we cannot survive without, or supply independently, or seriously question. Faced with this fact, the philosophical enterprises of sceptical doubt and rationalist reconstruction are doomed to failure on psychological grounds alone, and the attempts to pursue them can only generate and exacerbate anxiety.

[27] *EM* IX. 270.

When we turn to Hume's moral thought, we find the parallel insistence that we must recognize the dominance of the passions in our nature, and not risk misery by attempting to follow eccentric programmes of choice that frustrate them in the supposed interests of reason, or the mortifications of religion. Here again, we have to accept our nature, not violate it. Here Hume risks confusion in a fundamental respect: while there is nothing incoherent in describing our nature and then saying we must accept it and not violate it, this *is* incoherent if we are *unable* to violate it. To combine the descriptive with the normative without incoherence, it is necessary to permit freedom of choice in a form for which Hume's own account of liberty allows no space. The price of using the study of human nature as a guide to choice is the price of recognizing that it is part of our nature to be *able* to choose. But if this is admitted, we can then follow him in saying that if we make certain kinds of choice, we may ruin ourselves, and end up anxious, or incapacitated, or otherwise miserable, by frustrating our basic needs. Read this way, his system tells us that the polite society human beings had developed in property-owning Western Europe by his day, with all its protective artifices, meets the needs of human nature better than its alternatives. While this may be judged by some to be complacent or enervating, the experience of more radical programmes that are based on ideologies that attend less to the details of human nature, should make us hesitate to dismiss his advice too readily.

# 8

## Hume and the Freedom of the Will

HUME's views on freedom have been very influential; but they have
not been discussed by Hume scholars as much as his views on other
major themes. This is no doubt in part because, at least until very
recently, there has not been disagreement about where he stands.
The problem of free will is of course immensely complex and frus-
tratingly hard to articulate, and this essay is not offered as a serious contribution to its solution. I shall only try to comment on some
of Hume's arguments concerning it, on the connections these
arguments have with other parts of his system, and on the apparent
implications these arguments and these connections have for the
wider problem.[1]

### I

There has (again, until very recently) been a consensus among
Hume's readers that he provides us with a, perhaps *the*, classic
statement of what is commonly called Compatibilism. This is the
doctrine that there is no inconsistency in holding that human
actions are caused, and that they are sometimes free. This logical
(or conceptual) thesis is usually combined with two other claims about
matters of fact: that human actions *are* (always) caused, and that

[1] This essay, which sees print here for the first time, has been through a number
of versions, and in spite of appearances it has benefited from the comments of
many colleagues. It began as a contribution to the 1987 Hume Society conference in
São Paulo, Brazil. Professor Don Garrett replied to it, and some of his responses to
it have since been included in ch. 6 of Garrett 1997. Later versions have been read
to departmental colloquia at Calgary, Lethbridge, Western Ontario, and King's
College London. I am grateful to those present on these occasions for much intellectual help. I would also like to thank Charlotte Brown, Lorne Falkenstein, David
Norton, and Dale Tuggy for valuable comments.

they are, sometimes, free. I shall assume here that the term 'Compatibilism' refers to the combination of these three theses, though it is important to bear in mind that they are distinct. I should also add that all compatibilists I am aware of would agree that freedom, however it is to be understood, is a feature of only some human deeds or thoughts; and that compatibilists would typically say that one of the necessary conditions of freedom is that the causes of free actions lie within the agent rather than outside.

The competing view of freedom, which I shall follow common practice and call 'Libertarianism', is also a combination of three distinct claims: first, the claim that it is inconsistent to hold both that human actions can be free and that they are always caused—again, a logical, or conceptual, thesis; second, that some of them are indeed free; and, third, that in consequence these latter are in some manner, or to some extent, exempt from causation.

It is clear that both of these positions cry out for clarification. The libertarian is commonly accused of metaphysical obscurity in maintaining that free actions are exempt from causation, and the compatibilist needs to tell us how we are to determine when the cause of an action lies within an agent and when not, and whether there are clear criteria for determining which internal causes of human actions yield free acts and which do not, if only some do. I shall not attempt to answer any of these questions here.

Hume's direct discussions of freedom appear in two places. The first is in the *Treatise*, in Sections 1 and 2 of Part iii of Book II. Part iii of Book II is called 'Of the Will and Direct Passions' and Sections 1 and 2 are headed 'Of Liberty and Necessity'. No one would claim to know what Hume is about here without also drawing upon the argument of the next Section, 'Of the Influencing Motives of the Will', which includes the famous claim that reason is, and ought only to be, the slave of the passions. The second discussion of freedom is to be found in Section VIII of the first *Enquiry*, which is also called 'Of Liberty and Necessity'. This Section has been called 'one of his most Newtonian sections',[2] although he describes what he does there as a 'reconciling project' and begins it with claims that disputes about freedom are due to unclarities about words and ought to disappear when these unclarities are resolved. Certainly the tone of the *Enquiry* discussion is less aggressive than that of the corresponding Sections

---

[2] Jones 1982, 14.

of the *Treatise*; and since the *Enquiry* has more readers than the *Treatise* does (as Hume intended), it is standard to assume that what Hume is primarily about is much the same as what went on in the heyday of linguistic analysis in our own century, when philosophical problems were supposed to disappear when verbal or conceptual muddles about the key terms in which they were stated were resolved. This reading of what Hume is doing when he discusses liberty has been challenged recently by Paul Russell, who has produced the first substantial examination of Hume's theories on freedom and responsibility.[3] Russell argues that this reading is anachronistic, and misrepresents Hume's purposes. I have discussed Russell's work in detail elsewhere,[4] and can only make incidental reference to it in the present essay, which is, nevertheless, much indebted to it. For the moment I would merely say that while I agree that reading Hume as a twentieth-century analyst is indeed profoundly mistaken, it is nevertheless quite obvious that while pursuing his own purposes he makes conceptual judgements, and that his discussions of freedom contain such judgements at critical points. I shall therefore proceed for now as though the common reading of these discussions merely needs occasional correction, and that there is no good reason to withdraw the description of Hume as the classic compatibilist.

Hume's position has an easily traceable ancestry. What he says is anticipated in Chapter XXI of Hobbes' *Leviathan*,[5] and is intended as a response to the penetrating but confusing treatment of the idea of power in Section XXI of Book II of Locke's *Essay Concerning Human Understanding*.[6] Let us first look at the setting Hume's arguments have within his own system.

---

[3] Russell 1995.    [4] Penelhum 1998.

[5] 'LIBERTY, or FREEDOME, signifieth (properly) the absence of Opposition; (by Opposition, I mean externall Impediments of motion;) and may be applyed no less to Irrational and Inanimate creatures, than to Rationall . . . And according to this proper, and generally received meaning of the word, *A* FREE-MAN, *is he, that in those things, which by his strength and wit he is able to do, is not hindred to doe what he has a will to* . . . *Liberty*, and *Necessity* are consistent: As in the water, that hath not only *liberty*, but a *necessity* of descending by the Channel; so likewise in the Actions which men voluntarily doe: which, because they proceed from their will, proceed from *liberty*; and yet, because every act of man's will, and every desire, and inclination proceedeth from some cause, and that from another cause, in a continuall chaine, (whose first link is in the hand of God the first of all causes,) they proceed from *necessity*.' Hobbes 1909 edn., 161–2.

[6] Locke 1959 edn., i. 308–80.

## II

I begin by stressing that Hume does indeed have a philosophical system. His arguments cannot be appreciated if we do not recognize that what he says in one place is connected by a single vision with what he says in other places. So if, for example, we accept, as I think we should, that he is a sceptic, he is a sceptic with a system, however odd this may sound. He proclaims this, and makes clear what the nature of his system is, in the Introduction to the *Treatise*, where he tells us that '(t)here is no question of importance, whose decision is not compriz'd in the science of man' (*T* Int. xvi). The system is ancient in one way, and modern in another. It is ancient in that he is squarely in the Socratic tradition of offering philosophy as a way to a liberating self-knowledge. It is modern in that the self-knowledge it offers is to be achieved by using what he views as scientific (or 'experimental') method, a method that he considers to be analogous to Newton's.

In offering us a system dominated by a supposedly scientific method of understanding human nature, Hume is expressing his most fundamental conviction: that we are a part of nature and are not alien to it or capable of rising above it. His system is a naturalistic one, in Kemp Smith's language; and it is its naturalism, more than its empiricism, that makes it so influential in our own day. What Hume finds liberating in such a system is that it encourages us to accept a humbler vision of what is possible for us than the visions of its philosophical and religious competitors. These derive their initial inspiration from Plato, who held that as rational beings we can assert our essential independence of the natural order and the passions it implants within us. Hume thinks that this rationalist tradition, and the Christian tradition in which it was embedded in his own time, is a source not only of baseless metaphysics but also of erroneous moral objectives whose pursuit isolates us from the solaces that our social natures require.

Hume also believes that when the experimental method is applied to human nature, it becomes apparent that our natures are dominated by the passions, and that the claims made for reason by the competing systems he rejects bear no relation to its actual place in our lives. Both in the sphere of belief and the sphere of action, reason has a role, but it is a subordinate and instrumental one; it is the slave of the passions, and can neither overcome nor underwrite what they dictate to us. The famous dictum that reason is the slave of the passions can be viewed, in Kantian language, as a defiant and supposedly liberating, declaration of heteronomy.

It is therefore no accident that it is in Book II of the *Treatise*, 'Of the Passions', that we find the most detailed associationist descriptions of his system, or that his discussion of freedom is to be found there.

## III

I have said that Hume is indeed the classic compatibilist. Since Compatibilism has three parts to it, making a case for it will require making a case for each part. It will require a resolution of the alleged conflict between freedom and universal causality, or at least the causality of all human actions. It will require some argument for the reality of universal causality, or at least of the causality of all human actions. And it will require the compatibilist to show that some of our actions are in fact free. If the first and second requirements have been met, the third will not be hard. It is likely to be a matter of showing that the criteria of free action that have already been shown not to clash with the reality of universal causation, are indeed sometimes satisfied, and a simple appeal to common experience might well be enough for this. Hume deals with this third requirement in half a sentence.

The first two requirements naturally take much longer. Hume deals with the first by distinguishing between two supposed kinds of liberty—one which is manifestly compatible with universal causation and one that is not. He deals with the second by arguing that the sort of liberty that is not compatible with universal causation is a sort that we do not have, do not need, and indeed need to be without. Most of his discussion is centred on this last topic. I turn first, however, to his distinction between the two kinds of liberty.

He expresses the distinction in the *Treatise* by using scholastic names, names that do not reappear in the *Enquiry*. He distinguishes between liberty of spontaneity and liberty of indifference.[7] Liberty of spontaneity is the absence of impediments to the execution of one's

---

[7] For a helpful discussion of this distinction, see ch. 7 of Kenny 1975.

decisions. In the *Treatise*, Hume says that this is the sort of liberty that 'is oppos'd to violence' (*T* II. iii. 2. 407). While this phrase could be clearer, it presumably represents the claim that an action that is free in this sense is one that is brought about by the agent whose action it is, not by someone or something else; in Hume's psychology, this would probably entail that its proximate cause is a volition in the agent.[8] He immediately insists that liberty of spontaneity is the 'only . . . species of liberty, which it concerns us to preserve'. In the *Enquiry* we find the better-known description of this form of liberty as '*a power of acting or not acting, according to the determinations of the will*; that is, if we choose to remain at rest we may; if we choose to move, we also may' (*EU* VIII. 95). He says there that 'we can only mean' this when we speak of liberty, and adds that this 'hypothetical liberty' is possessed by 'every one who is not a prisoner and in chains'. This is the half-sentence I referred to above.

Liberty of indifference is said in the *Treatise* to mean 'a negation of necessity and causes'. Hume is concerned to convince us that it is a myth, although it is not always quite clear how much he thinks we need to be convinced. When he says that when we speak of liberty 'we can only mean' liberty of spontaneity, this suggests at first sight that he thinks we do not even believe that we have liberty of indifference, not merely that we do not need it. If this were what he thought, he would be hard put to it to show why there has ever seemed to be a problem of freedom at all, because it is obvious that liberty of spontaneity is fully compatible with universal causality. It consists merely in the absence of interference with the exercise of our choices, not the absence of causal determination in their formation. But we should not pay too much attention to his careless language here; for two pages before the *Enquiry* description of liberty of spontaneity he goes so far as to say that 'all mankind' have shown a propensity to deny that necessity extends to human action. So it is clear that Hume does not really think that all we ever mean by freedom is liberty of spontaneity. He thinks that we are inclined to believe we also have liberty of indifference, but that we are wrong about

---

[8] Hume's view on volitions appears at *T* II. iii. 1. 399. He seems to hold that volitions are impressions that function as the last in the sequence of mental causes that lead to action, and that we can all recognize their presence by introspection. This doctrine does not weaken his fundamental insistence that it is the passions rather than the reason that provide the motivating links in these sequences. See Bricke 1984 and Penelhum 1975, 111–17.

this. What he is trying to reconcile are the needs of a human science, which he sees as deterministic, and the needs of our moral thought and discourse, which we have at least a strong propensity to suppose requires liberty of indifference. He maintains that it does not require it; in fact, in his view, moral thought and discourse would be impossible if this form of liberty were a fact.

Before proceeding, however, we should notice another infelicity in his language. In telling us what sort of freedom we do have, he describes it as a *power* of acting or not acting. This seems to have him contradicting a striking claim he makes elsewhere, viz. at *T* I. iii. 14. 171, where he says while listing the 'corollaries' of his account of causation, that '(t)he distinction, which we often make betwixt *power* and the *exercise* of it, is . . . without foundation'. If, when I act spontaneously, I have the power to do something (e.g. to move) and the power to refrain (i.e. to remain at rest), it looks as though I must have the power to do whichever of the two I elect not to do as well as the power to do what I do elect to do. But this is only an apparent conflict. It is of the essence of Hume's understanding of freedom that we never have the power to choose in any other way than the way in which we do choose; and it is indeed this thesis that cashes out the metaphysical claim that there is no basis for the distinction between power and its exercise. The so-called 'power' that we nevertheless always have if we are not prisoners or in chains is a function, not of our mind-set prior to action, but of the circumstances in which we carry out what that mind-set has determined us to do. 'Power' is therefore not the right word for it. Perhaps 'opportunity' is. Undoubtedly, then, Hume commits himself here to the reality of unexploited opportunities; without it, it would be hard to attach any sense to the notion of alternatives to actions. But he denies, utterly, the reality of unexercised powers of choice.

## IV

So much for the liberty of spontaneity. If it is all we have or need, the reconciling project is a success. What about liberty of indifference? Hume interprets it as the supposed possession of a power to act in a way that is wholly or partly uncaused. I would like to specify it a little more carefully than this, following Hume's lead indirectly. When he tells us the sort of freedom we have, he says that 'if we choose to remain at rest, we may; if we choose to move, we also may'. I think that in believing we have liberty of indifference, we believe that at least sometimes, when we choose to remain at rest, we might (although we do not) choose instead to move; and that when we choose to move, we might (although we do not) choose instead to remain at rest. More generally, when we choose to act, we might choose instead not to act, or to act in some other way; and when we choose not to act, we might well choose instead to act. Hume denies these things. He is right, however, in my opinion, to suppose that most of us think we are free in this sense, and not only in his, and that arguments are needed to show we are mistaken.

I turn now to the arguments Hume offers. There are two parts to his attack. There is an argument to the effect that 'necessity' is as much a feature of the sphere of human actions as it is of the physical world. Russell calls this the 'necessity argument'. There is the complementary argument that liberty of indifference, which would consist of the absence of necessity, could not be distinguished from mere chance, and would make practical and moral judgement impossible by severing the indispensable connection between human actions and the agents who perform them. Russell calls this the 'antilibertarian argument'.[9]

The necessity argument seeks, fundamentally, to establish that explanation of human behaviour is of the same sort as explanation of physical events. It is this claim that cashes out his declarations at *T* I. iii. 14. 171 that 'all causes are of the same kind' and that 'there is but one kind of *necessity*, as there is but one kind of cause, and that the common distinction betwixt *moral* and *physical* necessity is without any foundation in nature'. In each case there is the constant conjunction of 'objects' (mental or physical events) and the inference of the mind from one 'object' to another. As we would expect, Hume draws here on the resources of his former analysis of causal relationships. In particular, he stresses that in ascribing 'necessity' to the moral sphere he is saying no more but no less than he says is involved when it is ascribed to the physical world: that in both there is constant conjunction plus inference. The parity he insists on

[9] Russell 1995, 11–12. The third argument which Russell distinguishes he calls the 'spontaneity argument'—that free actions are those which are unhindered and issue from causes within the agent. I have referred to this argument above, though not under this name. I am much indebted here to Russell's thorough analysis.

should be borne in mind carefully, since those who rather glibly say that Hume holds necessity not to be a real feature of the physical world at all, but to be projected onto it by the mind as a result of its habitual inferences, are likely to be slightly surprised by his repeated insistence on its reality in the mental sphere. His view, however, is that in both cases what is *there* is conjunction plus inference. Hence there is no reason to suggest either that moral and physical causation differ in kind, or that the former is less uniform than the latter is. Clearly libertarians have to deny he is right about this; equally clearly, they have a serious case to answer.[10]

Hume makes his case in a double manner. He says that we can and do find predictable sequences in human behaviour in the moral sphere, just as we do in the physical, and that there is no case for supposing human actions to be unpredictable or unexplainable in principle any more than physical events; just as we can show why the clock does not go right by finding the speck of dust in the workings, so we can explain why a polite friend is rude to us by by discovering he has not had his dinner. And he argues that it is a complete mistake to think that we can turn to introspection to support a belief in liberty of indifference. It is important to notice that his arguments for this last point gain effect from the fact that they parallel those he has used earlier in analysing physical causation to show that we cannot discern an objective necessity by introspection either. I think his arguments here are powerful and ingenious, and that he shows very effectively that we cannot prove we are free agents in a libertarian sense merely by looking within. In these post-Freudian days we are less inclined to try it, of course.

I turn now from the positive side of his case to the negative one: what Russell entitles the antilibertarian argument. It is not really separate. It consists in saying not only that we can predict and explain

---

[10] Compatibilists who look to Hume have a worry here that Russell has made clear for the first time. There is a tendency to think that one of Hume's purposes is to argue that since (in contrast to classical rationalist analyses) an accurate account of the causal relationship does not ascribe an objective necessitation to it, moral causation is free of compulsion. If this were Hume's purpose, it would seem to entail that if pre-Humean analyses were correct, caused actions would be compelled and Compatibilism false. While I do not agree that this shows Hume not to be a compatibilist, it does show that he does not use a common compatibilist argument that has gained prominence later. Hume's purpose is to insist on the universality of causal sequence and the inability of introspection to demonstrate its absence. See Russell 1995, chs. 2 and 3.

human actions, but also that we need to be able to do so; and that if liberty of indifference were a fact, we could not. We could not praise or blame anyone, or make plans that take human character-traits into account, if we could not connect what people do with the characters and personality-traits that lie behind their actions. For liberty of indifference would be the same thing as chance. The libertarian has to reject this, just as clearly as he or she must reject Hume's positive arguments for the equality of moral and physical causes.

V

When we examine Hume's antilibertarian argument, we find a surprising degree of dogmatism on a key metaphysical point. It comes out most clearly in this pronouncement:

> It is universally agreed that nothing exists without a cause of its existence, and that chance, when strictly examined, is a mere negative word, and means not any real power which has anywhere a being in nature. (*EU* VIII. 950)

This is offered as the major premiss in an argument that ends with the statement that 'liberty, when opposed to necessity, not to constraint, is the same thing with chance; which is universally allowed to have no existence'. Hume is not merely arguing from our success in finding explanations where we might not expect to, or from the similarities between physical and moral explanations; he is arguing from the alleged universality of causation.

It is striking that he should do this, since he is often thought, since Kant, to be sceptical about the common conviction that there is a cause for everything. I do not think there is any doubt that Hume shares this common conviction. Given his naturalistic epistemology, however, all we could properly expect him to offer in its support is an account of how it becomes entrenched in our basic repertoire of natural beliefs. But it is perhaps the most striking gap in his whole system of thought that he does not provide this.

The principle that everything has a cause is the subject of a famous section in Part iii of Book I of the *Treatise*: the one called 'Why a Cause is Always Necessary'. Hume argues there that this principle is 'neither intuitively nor demonstratively certain' but must 'necessarily [*sic*] arise from observation and experience'. But how does experience give rise to such a principle? Hume says that he will not answer this question directly, but will 'sink' it in the question of why we conclude that 'such particular causes must have such particular effects'. He adds, ''Twill, perhaps be found in the end, that the same answer will serve for both questions'. This looks like a promise, but he never fulfils it. It is a strange promise to make, for the two questions are logically independent.[11] The question he actually addresses is: Why do we think causes give rise to their effects with necessity, so that the same cause will always yield the same effect? One can give an answer to this without showing why we believe, and indeed without even believing, that every event has a cause. Every event that has a cause might well be necessitated by that cause, without its also being true that all events have causes. In my more daring moments I incline to think that Hume never quite grasps this, but I cannot argue that here. I would merely point out that both in Book I of the *Treatise* and Sections V–VII of the *Enquiry* Hume's psychological efforts are directed to explaining why we ascribe necessity to the cause-effect sequence, not to explaining why we ascribe universality to it. Similarly, the arguments of Sections 1 and 2 of Part iii of Book II of the *Treatise*, and of Section VIII of the *Enquiry*, show, if they are successful, that the same sort of necessity we find in the physical world obtains also in the realm of human thought and action. But neither shows that every event, physical or mental, must have some cause; nor do they show this taken together.

Let us look a little more at the arguments Hume gives for saying that 'the doctrine of necessity' applies to human action. He says firstly that we can infer or predict human actions from the motives, dispositions and characters of human agents, with a confidence that is comparable to that with which we can infer the movements of bodies. And he says in the second place that when people appear to act in unpredictable ways, we can postulate unknown causes from which their actions could have been predicted after all, had we known them; he compares this with the way in which we learn to explain unexpected physical events by reference to hidden causes—like the speck of dust that arrests the normal movements of the clock. MacNabb has suggested that it is in these arguments that we find

---

[11] See Penelhum 1975, 57–58 and Lewis White Beck's 'A Prussian Hume and a Scottish Kant' in Beck 1978, 111–29.

Hume's account of why we think that every event has a cause.[12] Some of Hume's language may suggest he thinks he is justifying that belief here; but even if his arguments are sound, they do not justify it, or explain why we believe it. They support what his other arguments support—the principle that 'such particular causes must have such particular effects': the principle 'same cause-same effect'.[13] This principle does account for the predictability of those events that are caused, but it does not establish, or explain our belief in, the principle that every event *has* a cause. We could live in a world where every cause produced the same effect each time it operated, but in which there were still some events that were not produced by any causes. (For arguments that would demonstrate the conceivability of such a world we have only to turn to Hume himself.) And a world like this would accommodate liberty of indifference. Similarly, even if it is true that when a cause does not seem to give rise to its usual effect, this is because some other cause has interfered, it could still be the case that some events are not caused at all. The principle that the same causes produce the same effects, and the principle that every event has a cause are logically distinct, and neither entails the other.

How serious is this for Hume's view of freedom? I find this hard to say, but I am inclined to think that to refute the belief in liberty of indifference he needs more than he provides. At least, this is true if I am correct in interpreting the belief in liberty of indifference to be the belief that sometimes when we have acted, we could have chosen not to, and when we have refrained, we could have chosen to act. For if this is true, it seems to imply that whatever led us to act or to refrain might not have done so: that in the very same circumstances, and with the very same influences, we might have acted differently. Prima facie, this does not only imply in its turn that the very causes that did operate might not have had the results they had (which would violate the principle 'same cause-same effect'), but also that we would then have acted independently of those causes, since, by hypothesis, they would have been the only ones operating; and this looks like a belief in the possibility of uncaused action. Hume himself certainly thinks that the belief in liberty of indifference requires this, or why the denunciation of chance? But if he thinks this, it is to the point to notice that he has not shown that every event has a cause, or why we believe it (if we do). He needs both

---

[12] MacNabb 1951, 56–7.      [13] I borrow this abbreviation from Beck.

predictability and universal causation, and at best he has only the former.

Does he even have this much? That is, do his arguments for the predictability of actions undermine the belief in liberty? I recall again that he maintains that we depend on regularities in human conduct, and that when people surprise us, hidden causes for their actions can be found.

What does the libertarian need? Not, I think, a world in which we cannot expect consistency in human behaviour. What the libertarian needs is a world in which, when we find such consistency, it can be praised or blamed because it is freely chosen. Hume gives us the example of a prisoner who has to accept that his guards will be constant and dutiful, so that he will go to the scaffold. A case like this, though based on observed regularities, does not refute a libertarian understanding. On that understanding, the guards' conscientiousness is freely chosen—because, for example, they calculate that they will suffer penalties if they let their prisoner escape. But on the libertarian view, they *could* do that, even though they do not, just as the bank teller *could* hold on to the money and be shot by the bank robber. An offer one cannot refuse is not an offer that one *cannot* refuse, although it is one that others can confidently predict one *will* not refuse.[14]

Now it is certainly logically odd to say that people can do things they can be predicted not to do, or could refrain from doing things they can be predicted to do, if one does not add that sometimes these unpredictable actions actually take place. If libertarianism is to be more than a hollow defence of logical possibilities, we have to have some real examples of these things. But it seems to me that we do have them, for we do find people, now and then, who have disobeyed orders at great cost, or have yielded to temptations that have never moved them in the past, or have declined unrefusable offers. Hume tries to head off a libertarian use of such examples. 'A person of an obliging disposition gives a peevish answer: But he has the toothache, or has not dined' (*EU* viii. 88). Yes; but in Hume's view someone who knew he had the toothache or had not dined would predict he would abandon his usual polite demeanour, and the libertarian has to say here that in spite of his distress he could,

[14] On this theme, see Baker 1974, 518, '(A)cting under duress is a clear case of action, because it is a special case of acting for a reason'.

contrary to that prediction, have sustained his usual demeanour had he so chosen.

It is true, however, that to defend the doctrine of liberty in this way is to reject Hume's assimilation of moral to physical causes. For Hume this would entail the abandonment of the expectation of a science of human nature, which he sees as justified by our success in predicting human action. But a belief in liberty does not entail such abandonment, only the abandonment of a Newtonian model of such a science. The predictability Hume emphasizes is a fact; but the libertarian understanding of it confines human science to *statistical* predictions, and accommodates the human power to surprise us, as a matter of principle. I do not say that anyone has shown this libertarian understanding of action, and of human science, to be true; but I suggest that Hume's detailed arguments have not shown it to be false.

## VI

So far I have only discussed the arguments Hume presents when explicitly addressing the problem of freedom. I would now like to look at some of the ways his views on this interlock with other key parts of his system.

(1) I begin with the connections his understanding of freedom has with his systematic and complex analysis of the passions, and some of the aspects of his moral psychology that derive from this. Russell's book makes it clear how that system generates Hume's interpretation of responsibility. Hume offers us a naturalistic (or psychological) account of how we in fact assess the responsibility of ourselves and others for our actions. We do this in the judgements that manifest moral approval and disapproval. These passions, which are central to Hume's ethical theory, are classed by Hume as calm forms of the indirect passions of love and hatred (*T* III. iii. 5. 614). Love and hatred, though they are occasioned, or caused, by specific qualities or actions of persons, have as their objects the persons themselves. Approval and disapproval, accordingly, are not directed at an agent's acts, but at the person behind them. More exactly, they are directed at the character or long-term mind-set, that generates them. For the mechanics of moral sentiment, so conceived, to work, we have to be able to infer the character of the agent from the acts we see him or her perform. This is a causal inference, which

depends on the existence of regularities similar in form to those we encounter in the physical world. It depends on the frequent conjunction of a certain motive and a certain sort of action. So the necessity argument (that there have to be causal regularities in the moral sphere as well as the physical) is designed to show not only that we need causal regularities to make our own decisions involving other people, but that we need these regularities in order to make judgements of praise and blame, i.e. to assign responsibility.

This explains an otherwise strange and counter-intuitive position that Hume adopts about moral praise and blame, viz. that they are not only directed to agents rather than to their actions, but that they are only felt and expressed when those actions flow from enduring qualities of character. In Hume's system, the indirect passions like love and hatred require a close and stable connection between the passion's cause and its object.[15] To recognize this connection is not of course to agree with Hume's position, which seems to me Procrustean; and I shall return to it.

(2) Hume's account of the passions gives him further weapons in the battle against libertarianism, which has a natural affinity for the rationalist understanding of human nature he rejects. Some libertarians are inclined to set great store by the fact that we are able to stand back and take stock of our desires and inclinations, and seem to be able to make choices that are contrary to them. This is often seen as a victory of reason over the passions, which are judged to be modes of *passivity* (or heteronomy). Hume's theory of the passions includes several doctrines designed to counteract this view, which poses an obvious threat to his science of man. There is his explanation of the sense of obligation as a form of self-hatred (*T* III. ii. 1. 479). There is the classification of prudence as one of the direct passions, namely the 'general appetite to good, and aversion to evil, considered merely as such' (*T* II. iii. 3. 417). And, most importantly, there is the doctrine of calm passions, which Hume uses to subsume motives that rationalists ascribe to reason under his associationist science of human nature. (Although the vocabulary is recent, I see no compelling reason why these doctrines could not have been augmented by a recognition of what Frankfurt has called second-order

---

[15] See Russell 1995, chs. 3 and 7; also *T* III. iii. 1. 575. It is a great merit of Russell's analysis to have made this position of Hume's more intelligible; although I am afraid that this merely amounts to our understanding better how Hume's system inclines him to hold it, rather than its having any greater inherent plausibility.

desires, such as the desire to rid oneself of the desire to take sugar or tobacco.[16]) It is impossible to consider here how plausible Hume's views on these matters are, but they are among his most considered and ingenious; and the moral for libertarians is to express doctrines of the autonomy of the will in forms that avoid coming as close as they often do to equating free choice with dutiful or prudential choice. For if libertarianism is true, free actions must also include those we perform when we yield to desire in the face of duty, or consciously take a holiday from the pursuit of the good.

(3) There is one form of such expression that Hume's system blocks in another place. I have suggested that if free actions are actions that we might have chosen not to do, this implies that some events might not be caused. This has been questioned. Some libertarians have argued that free actions are not uncaused events; they are merely are not caused by *other events*. They are caused *by the agent*, not by some event *in* the agent. The classic exponent of this view is Thomas Reid, and in the Sixties of our century it received exemplary expression in the work of Roderick Chisholm. I cannot explore the concept of agent-causation here, although it might seem to offer a more viable version of libertarianism. The obvious problem for anyone who introduces it is to relate agent-causation to event-causation. Reid, who agrees with Hume at least to the extent of holding that all causes are (in the end) of the same kind, holds that all causation is agent-causation, event-causes being causes only by courtesy and reflecting the workings of divine agency. This view, whatever its advantages, seems highly counter-intuitive today, no doubt as a result of Hume's influence. Chisholm, who seemed to countenance two distinct types of causation, has more recently tried to accommodate agent-causation into event-causation through definitions.[17] But it is noteworthy that Hume's system does not only prevent our even considering the possibility of agent-causation because he maintains that all causes are of the same kind. We are prevented from considering it for another reason. For we all know that Hume maintains there is no such thing as a self, or an agent, in addition to the impressions and ideas it has, and the bodily acts to which these lead. People are bundles of perceptions (at least in Books I and II;

---

[16] Frankfurt 1971.
[17] For Reid's views see Reid 1969, Rowe 1991 and Lehrer 1989, chs. 12–14. Chisholm's version of the agent-causation theory are to be found in Chisholm 1966; but see his more recent views in Chisholm 1976, ch. 2.

in Book III they become perambulating characters). They cannot
be *loci* of causation in their own right, for all the causes of actions
are events *in* the agents whom we hold responsible for them. I have
argued elsewhere that Hume's bundle theory does not lead him into
formal inconsistency when he speaks of persons and the way they
form their beliefs, or the way they use the idea of the self in the
indirect passions, since the idea of the series that I am, may itself
be an idea *in* the series it is an idea *of* (see Chapter 3); and I would
suppose that something similar could be said to accommodate the
centrality of character in his moral theory. But however we assess his
views on personal identity, we can see they are not a mere sceptical
consequence of his epistemology, but a key component of his science of man, with implications for his understanding of morality.

(4) It would be mistaken to conclude these reflections without
noting once again the importance in Hume's philosophy of the passage at *T* I. iii. 14. 170–72 where he draws 'some corollaries' from his
definitions of causation. These do not only represent a clear rejection
Aristotelianism in natural philosophy, but are in each case a major
affront to common sense, as Hume realizes. (The reason that so much
of Aristotle seems like common sense is of course that so much of
common sense is Aristotle.) Common sense does not readily acquiesce in the claim that all causes are of the same kind (so that there
is no real distinction between necessary and sufficient conditions, and
no formal or final causes); or that there is no distinction between
moral and physical necessity (so that actions are as predetermined
as physical events); or that there is no ground for distinguishing
between power and its exercise (so that my car has the power to reach
160 km per hour only when it is actually doing it). These are indeed
corollaries only if Hume's account of the genesis of the idea of necessity explains every legitimate occasion of its use.

Of course he does attempt to defend these claims. One might
well view the *Dialogues Concerning Natural Religion* as a lengthy
defence of the first, and I have already conceded the strength of some
of his arguments for the second. It is notable that he also makes an
attempt to render the last one less counter-intuitive than it seems
from its blunt assertion at *T* I. iii. 14. In Book II, at *T* II. i. 10. 311–16
(and again briefly at *T* II. ii. 5. 360–61) he attempts to explain the
fact that riches generate pride or admiration, whether or not their
owner spends them; riches being 'the power of acquiring the property of what pleases'. He continues:

It has been observ'd in treating of the understanding, that the distinction, which we sometimes make betwixt a *power* and the *exercise* of it, is entirely frivolous, and that neither man nor any other being ought ever to be thought possest of any ability, unless it be exercised and put in action. But tho' this be strictly true in a just and *philosophical* way of thinking, 'tis certain it is not the *philosophy* of our passions; but that many things operate upon them by means of the idea and supposition of power, independent of its actual exercise.

While continuing to maintain that this supposition is erroneous, Hume attempts to mitigate its importance by arguing that it is not due to the influence of any scholastic doctrine of free will, and is circumscribed by our expectations about the likely exercise of the powers that we and others have. I am not afraid when my enemy walks by with his sword at his belt, because I know he has reason to fear the magistrates and is unlikely to attack me. The pride and admiration generated by riches are due to our expectations of the pleasures they can be used to purchase. The miser's pride in his wealth is due to his overlooking the motives in his own nature that stand in the way of his using it; and any admiration that we may feel towards him is due to sympathy.

While Hume is, as always, accurate in his estimate of many of our motives, and while he is right that our hopes and fears are based on our past experience of one anothers' characters, it is hard not to find these accounts strained. One wants to say that what makes wealth so important in human life is that in giving us more opportunities it gives us, as we would all say, more *choices*. We tend not to will those things that we have no opportunity to pursue (although we may well *want* them); if their pursuit is open to us we may well refrain, either from duty or prudence or indifference; but that is by choice. My enemy does not leave his sword undrawn because he lacks opportunity, but because he elects to avoid the consequences of seizing it.[18]

## VII

I conclude with some comments on a part of Hume's system where his views on freedom seem to have results that he himself finds

[18] I am indebted here to David Norton for drawing my attention to these important passages.

unwelcome, and that reveal a deep inadequacy within them. I refer to a little-discussed part of his moral philosophy that we find in Section 4 of Part iii of Book III of the *Treatise*, entitled 'Of Natural Abilities'. The issue dealt with there is also discussed in the second *Enquiry*, in Section VIII and Appendix IV.

I agree with David Norton that in key respects Hume is a common sense moralist.[19] At least, it is an important part of his intentions in his ethical writings to show that his radical views on reason and the passions do not involve the rejection of common moral distinctions and judgements, but can be used to support them, as long as they do not have religious overtones. His naturalism in any case requires him to describe these discriminations as we find them, and to set severe limits on the amount of reformation they can be subjected to by the philosopher. The passages I want to consider now seem to reveal an area where his views on freedom interfere with the execution of this intention. He represents the resulting problem as a minor one, but I do not think that it is.

The problem is as follows. Approval is directed toward stable states of character. In expressing our approval of them, we call them virtues. Their negative counterparts are of course the vices. We admire the virtues in this way because we disinterestedly recognize that they are agreeable and useful to the person who has them or to others—in the language of the second *Enquiry*, we see they have utility. But the virtues are not the only qualities in people that are agreeable and useful. The same is true of natural abilities, or talents, such as wit, eloquence, or imagination. We admire these also, but not in quite the same way. We do not accord them *moral* approval. Why should we not, since they seem to satisfy the criteria for being virtues that Hume describes? Hume oscillates in the face of this problem between suggesting on the one hand that natural abilities might well indeed be classed as virtues, that is that there is no real difference between the sort of admiration they elicit and moral admiration, and saying on the other hand that although these are different, the distinction between the two sorts of traits is not 'very material'. In the *Enquiry* he suggests that determining the reason for the distinction between them is 'only a grammatical enquiry', or as we might put it, a mere matter of semantics. But he does rather go on about it, if this is what he really thinks. He does offer one important argument:

[19] Norton 1982.

that there is no case for holding that the virtues are acquired voluntarily and the talents are not, as some philosophers think. The
only truth in this position, he says, is that virtues and vices can be
modified by law and education, whereas talents can not.[20]

This implies that moral goodness is the mere result of good fortune, of what is now sometimes called moral luck; and has no relation to freedom except for the fact that we have to have liberty of
spontaneity to carry out the choices that our virtues lead us to make.
Of course there is some truth in Hume's claim that virtues and vices
can be modified in these ways, or upbringing and moral education
would be impossible, although if what he says were all there is to
say, we could not distinguish these from manipulation or indoctrination. But he is wrong to think that our talents (or our handicaps)
can not be modified by law or training. The fact that the work of
remedial language instructors, physiotherapists, or music teachers
has some success even with pupils of low ability, is enough to show
this. But even if Hume were right about these matters, it would merely
show that there was a practical point in expressing approval of virtues
that was absent in the case of talents; it would not reveal any differences in the grounds we have for praising them.

I think we can make better progress in discerning the differences
between natural abilities and virtues by noticing in the first place
that natural abilities can be exercised both well and badly by those
who have them, whereas virtues can not. Wit, grace, or physical
beauty, can be used to make cruel jokes, entrap innocent victims, or
distract attention from evil purposes, and when these things happen
the resulting actions are vicious, not virtuous. No one can similarly
misuse his or her own virtues.[21] (Of course one person can misuse the
virtues of another person, as when corrupt leaders hide behind their
ministers' honesty or their bodyguards' courage, but that is another

[20] Hume makes this suggestion at *T* III. iii. 4. 609, though he does not repeat it in
the parallel discussion in Appendix IV to *EM*. In both discussions he is concerned
to reject the suggestion that the distinction between virtues and talents (and between
vices and handicaps) can be made on the basis of the voluntariness of the former
and the involuntariness of the latter. The suggestion that the distinction could be
justified on a future-looking basis is similar to the view of C. L. Stevenson that
'ethical judgements look mainly to the future'. See the essay 'Ethical Judgements and
Avoidability' in Stevenson 1963, 138–52 and ch. 14 of Stevenson 1944. Stevenson's
ethical theory is the closest in the twentieth century to that of Hume.

[21] Compare Aquinas, *Summa Theologiae*, 1a2a 55, 4, where he defines virtue as 'a
good disposition of the mind, by which we live righteously, of which no one can make
bad use'.

matter.) Hume has to assume that talents will always be used well when he suggests that the distinction between them and the virtues is merely semantic.

But this only carries us a small distance. Even though praise for talents may not be moral praise, we must bear in mind that we give moral praise to virtues that their owners have not had much hand in creating. Most virtuous people will thank their parents or their teachers for their good habits. So to begin again: if virtues and abilities are both influenced by prior factors like upbringing and education and heredity, why is there such a clear difference between their evaluative status? Here I think that by concentrating on the issue of origins, Hume has diverted attention from the place where the voluntary element in virtue is to be found. A virtue is indeed a disposition to act well regularly. Hume emphasizes the epistemic implications of this: that it enables us to predict how the possessor of the virtue is likely to behave. But this is only part of the story. The very predictability is one of the grounds for the praise; or the blame. George Washington is praised for telling the truth *regularly*. Don Juan is condemned for debauching women *at every opportunity*. We also, contrary to what Hume maintains, praise or condemn people for isolated acts that are out of character: the very fact that the agent's normal predispositions have been ineffectual this time may be a reason for applauding or condemning what the agent has done.

I submit that we cannot make sense of this dual fact, that both regular and irregular good acts may be praised, without introducing the libertarian judgement that what makes both the predictability and the surprisingness praiseworthy is the fact that in either case the agent has had the power to act otherwise, and that when the virtue is manifested that power has not been exercised, and when a good but unexpected action has been done, it has been. A virtue is a regular disposition to perform good actions *that one might well not perform*. Hume thinks that the notion of an unexercised power is without foundation; but it is essential to the concept of virtue. I believe, therefore, that Hume's views on freedom do not allow for a fundamental condition of the very moral evaluations he is at such pains to describe.

# 9

---

## *Hume's Scepticism and the* Dialogues

THE question of whether Hume is a sceptic and, if he is, what sort of sceptic he is, is probably the most vexed problem of the subtle subscience of Humeneutics. I will say at the outset that I think Hume is a sceptic, but a sceptic of an aberrant kind. I shall try in what follows to indicate what I take the nature of his scepticism to be, the place that it has in his philosophical system in the *Treatise* and the first *Enquiry*, and the extent to which it leads him into inconsistencies. I shall then attempt to use the results to interpret the *Dialogues Concerning Natural Religion*.

### I

There are still well-informed philosophers who find it odd that anyone should even suggest that Hume is not a sceptic. To most students of philosophy the two paradigms of scepticism are the Descartes of the first *Meditation* and the Hume of the fourth and fifth sections of the first *Enquiry*. But it has come to be quite widely held that Hume's views, rightly understood, are not sceptical at all.

The former opinion is the one held by many of Hume's own contemporaries, particularly Reid and Beattie, and presented at length by T. H. Green in his introduction to the Green and Grose edition of Hume's Philosophical Works. It is taken as nearly self-evident by many students because they are confined in their studies of Hume to the first Book of the *Treatise* and to Sections IV–VII of the *Enquiry Concerning Human Understanding*, of which it is the most natural and obvious reading.[1] The attendant understanding of

---

[1] Hume discusses scepticism in the *Treatise* I. iv. 1 and I. iv. 7; in Section XII of the first *Enquiry*; in Part I of the *Dialogues*; in the essay 'The Sceptic'; and in the *Letter from a Gentleman*. Some essays of particular interest on this theme are Robison

Hume represents him as the thinker who drew out the implications of Locke's 'Way of Ideas' and showed how it leads inexorably to unanswerable doubts about induction, perception, and self-identity. The latter opinion of Hume is due primarily to the work of Norman Kemp Smith, who represents Hume as a *naturalist*: someone whose main objective is to reveal those forces in human nature that govern our factual beliefs, our emotions, and our moral lives, and to show the inadequacies of rationalist interpretations of them.[2] As seen in this interpretation, Hume becomes a common-sense philosopher, not a subverter of common sense; for he represents all of us, himself included, as inescapably committed by our very natures to certain beliefs and to certain emotional and evaluative responses to our physical and social environment.

The basis of a solution is surely that the Reid-Beattie interpretation and the Kemp Smith interpretation are not incompatible. If Hume's objective is to reveal the sources of our beliefs and evaluations in human nature, it is a perfectly proper part of such an inquiry to argue that these beliefs and evaluations do not result from our having discovered good reasons for them, and are unaffected by the subsequent revelation that no good reasons for them exist. Such a conclusion would imply that one should seek their causes elsewhere. Conversely, if Hume decides that our most basic beliefs concerning matters of fact are beliefs for which there are no good reasons, it is perfectly consistent with this to go on to ask what it is about us that makes us hold them nevertheless, and whether it is possible for us to suspend them or abandon them. I would suggest, then, that Hume is both a sceptic and a naturalist: that he does say that our basic beliefs about matters of fact are devoid of rational justification, that he offers us

1973, Brett 1974, and Stove 1975. The arguments in this essay are an extension of interpretations offered in Penelhum 1975. Since this essay was written there have been important contributions to our understanding of his position on this difficult issue from which I hope I have profited. I would particularly wish to mention Fogelin 1985, Stroud 1977, Wright 1983 and 1986, Bell and McGinn 1990, and Norton 1993. There have also been important scholarly studies of the classical Sceptics and their influence in modern thought; among these are Burnyeat (ed.) 1983, Annas and Barnes 1985, Popkin 1979 and 1980, and Hankinson 1995. Two influential works by contemporary thinkers are Stroud 1984 and Strawson 1985. I returned to these matters myself in Penelhum 1983 and ch. 2 of Penelhum 1992. My assertion in part II of this essay that Hume was acquainted with Sextus is certainly over-confident; Julia Annas has made clear in a recent essay how limited his understanding of the actual Pyrrhonist tradition was. See Annas 1994.

[2] Smith 1905 and 1941.

detailed accounts of how we come to hold them and why we cannot
abandon them, and that these accounts are applications of a general
understanding of human nature that is applied elsewhere to our emotional lives and to our moral and social evaluations. It is an integral
part of such a position that this general understanding of human
nature represents us as creatures of passion, not of reason; but since
Hume says this over and over, there is surely no obstacle in the way
of using this as the connecting link between the negative and the
positive parts of his system. Hume's scepticism is not something
incompatible with his naturalism. It is an integral part of it.

This position implies two propositions that I think are true but
cannot argue here. The first is that Hume does indeed say that
induction has no rational grounds, that our belief in distinct and
continued existence cannot be given rational justification, and that
our ascription of identity to ourselves is without foundation. The
second proposition that my position implies is that Hume's primary
aims are psychological rather than philosophical: that his complex
and exciting arguments about the rationality of our beliefs are
propaedeutic to a psychological examination of the sources of the
cognitive and affective commitments our natures cause us to make.
This does not imply that Hume *confuses* psychological and philosophical considerations with one another. On the contrary, his
objectives cannot be stated without distinguishing them carefully;
and he seems to me to be the first major philosopher to make the
distinction between them. To argue that he confuses them on other
than some individual occasions is to miss the whole point of what
he is doing. Hume's naturalism is a combination or mixture of philosophy and psychology, with the latter predominating. The scepticism
is the main thrust of the epistemological part of the philosophical
propaedeutic to his psychological account of the sources of our
cognitive commitments. Its purpose is to show us that it is not
because we have good epistemological reasons to do so that we make
these commitments, since ordinary men do not have such reasons,
and philosophers have been unable to invent any.

## II

So far I have been arguing that Hume's scepticism is closely integrated with his naturalism, but I have not said much about the nature

of either. I now must do this, for one of Hume's best-informed interpreters, Richard Popkin, has identified them.[3] He reminds us that
one of Hume's overt concerns is to define the relationship between
his own scepticism and that of the Pyrrhonians; and he argues that
Hume, partly through misinterpretation, arrives at a position that
is in fact merely a consistent version of theirs. While I find this
illuminating, I do not think it is quite right.

The major source for our understanding of ancient scepticism is
the work of Sextus Empiricus, particularly his *Outlines of Pyrrhonism*.
There is clear evidence that Hume was acquainted with Sextus.
In spite of the title of his work, Sextus wrote about five hundred
years after Pyrrho, and between them the Sceptical school had gone
through more than one major cycle of change. In spite of these
changes, the basic intent of scepticism in the ancient world has to
be seen as the same as that of the contemporary ethical schools
of Epicureanism and Stoicism: that of cultivating an appropriate
moral attitude in the face of a world in which happiness could no
longer be identified with some objective that depended in any way
upon external, social circumstance. Pyrrho's contribution was to urge
the cultivation of noncommitment, or suspense of judgement, in the
face of both the conflicting theoretical claims of competing schools
of thought and the conflicting moral and religious claims of competing societies or creeds. This suspense of judgement would lead
to unperturbedness, or *ataraxia*. Since this is the antithesis of the
turmoil of the passions, the term *apatheia*, or absence of passion,
appears to be more or less equivalent to it and is also used. When
we come to the statement of the end of scepticism in Sextus, the
objective is qualified significantly: 'We assert still that the Sceptic's
End is quietude in respect of matters of opinion and moderate feeling in respect of things unavoidable.'[4] He explains the meaning of
'things unavoidable' by saying that even the sceptic is sometimes
cold or thirsty and cannot avoid being affected by such discomforts.
But he is able to be less disturbed by them than his fellows because
he makes no judgement about whether or not they are 'evil by nature'.
This seems to mean that the sceptic cannot avoid committing himself
on how things feel or seem to him, but he can avoid committing
himself on how they really are. His commitment will therefore be
to the moment, not to some dogma that attempts to judge the moment

---

[3] Popkin 1951.      [4] Sextus Empiricus 1967 edn., 19.

*sub specie aeternitatis.* Sextus recognizes (whether Pyrrho did or not) that nature gives us both sensations and intellectual responses to them, and that if the sceptic, like the Stoic, was to offer his way of life as living according to nature, then some assent to sensation would have to be allowed for—because the sceptic, unlike the Stoic, could not judge what nature required in terms of some cosmic metaphysic. The sceptic also has to recognize practical necessities and to participate in the daily affairs of society. Sextus sums up the life of the Sceptic as follows:

Adhering, then, to appearances we live in accordance with the normal rules of life, undogmatically, seeing that we cannot remain wholly inactive. And it would seem that this regulation of life is fourfold, and that one part of it lies in the guidance of Nature, another in the constraint of the passions, another in the tradition of laws and customs, another in the instruction of the arts. Nature's guidance is that by which we are naturally capable of sensation and thought; constraint of the passions is that whereby hunger drives us to food and thirst to drink; tradition of customs and laws, that whereby we regard piety in the conduct of life as good, but impiety as evil; instruction of the arts, that whereby we are not inactive in such arts as we adopt. But we make all these statements undogmatically.[5]

This means, I think, that the sceptic as Sextus describes him accepts that he has to act, has to respond in some way or other to his sensations, and has to conform, or not to conform, to customs. In such a situation he will respond to his sensations with the natural or easy assent to which he, like all other men, is inclined, and he will conform to those customs and values he finds prevalent around him. But this will not be because he thinks, as other men do, that his sensations are appearances that reveal realities, or that the customs and values of his fellows embody moral truths. Nor does he think they do not: he suspends judgement either way. But since he suspends judgement either way, there is nothing to stop him from conforming in the easiest and most comfortable way possible. What is essential here is that the conformity, even if it does represent a change from the ascetic withdrawal that has sometimes been ascribed to Pyrrho himself, does not represent a departure from the basic thesis that quietude comes from suspense of judgement. It seems to me to depend upon it as much as ever; for only in the absence of judgement can one be confined to one's affections by the immediate exigencies of the moment.

[5] Sextus Empiricus 1967 edn., 17.

To return to Hume: Popkin suggests that Hume misinterprets classical Pyrrhonism and that the position he himself adopts, though not identical with Pyrrhonism, is in fact a more consistent version of it than the one Sextus presents to us; and he says that his Humean scepticism is identical with what Kemp Smith calls naturalism.

Hume does indeed seem to misinterpret Pyrrhonism—if we take this to be the views of Sextus. At least he ignores the practical accommodations Sextus allows the sceptic, and the natural assent to appearances. But I do not see this as a fundamental misunderstanding. For Sextus's position still requires an inner suspense of judgement about the conformity of appearances to reality, and it is precisely this that Hume says we are not at liberty to exercise. 'Nature, by an absolute and uncontrollable necessity has determin'd us to judge as well as to breathe and feel,' (*T* I. iv. 1. 183). He does not say that the Pyrrhonists' *arguments* are unsound; he even adds some of his own. But he insists that the suspense of judgement they recommend is beyond us. We cannot even say, with Sextus, 'Yes, I realize that there is no good reason to suppose that my sensations are veridical, but I will do what comes naturally and act as though they are.' Neither the plain man nor the philosopher can refrain from believing that they *are* veridical. We cannot make our assertions *un*dogmatically.

So I think that the form of scepticism Hume *does* adopt, though it is very close indeed to what Popkin finds in Hume, is more at variance than Popkin thinks it is with the views of Sextus. The Humean sceptic, according to Popkin, recognizes the psychological impotence of Pyrrhonian arguments and dogmatizes where it is natural to do so, in full recognition of his dogmatism and of the groundlessness of it. He also accepts that nature does, for some of us, encourage doubts and uncertainties at least for short periods, so that one is still following nature if one engages in the attendant suspense of judgement if one can. So the Humean sceptic is hesitant and dogmatic by turns, as nature encourages him. Such a thinker is bound to oscillate between a more suspenseful mood while he is doing philosophy, and a more dogmatic mood when playing backgammon. But he will follow nature more consistently than the classical Pyrrhonian, who will be trying to suspend judgement in the most unnatural way, both in his study and out of it. That way is not the way to *ataraxia*, but to madness.

This sort of sceptic, alternating from nature between suspense and dogmatism, is indeed the Hume of the seventh, and concluding, section of Book I of the *Treatise*: the Hume who is openly and endearingly, and I think unironically, torn between sceptical doubt and common-sense dogma. But there is one respect in which Popkin is superficial. He says that the classical Pyrrhonian will not achieve *ataraxia* by suspending judgement, because the attempt to suspend judgement constantly is unnatural. This may be so; but it does not seem to me to be this that Hume sees as the undesirable feature of sceptical doubt. He regards it as independently disturbing, even when it is the result of the indulgence of a natural inclination to philosophize. That sort of inclination *is* natural, but it is also hazardous. There is evidence that Hume did find philosophical perplexity conducive to exhaustion and melancholia. He says this, more or less, in the *Treatise*:

> But what have I here said, that reflections very refin'd and metaphysical have little or no influence upon us? This opinion I can scarce forbear retracting, and condemning from my present feeling and experience. The *intense* view of these manifold contradictions and imperfections in human reason has so wrought upon me, and heated my brain, that I am ready to reject all belief and reasoning, and can look upon no opinion even as more probable or likely than another. Where am I, or what? From what causes do I derive my existence, and to what condition shall I return? Whose favour shall I court, and whose anger must I dread? What beings surround me? and on whom have I any influence, or who have any influence on me? I am confounded with all these questions, and begin to fancy myself in the most deplorable condition imaginable, environ'd with the deepest darkness, and utterly depriv'd of the use of every member and faculty. (*T* I. iv. 7. 268–9)

Consequently, I think that it is not the unnaturalness of sceptical doubts but their capacity to produce anxiety that makes Hume say the wise sceptic will keep them in their place. In the *Treatise* this seems mostly to amount to a decision to indulge in philosophy only when so inclined, and to escape from its tribulations into social life when they become too much. But this recognition of the hazardousness of philosophy leads him in the first *Enquiry* to a more formal attempt to limit scepticism, by limiting the subject matter of philosophical reflection as well as the psychological occasion of it. I refer, of course, to the introduction there of the concept of *mitigated scepticism*, which Hume recommends to us as a mode of thought whose virtues can be made obvious to us if we have learned humility about the powers of our reason from indulgence in the

Pyrrhonian variety. I do not agree with Popkin that this later version of scepticism is the same as the earlier.[6]

Hume characterizes mitigated scepticism in three ways. First, it embodies a humility about the powers of reason, which may be a fruit of the study of Pyrrhonian arguments against it. Second, it 'confines itself to common life', and its decisions are 'nothing but the reflections of common life, methodized and corrected'. The only argument he offers for this restriction is this one: 'While we cannot give a satisfactory reason, why we believe, after a thousand experiments, that a stone will fall, or fire burn; can we ever satisfy ourselves concerning any determination, which we may form, with regard to the origin of worlds, and the situation of nature, from, and to eternity?' (*EU* XII. 162). Finally, he deduces from this restriction that the sceptic will confine himself to 'abstract reasoning concerning quantity or number' and 'experimental reasoning concerning matter of fact and existence'. This counsel of humility leads him to his final famous peroration about committing writings that are more ambitious than this to the flames.

I will try at this point to summarize what I take to be Hume's overall position with regard to scepticism. (1) He agrees with the Pyrrhonians that the beliefs of common life and the constructions of divinity and school metaphysics are devoid of rational justification. (2) He disagrees with the Pyrrhonian sceptics in their recommendation that the philosopher should in consequence withhold assent from the beliefs of common life and the constructions of divinity and school metaphysics alike. He has at least three reasons for saying this. (a) It is psychologically impossible for us *not* to assent to the beliefs of common life. (b) The sceptical attacks on these beliefs, though admitting of no answer, also produce no conviction: so not only is the assent to those beliefs something we are unable initially to withhold; it is also something that cannot subsequently be withdrawn. (c) Even if the assent could be withheld or withdrawn, to do so would produce not the inner calm and unperturbedness the Pyrrhonian pursues but the very anxiety he is seeking to avoid. In this respect, the questioning of the sceptic is in the same position as the constructions of the theologian and the metaphysician. Consequently, one is as hazardous to our peace of mind as the other. (3) The result of this is a recommendation to indulge our propensity to philosophical

---

[6] Popkin 1951, Chappell 96.

thought, if we personally have such a propensity, to the minimum. This recommendation takes different forms. (a) In the *Treatise* it amounts to a recommendation to indulge in philosophical speculation only on those occasions when we are minded to do so, and even then to treat it as a pastime in which nature has disposed us to participate. Its hazards are to be dealt with by making sure that we also participate actively in those social pursuits that will distract us from the rarefied doubts and wonders that beset us in our studies. What he says here has to be connected with his moral diatribes against the 'monkish virtues' of the ascetic: the ascetic wantonly cuts himself off from those activities that are nature's cure for the mental distempers into which philosophy can lead us if we take it too seriously. (b) In the *Enquiry* this on-again-off-again policy is replaced by the positivist recommendations of mitigated scepticism: instead of trying to contain philosophy by rationing the amount of time we spend on it, we should contain it by confining its subject matter, so that it is critical and descriptive, not revisionary or speculative. Philosophy, thus understood, would become the journeyman study of those processes of reasoning we must use in common life and in science, where we presuppose and do not question the regularity of nature, the reality of the external world, and the identity of the self, and do not attempt to get above ourselves by treating of God, freedom, and immortality. Examples of this sort of activity would be his own comments on how we should estimate probabilities or judge of causes and effects.

## III

The most obvious criticism of what Hume says concerns the consistency of mitigated scepticism. How can he recommend that we confine ourselves to the reflections of common life, when their presuppositions are as incapable of rational justification as the pretensions of metaphysics? Surely Hume should either indulge both or reject both? How can scepticism consistently *be* mitigated?[7]

I think Hume's answer is as follows. Although it is true that the natural beliefs of common sense and the speculative constructions of

---

[7] The best expression of this criticism is G. E. Moore's essay 'Hume's Philosophy' in Moore 1922, 147–67.

metaphysics and religion are alike devoid of rational justification; and although it is also true that human nature admits within it forces that make it natural, in some manner or other, to engage in both; the forces that impel us to adopt the beliefs of common life are found in all men, whereas those that lead us into metaphysics or into religion are found only in *some* men. Metaphysics is a relative rarity, indulged in only by philosophers. Religion is not a rarity in the same way, but the forces that produce it are *pathological* forces, such as the superstitious fear of the unknown, and fortunate men in civilized communities can be free from them. So the real reason for restricting philosophical thought to the affairs of common life is that our pursuit of those affairs is the result of beliefs that none of us can avoid having, whereas the fancies of the metaphysician and the theologian can be avoided with a bit of luck and judgement.

Offering this as Hume's answer is somewhat speculative. I do not mean by this that there is any lack of clear evidence that Hume regards the urges to metaphysics or religion as less than universal. He frequently indicates that our common beliefs owe nothing of their origin to the metaphysician. In the concluding passages of Book I of the *Treatise* he speaks somewhat enviously of those honest gentlemen who 'in *England*, in particular . . . have carried their thoughts very little beyond those objects, which are every day expos'd to their senses'. (*T* I. iv. 7. 272) The whole burden of the *Natural History of Religion* is to reveal the special psychopathology of religion as something we should evade if we can. What makes it speculative to offer this as Hume's answer to the common criticism that he has no grounds on which to distinguish the methodizing of natural beliefs on the one hand and the construction of metaphysical and theological systems on the other is that he does not explicitly offer this as his reason for recommending mitigated scepticism to us. On the contrary, the reason he gives is the strange one I have already quoted—that if we cannot give rational grounds for believing that a stone will fall, or fire burn, we cannot claim to settle problems about the origin or future of the world and ought therefore to have learned caution from our failure to justify our natural beliefs. Now this is an odd argument. Why should the failure to produce good reasons for thinking that fire burns teach us to be cautious? Since it shows us that we must inevitably ignore the absence of evidence and jump to conclusions without it, surely it should teach us that we have no sensible choice but to throw caution to the winds? But the moral looks different if we take into account what I have argued Hume believes about our psychological capacities. For the unjustifiability of our natural beliefs *can* teach us caution if it makes us see that we are so prone to believe unjustified propositions that we ought always to avoid intellectual commitments *where we can*. And nature does permit us to avoid them in the case of metaphysics or religion, by allowing us to be incurious or to suppress the curiosity we have. The evidence for our having the capacity to do this is that some men manage it.

If this is the right interpretation of what mitigated scepticism teaches us, then it is clearly not the same as the view Popkin finds, correctly, in the *Treatise*, where the wise philosopher philosophizes from time to time because it comes naturally to him to do so. Instead of saying, as he does there, that the best way to peace of mind is for those who like doing that sort of thing to do it, and the rest not, we now find Hume saying that everyone, however minded to philo-sophize, should keep to the 'proper subjects of science and enquiry'. The difficulty is that even though some men are incurious about metaphysics and are free of superstitious anxiety, it might still be impossible for *other* men, such as you or I or Hume, to avoid wondering about the origin of the world or the immortality of the soul. Even though some commitments may be universal and some not, it might still be that those who are committed to the latter are as unable to avoid their commitment as they are to avoid the com-mitments that everybody else makes. Our inabilities may just vary; and the cautious advice of the mitigated sceptic may be advice that can be taken only by those who do not need it.

So the mitigated scepticism of the *Enquiry* accords less well with Hume's philosophical psychology than the quasi-Pyrrhonism of the *Treatise*, however much Hume the positivist and secularizer may wish to resort to it. I shall suggest shortly that Hume modifies it in the *Dialogues*. For the moment, however, I must return to the position of the *Treatise*.

## IV

I have so far suggested that Hume rejects the recommendations of classical Pyrrhonism for three reasons. (1) He does not think we are able to withhold assent from the beliefs of common life. (2) He does not think that anything Pyrrhonists may say can enable us to *withdraw* assent from these beliefs once we have acquired them. (3) Suspense of judgement leads not to peace of mind but rather to anxiety.

I have little to say about the third of these propositions. It seems to me that the effect of philosophical perplexity upon human nature is unlikely to be uniform, and that Hume may be right about its effect on some people and wrong about its effect on others. But for his opinion to be based on experience (as I have suggested it is), and for it to form the basis of a recommendation that we indulge ourselves in philosophy in modest doses, it is obviously necessary to modify the doctrine that we cannot withdraw our assent to the beliefs of common life. If we could not do it at all, we obviously could not be distressed by doing it, or be urged to do it only in moderation. What Hume has to say, and does say, is that those who can be afflicted by philosophical doubts can be spared their distressing consequences because these doubts are only short-lived and cannot survive the transition from the study to the world outside.[8]

I turn now to the other two contentions. Hume has a moderately complex argument, I think, in support of the claim that we cannot *not* assent to the beliefs of common life.[9] I suggest that it goes as follows. There are no good reasons in favour of the beliefs of common life. Hence we do not hold those beliefs because we have such reasons. The only reasons that have been offered are all bad ones; they are known only to the philosophers who have invented them; and the philosophers themselves have held the beliefs they have attempted to justify before inventing their reasons. Hence not only is our assent to our natural beliefs not dependent on our having good reasons for them; it also is not dependent on our having bad reasons for them that we think are good. Therefore, we hold these beliefs not for reasons at all, but only because of *causes*, such as laziness, custom, or habit.

I think this argument is unsuccessful.[10] Hume is clearly right in insisting that philosophical arguments have no share in the genesis of our natural beliefs, but he does not succeed in showing that *reason* has no role in their genesis. Even if we agree that we have no good reasons for them, it might still very well be the case that we *thought* we had good reasons. To prove that to be untrue Hume

---

[8] See, for example *EU* XII. 160: 'All human life must perish, were his principles *universally and steadily to prevail*' (my italics). The strongest statement of the view that scepticism is only skin deep is to be found in the (admittedly suspect) *Letter from a Gentleman*, where it is dismissed as a 'jeu d'esprit'.

[9] I am here extrapolating from many places, but especially from *T* I. iv. 2.

[10] I am indebted here to some comments by Gary Colwell.

would have to show, as he realizes, that the only reasons that have ever been thought of are those that the philosophers have thought of. But this is very implausible, even on Hume's own accounts of the origins of our beliefs. What Hume calls custom or habit is manifested in our inferences from the past to the future: right or wrong, surely our doing this is something that we *think* to be rational? Our belief in the distinct and continued existence of our perceptions may be due, as he says, to the constancy they show and the fact that assuming their continuance makes it easier to anticipate them: but right or wrong, surely we *think* this basis is rational? And our belief in personal identity may be due to our confusing successions of related perceptions with continuous unchanging ones, but surely the ascription of identity in such circumstances is *thought* to be rational when we make it?

Hume's argument in support of the claim that our assent to the beliefs of common life cannot be *withdrawn* is, I think, this. The Pyrrhonian sceptic shows us quite successfully that there are no good reasons in favour of these beliefs. But since these beliefs are not there because we have ever thought there are such reasons, we are naturally unaffected by the revelation that no such reasons exist. The Pyrrhonian's arguments are unanswerable, but they are also impotent, or 'vain'.

I think this, also, is a bad argument. Even if it were true that my beliefs are not due to my thinking they have good reasons, it by no means follows that when I am shown that they have no good reasons, they will remain unaffected. The discovery of their lack of epistemic respectability may nullify all the causes that have produced them. There is, in any case, some clear evidence that the encounter with Pyrrhonian arguments does at least have some shock value: even if we are no more rational than Hume says we are, we at least mildly aspire to be. Hume's recognition of this fact appears in his qualification, already noted, of the doctrine that sceptical doubts are ineffectual. He says instead that they produce only a 'momentary amazement and confusion' and that involvement in daily affairs destroys their effects (*EU* XII. 160).

## V

I shall now try to explore the question of how correct Hume is in his negative estimate of the *efficacy* of Pyrrhonian doubts. Is he right to hold that they cannot cause us to withdraw our natural assent once it is given?

We must first put aside a number of irrelevant arguments. They all come from common, and reasonable, philosophical responses to the Pyrrhonian arguments as Hume himself presents them.

(1) There is, first of all, the common-sense response that comes from Reid and Moore. This consists of saying that because our common beliefs are true, and indeed because we *know* that they are true, the Pyrrhonian arguments Hume considers to reveal their lack of rational bases must be defective. For present purposes such arguments can all be admitted; yet they get us nowhere. For all they would show us is that the Pyrrhonian is engaged in producing arguments to undermine the status of propositions that he and we know quite well to be true. But this would not show, at all, that he and we could not be made doubtful about these propositions by these arguments. For we can be doubtful about things that we know perfectly well— even while saying too loudly, along with Moore, that we know that we know them. It is very likely, as Hume sees, that we may in such circumstances oscillate between two inconsistent attitudes—so that sometimes we really are quite doubtful and other times really are quite free of doubt. I defer for the moment the question of whether or not someone who oscillates like this can be said to know, or to believe, the propositions he oscillates in attitude toward, all the time. My point for the moment is the simple one that all that the arguments and asseverations of a Moore can do is prove that our doubts must be *mistaken*. This in no way shows that the doubt is *unreal*.

(2) Next, there are arguments deriving from Kant and Wittgenstein, which are designed to show that the doubts of the Pyrrhonian are *incoherent*. I shall follow a common practice and call these transcendental arguments, though I am not very clear what this title means. These arguments are supposed to show that there is something inescapably wrong with the Pyrrhonian's difficulties. They usually proceed by trying to persuade us that someone who worries about whether or not there is any good reason to assume that his sensory experiences correspond to realities implies, or presupposes, in posing his question, the ability to distinguish between mere sensations on the one hand and real things on the other; or that someone who wonders whether or not he is the same person that he was last week can wonder about this only if he is the same person and could not wonder about this if he were not. I find these arguments very

difficult to assess. But I am willing to accept that they show what they are supposed to show. It just seems to me, once more, to be irrelevant to the questions of the efficacy of the Pyrrhonian sceptic's doubts. For this does not depend psychologically upon the coherence of the sceptic's reasons. If a transcendental argument succeeds, it presumably shows that the Pyrrhonian's doubts cannot be coherently argued for, or even expressed, unless the propositions he doubts are in fact true, *or* unless he is in some manner committed to them, *or* unless he already knows them. I am even willing to agree that if a Pyrrhonian were to concede that some such argument is successful, he would, in some cases at least, cease to doubt the things he doubts now. But none of this shows that before the incoherence is revealed (and if we need a transcendental argument to reveal it, it will not be obvious) we cannot genuinely doubt the propositions that the Pyrrhonian questions.

(3) Finally, very briefly, it has sometimes been argued that the doubts of the Pyrrhonian are really pseudodoubts for a linguistic reason. This reason is that when the propositions that the Pyrrhonian questions are subjected to philosophical analysis, they can be shown to be reducible to propositions of an order that the Pyrrhonian has exempted from his questions. For example, it has been argued that the assertions about physical objects or persons that the Pyrrhonian says he is doubtful about can be translated into, and therefore are equivalent in meaning to, statements or sets of statements about sensory experiences to which the Pyrrhonian can assent. I think this sort of argument, even if it is successful, is also irrelevant to the question of the efficacy of the doubts the Pyrrhonian has. For it is quite possible for someone to be certain and doubtful about two propositions that are identical or logically equivalent, at least if he does not realize that they are. No doubt this will lead to inconsistencies in his actions and responses; but these can exist, and are in the circumstances quite intelligible.

## VI

Having put these arguments aside, I return to the question of the efficacy, the psychological reality, of the doubts of the Pyrrhonian. Hume says that at best these doubts are very short-lived and are dispelled at once by the exigencies of common life.

We can all agree that in some sense it is true that philosophical doubts are much easier to sustain in the study than in the market-place. The question is what this *shows*. To start with, it does not show that the doubts are not real ones while I nurse them in the study—unless one insists, questionbeggingly, that a doubt that is dispelled by a departure from the study is not a real doubt solely because of this. But let us make a minimal concession: let us admit that a real doubt has to affect our subsequent attitudes to some extent. The question is to what extent and in what ways. I would submit that a doubt that is conceived and nurtured in the study and then persists outside it, even in the form of an occasional question or hesitation, is still a real one, though a psychologically weak one —especially if a return to the study revives it readily.

Let us make a comparison with positive religious commitments, which I may regularly nourish in the church or the closet, and which may pale as I encounter the day-to-day demands of the secular world. Here I would suggest that the fact that I come to have my religious attitudes weakened, and come to have my doubts freshened, by these circumstances does not show that I did not really believe what I said to myself in the closet or in the church. I see no significant difference in the case of Pyrrhonian doubt. If I convince myself that it is doubtful that there are any real material objects while I am in the study and then find it difficult to feel doubtful for long about this while I am in the marketplace, the diminution of my hesitancies does not show that my doubts were unreal before I got there.

We can now add to *this*. Just as someone who has faith can, as a matter of personal policy, try deliberately to contend with the doubts that may flood in upon him when he leaves the closet or the church for the hurly-burly of the secular world, and can try to deepen and strengthen the attitudes that are the expressions of the convictions he has in faith, so one could (could one not?) deliberately sustain the doubts that one has argued oneself into in the study when one leaves the study for the backgammon table and the affairs of common life. Just as one can fight off doubts, so one could (could one not?) try to fend off convictions. After all, all one would need for a motive would be the reflection (true or false) that the best place to arrive at a knowledge of reality is in the calm and detached situation of the study, where one is capable of objectivity and able to apportion the impact of one's experiences to their epistemological status; or one might be swayed by the reflection (true or false) that the more involved in affairs one is, the more one is disturbed by them emotionally and intellectually. Reflections of this sort would be enough to supply one with a motive for not yielding to the blandishments of what other, less discriminating people call realities. After all, they do not have the benefit of reflection and study the way the philosopher does.

So far, then, I would suggest that the doubts the Pyrrhonian nourishes in the study need only a very limited persistence outside it to be classified as psychologically genuine; but they can in any case be sustained in the face of the impact of common affairs as a matter of deliberate policy, in the way in which someone who has a commitment of faith can sustain it in the face of those features of human life that serve to weaken the attitudes that faith generates, and to create doubts. I would now draw the conclusion that for as long as the sceptic is trying, with some success, to sustain his doubts in the face of the blandishments of common affairs, his situation is not the one that Hume suggests, in which he oscillates from scepticism to dogmatism between the study and the marketplace, but is one in which he remains doubtful, in a quite real sense, all along—one in which the common convictions are to some real degree fended off by the repetition of philosophical reflections. If this is true, then the sceptic's situation is the one that Sextus recommends to us, and that Hume seems to consider to be impossible, namely, one in which we suspend judgement on the very practices and commitments that other men make dogmatically, and with which we fall in on the surface.

This will no doubt immediately raise an objection: surely the so-called sceptic is really abandoning his suspense and hesitation altogether the first time he avoids an obstacle or sits on a chair or answers to his name in a roll call. For such actions would be things he would be *no more inclined to do than not* if he really had the doubts that he professes to have. Just to get into common affairs and to function within them is to abandon these hesitations. This objection is mistaken; and the mistake is one that Hume makes, but Sextus does not. Remember again that the question before us is not the overall consistency of the sceptic's opinions, but the reality of his doubts. For his doubts to be real, all that is necessary is for him to make the ordinary day-to-day responses to his situation without interpreting these responses in the common-sense manner. When it indeed appears to him that there is a bus approaching and that he is in its path, his response will be the same as everyone else's, but he will interpret it as one in which he controls the sequence of sensory experiences that he has, rather than as one in which he has stepped out of the way of a bus. For his doubts to be real, it is not necessary that the attempt to express what he thinks he is about be successfully made without confusions or inconsistencies. Nor is it in the least bit necessary, for his doubts to be real, that we, in talking about him, manage to describe what he is up to without committing ourselves to the reality of the external world, the rationality of induction, and the rest. All that is necessary is that the confusions he may be involved in, or the commitments we may have to make, are less than obvious *to him*.[11]

So Hume's denial of the reality of the sceptic's doubts is too hasty. It does seem possible for the doubts to persist, as a result of deliberate effort and reflection, into the affairs of common life, so that we are able to sustain the uninvolved participation in human affairs that Sextus recommends and that Hume says is beyond us. He may be right in suggesting that doubt and hesitation are worrisome and not liberating. But that would merely show that we would be imprudent to foster them. It would not show that he could avoid the worries by taking refuge in the supposed inability of human beings to sustain the doubts that lead to them.


## VII


I turn now to the *Dialogues Concerning Natural Religion*. It is my purpose here not to try to resolve all the calculated ambiguities of that work but merely to suggest that an understanding of the sceptical strain in Hume will assist us in resolving them. I must state at the outset that I agree with those scholars, from Kemp Smith on, who identify Hume with Philo. I do not agree, however, that such an identification makes the import of the *Dialogues* clear. He appears to change his position in Part XII in certain fundamental respects, and any interpretation of the *Dialogues* must either show that this change is only apparent and not real, or do something to explain it. My own view is that it is real enough and represents one more attempt on the part of Hume, as a sceptic, to assess the psychological weight of his own negative arguments. I shall try to make a case for this and estimate the success with which Hume has done it.

[11] This objection is close, of course, to that dismissed in V (1).

I can say nothing here about the detailed arguments of Parts II to XI. I follow most contemporary readers in thinking that in these arguments Philo demolishes the empirical or experimental theism that Cleanthes represents. He shows, in other words, that if one uses the evidential canons to which Cleanthes insists on appealing, there is no good reason to accept the theistic conclusions that Cleanthes finds so obvious. I will concentrate instead on Part I, which none of us seems to read, and on Part XII, which none of us seems to understand.

Philo comes on the scene in Part I agreeing with Demea about the 'weakness, blindness, and narrow limits of human reason'. He adds a sceptical turn of his own: since reason is prone to 'uncertainty and needless contrarieties, even in subjects of common life and practice', it is clearly unable to decide 'the origin of worlds'. Cleanthes takes him to task for the implied suggestion that religious faith should be founded on philosophical scepticism and says that no philosophical sceptic can be in earnest. Pyrrhonians, he says, are like Stoics in assuming that 'what a man can perform sometimes, and in some dispositions, he can perform always, and in every disposition'. In making this criticism of Pyrrhonism Cleanthes is only repeating what Hume himself has said about it in the *Enquiry*. Unsurprisingly, if Philo is Hume, Philo agrees: the sceptic must engage in common life like other men, and if he should pursue his philosophical inquiries beyond the necessities of common life, this indulgence is excusable because it is based upon our universal urge to generality and principle. 'What we call *philosophy* is nothing but a more regular and methodical operation of the same kind.' But 'when we carry our speculation into the two eternities . . . we have here got quite beyond the reach of our faculties.' To depart from the topics of common life is to abandon the correctives that restrain the doubts of the sceptic; these doubts become at least as legitimate as the dogmatist's speculations once these correctives are removed (*D* I. 131–5).

Thus far Philo is an exponent of the mitigated scepticism of the *Enquiry* who dissociates himself from Pyrrhonism and holds that philosophy should confine itself to the concerns of common life. He now has to face an obvious criticism from Cleanthes that such a restriction ought to restrain him from scientific inquiry as well as from metaphysics, since the plain man is as baffled by Newton as he is by Plato. He does not answer this immediately. The reason is obvious enough: the answer is to be found in the detailed arguments of Parts II to XI. These arguments show that the procedures of scientific inquiry cannot yield theological results, and that it is only scientific enquiry, not natural theology, that proceeds by methodizing and correcting the reflections of common life. What he does do immediately is comment on some historical remarks that Cleanthes has just made. Cleanthes has said that before the time of Locke, Christian apologists regarded reason as the enemy of faith and consequently were prone to find allies, however dubious, among the Pyrrhonists. Since Locke, however, sceptics have been assumed to be atheists, and faith has been held to be 'nothing but a species of *reason*', (*D* I. 138). Cleanthes himself is patently a follower of Locke. Philo's comment is that 'the priests' will always seek to consolidate the faith by any means that lies to hand, and that in recent ages they could no longer depend on 'education' (indoctrination) to establish it; hence they now see reason not as a presumptuous enemy as before but as the only 'principle to lead us into religion'. I shall return to this passage shortly, but it does carry one obvious implication: if Philo can succeed, as he later does, in showing that Cleanthes is mistaken in believing reason to be the ally of priestly religion, then Locke's predecessors will have been right to think its natural ally to be scepticism.

Part XII opens after Demea's departure, with Philo retreating, at least nominally, from the 'careless' scepticism of the previous ten parts. Throughout Part XII he repeatedly asserts his acceptance of 'a purpose, an intention, or design' and his 'veneration for true religion'. There is no denying that this is at least verbally inconsistent with the negativity of everything that he has said since Part I. Kemp Smith labours very hard to show that the inconsistencies can be dissolved and that Philo does not mean a word of it (*D*. 120–23). I think Nelson Pike has succeeded in showing that this line of argument is not wholly successful,[12] and I have tried elsewhere to steer a middle course between their interpretations.[13] I confine myself here to considerations that bear on the major theme of this paper.

Undoubtedly, Philo's protestations are expressed in language of carefully contrived ambiguity. Purpose and design strike everywhere 'the most careless, the most stupid thinker'; the existence of God

---

[12] See Pike's edition of the *Dialogues*, 1970. I am much indebted to his argument throughout.

[13] See Penelhum 1975, 189–96. For a well-argued statement of an interpretation different from the one offered here, and now extended, see Gaskin 1974, 1978, 1988.

must be left undisputed since it is supported 'by all the arguments which its nature admits of, even though these arguments be not, in themselves, very numerous or forcible . . . and no understanding [can] estimate their cogency', (*D* xii. 214, 216). Further, his final statement of the 'whole of natural theology' is something he himself says is 'somewhat ambiguous', namely, '*that the cause or causes of order in the universe probably bear some remote analogy to human intelligence*', (*D* xii. 227). All of this must be emphasized. But it must also be emphasized that Philo does nevertheless accept *some* of what Cleanthes has been arguing for, namely, that the order in the universe does have a cause or causes that are somewhat like human intelligence—when he has shown decisively in what has preceded that Cleanthes' arguments do not show even this much to be a more likely view than any other. He still differs from Cleanthes, however, in three fundamental respects. First, he continues to deny that this proposition can be extended from human intelligence to other human qualities. Second, he insists that 'it affords no inference that affects human life'. Third, he spends a great deal of Part XII arguing that the evils of institutional and revealed religion set it apart from 'the philosophical and rational kind'—whereas Cleanthes obtusely continues to insist that all 'false' religion needs to bring it into conformity with 'the true' is a little soap and water.

I incline to the view that these considerations show Philo (that is, Hume) to be genuine in his acceptance of this conclusion of natural theology, in part because it does not seem to him to matter whether one accepts it or not. When all the appropriate disclaimers are built in, it is, as he says, a merely verbal matter whether one stresses, with the atheist, that the analogy is remote or stresses, with the theist, that even a remote analogy is still an analogy. What does matter, however, is whether or not one goes on to use the acceptance of the analogy as a ground for adherence to some form of institutional religion, for which Philo has nothing but abhorrence. Cleanthes keeps on *saying* he does. But Philo (Hume) knows better. He sees that Cleanthes' sort of civilized rational theologian will attempt to preserve what he perceives as his rationality by drawing no practical consequences from his theism that could not equally well be established without it. To Philo (Hume) the very practical and doctrinal emptiness of natural religion, thus understood, is a reason not for rejecting it but for giving it a 'plain, philosophical assent'. The last speech of Philo is to be seen, I suggest, as in part at least a message to the atheist to recognize in Cleanthes' sort of theologian a social and practical ally in the battle against the Demeas of this world who think religious beliefs ought to have specific consequences that unbelievers cannot arrive at for themselves. Cleanthes, of course, cannot be expected to understand any of this: but the good, secularizing influence he exercises on his fellow believers is best fostered if he does not. With enemies like Cleanthes, unbelievers do not need friends.

Even if all this is plausible, it does not account for all the nuances of Part XII. In particular, we still need to do more to determine what Philo means by that famous final statement: 'To be a philosophical sceptic is, in a man of letters, the first and most essential step towards being a sound, believing Christian,' (*D* XII. 228).

To some degree this is plain enough. One thing Philo means is that his arguments in Parts II to XI have undermined all Cleanthes' claims to deduce any doctrines from the design hypothesis except the vague deistic pronouncement that constitutes the very unreligious religion that he and Philo share. But this cannot be all. For even this common doctrine is more than the Philo of Parts II to XI seems to accept. His final statement must mean more than just this.

We can find a clue, I think, in the comment of Cleanthes that immediately precedes Philo's suggestion that theists and atheists differ only verbally (*D* XII. 216). Cleanthes says that the analogy of the world to 'a machine of human contrivance' must 'immediately strike all unprejudiced apprehensions' and that a sceptical critic can do no more than 'start doubts and difficulties' in order to make us suspend judgement; yet this suspense is impossible for us. Philo replies that indeed it is impossible and that since the analogy is undeniable, the causes of the world and of machines must be analogous also; the only dispute remaining will then be the 'verbal' issue of whether the fact of the analogy is of more importance than its remoteness. Again we must note that the very suspense that *Philo* tells us here is impossible is nevertheless the logical outcome of his own negative arguments in Parts II to XI. Here he accepts that there *is* analogy between the cause or causes of order in the world and human intelligence. It is the subsequent implications of this acceptance that lead into the verbal disputes. This amounts to an admission that all he has done hitherto is to start the 'doubts and difficulties' Cleanthes has referred to and that the perception of design in nature is not destroyed by them.

Now Hume surely thinks that Philo has succeeded in refuting all Cleanthes' *arguments* for the design hypothesis, as indeed he has. But if this is so, Philo's concession in Part XII can only represent an admission that the perception of design in nature is a prephilosophical interpretation of it—a natural belief that is not established by argument but that, for that very reason, is not eliminated when arguments in its favour are refuted. Hence all that Philo's doubts and difficulties can achieve is to prevent our drawing specific moral or religious consequences from it. This is of course of vital importance, but it is less than Philo's own arguments suggest. Hume seems to be committed to the existence of a vague universal deism that he does not think the arguments of mitigated scepticism can wholly eradicate, even though they can render it harmless in practice for the 'man of letters'. Once again he has felt obliged to concede the psychological impotence of his own sceptical arguments.

But the concession, though a major one, is one that Philo has meticulously circumscribed. It amounts to an admission that men are unable to refrain from ascribing some degree of teleology to the cause or causes of nature, but it prevents any rational speculation about the specific character of that teleology. Such further speculation will be the handiwork of the 'haughty dogmatist' who is 'persuaded that he can erect a complete system of theology by the mere help of philosophy'. Sceptical arguments may not produce total suspension of judgement, but they can inhibit us from following in his footsteps. Philo does not stop here, however; he goes on to say that, faced with the 'obscurity' of natural theology, a 'well-disposed mind' will 'fly to revealed truth with the greatest avidity' in order to rescue itself from its ignorance. Sceptical humility about the powers of reason will lead such a mind to embrace the claims of revelation.

One has to be very gullible indeed to suppose that Hume himself has such a well-disposed mind. Philo's own recent comments about the evils of popular religion, and Hume's onslaughts upon it in the *Natural History of Religion*, block any such line of interpretation. But in spite of this it seems that Hume is concluding that those apologists who have seen scepticism as the ally of religion have shown a clearer understanding of who their natural allies are than those who have followed Locke and Cleanthes in urging the reasonableness of Christianity. For to such dogmatists revelation is, in Philo's phrase, an 'adventitious instructor', which can in the long run be dispensed with. Although scepticism cannot *establish* the claims of revelation, it can make it crystal clear (to the well-disposed mind) that there is no philosophical substitute for what it offers. So Philo's last remark has, as its secondary meaning, the conclusion that Lockean theologians are looking for support in the wrong place.

In summary, I suggest that the calm and reflective Philo of Part XII concedes that his own negative arguments have not been enough to prevent our natural acceptance of some principle of design in nature, but he does consider them enough to prevent this acceptance from serving as the basis for practical inferences or moral speculations. A sceptic who recognizes the inevitability of a 'plain philosophical assent' to this principle can reach a practical accommodation with the humane secularizing theologians who urge it upon him. He also sees that those who are prone to those pathological forces that he sees at work in popular religion can readily point to the sceptic's own arguments as a reason for succumbing to them, even though he does not believe that we are all in this psychological predicament.

## VIII

How far does Philo's final position represent a modification of Hume's scepticism as we encounter it in his earlier writings? I think that in one important respect it involves a return from the position of the *Enquiry* to that of the *Treatise*. In the *Enquiry* Hume advises us to keep off theology and stay with the affairs of common life. Philo's arguments in Parts II to XI must no doubt be read as demonstrating the wisdom of that advice and as showing us the chronic inconclusiveness of theological speculation. But Philo's final position involves the concession that in spite of this we cannot be prevented from committing ourselves to the first principle that natural theologians, with their bad arguments, are labouring to establish. All that mitigated scepticism can do is render it practically and psychologically harmless. So we cannot wholly keep away from natural theology; we should, instead, indulge it to the extent of giving its first principle a 'plain, philosophical assent'. Indeed, it would seem that Hume is even suggesting once more that if we attempt to remain in a state of intellectual suspense with regard to it, as a 'careless' (or Pyrrhonian) sceptic would have us do, we open our minds to the very anxieties for which the dubious blandishments of revelation might seem to be the only cure. So the best solution is to say yes and then trust that the resources of common life (which the secularized theologian values as much as we do) can serve to protect us against indecision and false religion.

But although Philo's position does involve this degree of mitigation of mitigated scepticism, it does not involve its abandonment. There seems no reason to question that Philo does consider his arguments to block the way to 'dogmatism', that is, to philosophical speculation that proceeds beyond the minimal natural theology he regards as unavoidable. Indeed, while he has extended the scope of natural belief beyond the affairs of common life, he has done nothing to encourage us to philosophize one inch past the point where natural belief peters out. That remains 'haughty' dogmatism; and the prudential veto of the *Enquiry* has been not removed but, in Hume's view, strengthened, by the acceptance of the proposition into which 'the whole of natural theology' resolve itself. This would seem to be Hume's final answer to Butler, with whom Mossner has plausibly identified Cleanthes.[14] Butler assumes that his readers will accept that the world is created by an intelligence, and he argues in the *Analogy of Religion* that anyone who accepts this ought to accept as probable that this intelligence is moral, that it provides for our future survival, and that it guides the universe providentially as Christianity teaches us. Philo, on the contrary, ends the *Dialogues* by conceding the premise of Butler's argument and denying all its conclusions: to accept the being of God is to go nowhere in theology. For that very reason the inability of sceptical argument to shake us free from this acceptance need not alarm a man of letters in the least.

## IX

If this is indeed Hume's final position, what are we to make of it? I will begin by assuming for the sake of argument that Hume is right when he says that negative arguments like Philo's cannot eliminate our acceptance of intelligent design. If this is true, it leaves two major difficulties. First, there is an obvious problem of consistency. Mitigated scepticism does not prohibit us from engaging in the reflections necessary to common life merely because these reflections are based on beliefs that cannot be philosophically justified. It is of the essence

[14] Mossner 1936.

of mitigated scepticism that one accepts what one must and proceeds from there. If one now extends the list of unavoidable beliefs to include the belief in intelligent design, parity of reasoning ought surely to permit us to explore the whole of natural theology. The second, and more important, difficulty seems to me to be this. Hume has given no reason to think that, consistency aside, we *can* stop in our tracks where he recommends that we stop. If we cannot not think there is intelligent design, it might be hard for any of us, and impossible for some of us, not to wonder what sort of mind lies behind it. There might be some plausibility in recommending self-denial if we could refrain from postulating design in the first place; but the case is immeasurably weaker if one concedes that we cannot do even this. So Philo's concession, even if logically consistent with mitigated scepticism, is psychologically at odds with it.

But these criticisms assume that Hume needs to make the concession in the first place. I now wish to question this. Earlier I argued that Hume is wrong to suggest that the Pyrrhonist's doubts about the beliefs of common life cannot be sustained, and wrong to think that the Pyrrhonist's practical accommodations cannot be accompanied by an inner suspense of judgement. I would now like to apply this to the one proposition of natural theology. Hume seems to think that we cannot suspend judgement about that proposition, but that, to our good fortune, we can see it is harmless and reach a practical consensus with the unsuspecting theologian. But its harmlessness would depend on our being able to restrain our tendency to dogmatize beyond it; and why do we *have* to accept it at all? The sort of practical consensus that Hume desires is surely more likely if we are able to suspend judgement inwardly but accommodate ourselves outwardly, in the manner of Sextus. Hume is once again underestimating the capacity of the sceptic to sustain his own doubts in the face of the psychological pressures to believe. He is underestimating the psychological power of his own critical arguments. No doubt this is due in part to his dislike of the dogmatism of the atheists of his day, and also to his own sense of isolation in the face of the nearly universal orthodoxy that surrounded him. But in our day, when agnosticism is commonplace and practical agreement between believers and unbelievers about the affairs of common life very frequent, the matter looks different. Indeed, suspense of judgement about theological questions is no longer confined to men of letters. And Hume, in spite of his self-doubts, has had as much to do with this as any other single person.

No doubt some will say that these criticisms are criticisms of a position Hume does not hold, that he is as much an agnostic as those of our contemporaries who learn their atheology from him. I can only submit that this reading, tempting though it is, cannot supply an adequate account of the text. I think the text has to be read in the light of Hume's attempt to take the measure of the sceptical tradition, in particular its insistence on the inability of reason to establish truth and its recommendation to universal doubt. His acceptance of the one and his denial of the other lead him into difficulties that follow him to the very end of his career.

# 10

## Natural Belief and Religious Belief in Hume's Philosophy

THE most widely held view of Hume, in his own day and since, has been that he is a deliberate secularizer: that he seeks to persuade us that there are no good reasons to hold religious beliefs. With minor reservations that will become obvious, I think this is true. Probably the next most widely held view of Hume is that he is, at least in one key respect, a sceptic: namely that he considers our most obviously indispensable beliefs, such as that in the continued and independent existence of objects of perception, to be held by us not because we have good reasons for them, but because of the power of the 'sensitive' part of our natures. This view of him is also, I think, clearly true. There is an obvious tension, however, between these two opinions. One would expect someone who held that key human beliefs were not due to reasons, to be less persistently determined than Hume is to show the *absence* of such reasons in the case of religious beliefs, since such a determination suggests this absence is peculiar to them. Hume is quite aware of this tension, and is still engaged in dealing with it at the very end of his career, in the enigmatic closing passages of the *Dialogues Concerning Natural Religion*.

These passages present notorious problems. In terms of the tension just referred to, they can be described as follows. The most plausible way of reconciling what Hume says about religious and natural beliefs is by noticing that he thinks their causes are quite different. The causes of religious beliefs are pathological and, with luck, education and reflection can overcome them; so religious belief is not inescapable in the way natural belief is. This interpretation is strongly supported by the *Natural History of Religion*. It is also supported indirectly by the *Dialogues*, up to the end of Part XI, since they are intended to show that if the natural beliefs are true, that does not give any better rational support to theism than to its many alternatives. But Part XII confuses all this. For in it Hume seems to embrace a form of theism (or deism) without supplying any reasons for it beyond those which he has been busily undermining hitherto. This suggests he thinks there may be some non-intellectual basis for theism in our natures that we cannot avoid after all. Amid the theories that have been offered to explain Part XII, I have hitherto inclined to the view that Hume does finally accept some form of theism as natural, and seeks to modify the impact of this on his system by distinguishing it sharply from popular, or pathological (in the code-language of the text, 'false') religion.[1]

This, I now fear, needs emendation, and this paper extends the debate. The excuse is the intrinsic importance of these details for understanding the thrust of Hume's system, and for the wider issue of the status of the beliefs Hume discusses. I shall try to do two things: to come as close as possible to an accurate account of the position Hume gives to Philo in Part XII, and to spell out more carefully than before what Hume tells (or shows) us there about the appropriate attitude towards religious questions for the 'man of letters'.

I want to suggest that light can be thrown on the second matter if we take proper account of the fact that Philo's speeches contain a parody of an apologetic position which had, in various versions, a number of important adherents in the hundred years before the *Dialogues* was written. This is a form of fideism, or theologically faith-centred apologetic, that is supported by attacks on reason derived from the Sceptical tradition in its Pyrrhonian or Academic forms. For convenience I shall call this Sceptical Fideism. The Sceptical Fideist seeks to commend faith to us by emphasising the impotence of reason, both in general, and in specifically theological matters.

The term 'Fideism' is often used alone here. I think, however, that it is important to distinguish those who reject attempts to offer rational credentials for faith, or who reject philosophical defences of it, because they are influenced by Sceptical doubts about the powers of human reason, from those who reject them on overtly theological grounds, such as the claim that even if human reason were inherently competent to propound truths about God, human thought-processes unaided by grace are too corrupted for us to accept them. I therefore use 'Fideism' as a generic form embracing both

---

[1] See Chapter 9.

groups. I would, however, class as Sceptical Fideists any thinkers who reject philosophical apologetic for reasons which can be found in the Sceptical repertoire but which they do not recognise to have this historical origin.

Philo explicitly endorses Sceptical Fideism in his last speech:

> To be a philosophical sceptic is, in a man of letters, the first and most essential step towards being a sound, believing Christian . . .

What are we to make of this? I do not think this is a question that can be answered very briefly, even if one agrees with Kemp Smith and others (as I would) that Philo is to be taken as speaking for Hume throughout the *Dialogues*. Three matters, at least, have to be weighed before this remarkable sentence can be interpreted plausibly. First, we have to assess the special problems of interpretation that arise for the reader of Part XII, where these fideistic sentiments surface. Second, we have to take account of relevant views on religion which Hume expresses in other places, particularly the *Natural History of Religion*, and (more hazardously) of his relationship to the Sceptical tradition elsewhere in his philosophical system. Third, we need to look at some of the variations in the Sceptical Fideist tradition itself.

I

I shall assume that Philo represents Hume throughout the *Dialogues*, though not, of course, that this proves his own opinions to be found *only* in Philo's speeches, or that the dialogue form is not used to convey reservations or qualifications about what Philo says. I shall also assume that there is a real problem of interpretation in Part XII: that there is a definite change in the position Philo adopts there from the stance he has assumed earlier. This change, which is not offered by him *as* a change of mind, consists in the apparent acceptance of the major part of the conclusion for which Cleanthes has been arguing all along: namely that the orderliness of nature bespeaks design by intelligence. This change remains when all allowance is made for ironies in expression, qualifications of doctrine, and slyness of choice of examples. I do not think that Kemp Smith's labours establish that Philo's acceptance here is not genuine; they show rather that what Philo accepts has no religious import and justifies no speculative inferences. In particular, although Philo admits that the orderliness and adjustment of means to ends throughout nature force us to ascribe them to intelligence, he does not agree that this justifies our embracing the dogmas and ceremonies of popular religion, or that it warrants our ascribing moral attributes to the mind, or minds, that may possess this intelligence. So the 'philosophical and rational' religion that Philo, with an exasperating air of obviousness, professes throughout this Part, is a wholly unreligious and untheological kind of religion. Some of the irony and indirectness of the writing, I have suggested, is due to Hume's wish to consolidate this fact in the reader's mind as unshockingly as possible. In the text itself, it represents Philo's attempt to get it past the social and religious defences of Cleanthes. But unreligious or not, Philo does accept the primary claim that Cleanthes has been urging upon him.

This last is very close to the reading of Part XII that is offered by J. C. A. Gaskin.[2] There is, however, one major point of difference that separates the interpretation I have offered previously from the one which he offers. In attempting to make Philo's anaemic deism cohere better than it otherwise seems to do with Hume's philosophical system, I have classified it as one of the natural beliefs,[3] that is, as one of those convictions that Hume thinks we have as a result of psychological causes that we cannot eradicate. Viewed this way, Philo's acceptance of design is one more example of Hume's recognition that although sceptical attacks on these beliefs expose the absence of rational grounds for them, they cannot dislodge them. Gaskin maintains that the belief Philo admits to is *not* in this category, but is what he calls a reasonable belief, that is, one which 'occurs or fails to occur or is modified as the involuntary accompaniment of an honest assessment of the evidence' (Gaskin 1978: 131). After careful reflection, I now feel that neither position can stand unamended.

Gaskin's case against classifying Philo's theism as a natural belief is a weighty one. He has two main arguments. The first, supported by what Hume says in the *Natural History of Religion*, is that belief in a deity does not qualify for this status because it is not *universal*. The second, supported by the trouble Hume takes in Part XII to

---

[2] Gaskin 1978, chs. 8 and 10. This essay responded originally to Professor Gaskin's first edition; in his second edition he comments on my arguments here; see Gaskin 1988, ch. 7.

[3] Needless to say, I was not the first to do so. See R. J. Butler 1960.

emphasize the trivial and ancillary role of 'true religion', is that Hume manifestly does not think that belief in a deity is *requisite* for participation in the affairs of life. The positive evidence in favour of this is to be found in the way Philo expresses his assent, in particular the way he describes what he is assenting *to*. He says not just that he is assenting to the existence of a deity, but that he is doing so because of the evidences of design; and while he piles on the qualifications about the degree of analogy that there might be between divine and human intelligence, he says explicitly that the evidences of design require us to agree there is *some* degree of analogy. In other words, he describes himself as assenting *to an argument*. He also says that the assent he gives, and recommends, is a 'plain, philosophical assent', and consists in agreeing 'that the arguments on which is it established exceed the objections which lie against it', (*D* XII. 227). This is certainly the language of judicious philosophical evaluation.

But there is still a major difficulty, and it is the problem with which we began. What Philo so blandly agrees to in Part XII is still a crucial part of what Cleanthes urged on him in Part II, and Philo presents it in a form which repeats the structure of that original presentation. There are indeed many hints of insincerity. (One need only mention the rotting of the turnip, or the absurd lingering detail of the physiological evidences from Galen.) But the hard fact remains that what Philo tells Cleanthes he has never seriously questioned is the very argument he has previously been urging to be a bad one; and the reasons he has offered for this negative judgement are reasons which, in common with most readers I know, I find it hard to think Hume did not himself accept—and which are, in any case, nowhere refuted by Cleanthes or taken back by Philo. If Hume judged the belief in design to be reasonable, it would be strange for him to leave it stripped of all credentials in this way.

Before returning to this interpretative stalemate, let us look at some alternatives and an objection. (a) One alternative is, of course, that of Kemp Smith: that the ironies and ambiguities of Part XII are signals from Hume that he, or Philo, does not mean it when he says 'Yes'. The ambiguities need to be taken with the utmost seriousness, and are only *partly* accounted for by our taking them to show that Philo's deism is religiously lifeless. But we should recall that the dialogue form, especially with the inclusion of Pamphilus and Hermippus, would allow Hume many devices for conveying his own rejection of Cleanthes' position without having Philo put on an appearance of accepting it. If Kemp Smith's reading is the right one, then Part XII becomes a needlessly obfuscatory exercise on Hume's part, and a place where his artfulness has got the better of him. (b) Another alternative is that of Nelson Pike.[4] He argues that we can explain the appearance of change in Philo's position by recognizing that the argument he agrees to in Part XII is not the same argument that he has been attacking hitherto: that he now assents to an *immediate* inference from orderly phenomena to divine intelligence, not to Cleanthes' earlier argument, in which the inference is mediated by an analogy with human intelligence. Pike supports this suggestion by a reference to Cleanthes' example of the voice from the clouds in Part III. The distinction between the immediate and the mediated design argument, and the interlude in Part III, both deserve special study; but I cannot find the text of Part XII lends itself easily to this reading. If we read Philo's speeches (especially paragraphs 6 and 8 of Part XII) we find that the reasoning to which he says he is assenting is the analogical reasoning he has attacked all the way through. It is undoubtedly true that the qualifications with which Philo hedges the analogy indicate that Hume felt the Design Argument's power did not come from the reasons Cleanthes offers for it; that, indeed, is our puzzle, since he makes Philo assent to it nevertheless. But that does not show he, or Philo, thinks that the immediate argument is a better argument. Of this there is no sign.

(c) One natural objection to the claim that Philo's earlier criticisms of the Design Argument are never answered is to point to a passage at the end of Part X. Here Philo draws an important contrast between what he has just said about the alleged moral attributes of God and his earlier attacks on God's natural (or intellectual) attributes. He confesses that although his attacks on the moral attributes amount to a 'triumph', those on the natural have been 'mere cavils and sophisms', for which he has needed all his 'sceptical and metaphysical subtlety' (*D* x. 201–2). This is the most explicit advance warning of Philo's final position. But it also contains no answer whatever to these alleged cavils and sophisms—for the simple reason, in my view, that Hume thinks they are unanswerable. What it signals is Hume's acceptance (surely reluctant?), that even though they are unanswerable, they are like the sceptics' attacks on our natural beliefs in being impotent—whereas the evidence of evil

---

[4] See his edition of the *Dialogues*, 1970, 204–38.

in the world demonstrably forces the theist to change his ground on the moral attributes of God. In this case of divine intelligence, the theist has merely to refer us once again to the intricacies of nature, and it is as though we had never heard how inadequate a reason they give us to infer it.

Where does this leave us? I suggest that the minimal deism of Part XII is accepted by Philo as the inescapable conclusion of an argument which he has shown, and knows he has shown, to be a complete philosophical failure—except in the one respect that when we encounter it we cannot help assenting to its conclusion! In this respect minimal deism is like the natural beliefs: we can be momentarily disturbed by sceptical objections, but not seriously shaken from holding it. But it is *un*like the natural beliefs in that, as far as the *Dialogues* go at least, it is not a belief that is *arrived* at without reasoning. It is also unlike them in that those who do not encounter such reasoning (which includes most people in most cultures, according to the *Natural History*) do not believe in minimal deism. These special features of its origin make it possible for the man of letters to accept it but compartmentalize it in a way not possible for us with the natural beliefs.

To return to Gaskin's interpretation of Philo's deism as a reasonable belief: the considerations raised here require this to be modified considerably; but if his definition of a 'reasonable belief' is taken strictly, Philo's deism will indeed still fit. For if we hold some belief because of *reasoning*, even though that reasoning is bad (and ought not, by philosophical standards, to persuade us), this would seem to conform to the wording of the definition. If this is enough to make it a reasonable belief, Philo's deism presumably is one: it has been brought about by reasoning, but it is not dislodged when the reasoning that has brought it about is shown to be bad. This is a special use of the word 'reasonable'. While it is normally acceptable to call a belief reasonable if the person who holds it does so for reasons which are bad, but which he erroneously thinks are good, what we need here is to stretch the concept to cover a case where the person himself cannot abandon the belief even though he recognises the inadequacy of the original reasons.

If the above is correct, and Philo's deism does not fit easily either into the category of natural belief, or into that of reasonable belief, it is an anomaly in Hume's system. Since, in my view, the tension between Hume the naturalist and Hume the secularizer is inevitable, it is not surprising there should be an anomaly here. In the rest of the paper I explore some of the ways in which he tries to ease the tension, and I thus try to make the reversal of Philo's stand more intelligible.

II

I begin with some brief comments, first, on relevant features of Hume's other writings, beginning with the *Natural History of Religion*, and continuing with some of his judgements on scepticism in the *Treatise* and the first *Enquiry*.

In the Introduction to the *Natural History* Hume distinguishes carefully between the 'foundation in reason' which religion may have, and its 'origin in human nature' (*NHR*. 21). As is typical of his procedure, he pays uncritical lip-service to the alleged fact that 'the whole frame of nature bespeaks an intelligent author'. That this is only lip-service we can see from what he says about the quality of this foundation when he examines it in the *Dialogues*; but the purpose of the *Natural History* is only to examine the origins of religion in human nature. It is in this context that he tells us that 'perhaps' religion is not universal; so that the forces he is to examine are not forces which always prevail in us in the manner of those which produce our natural beliefs, and some lucky people may escape them or be weaned from them by what he calls 'an extraordinary concurrence of circumstances'. It is not to be doubted that Hume includes himself among this favoured minority. It is not quite clear, however, what this shows about the extent of the minimal deism Philo espouses (which *is*, of course, the recognition that the whole frame of nature bespeaks an intelligent author). If one wishes to class it as a natural belief, one has to discount altogether the reference to its foundation in reason, since that is not how natural beliefs arise, but retain the sharp distinction between it and all forms of actual religion, since the latter are not universal. Two things make it hard to decide whether this is possible: on the one hand, what Hume tells us is probably not universal is 'the belief of invisible, intelligent power'—a phrase broad enough to include the amorphous deity of Philo; on the other, in the *Natural History* he insists that what the whole frame of nature bespeaks must obviously be a *single* intelligent author, and the unity of the deity is one of the natural characteristics about which

Philo is careful to remain uncommitted. On balance, however, I incline to think that in the *Natural History* Hume not only makes it impossible, deliberately, to classify popular religious belief as natural, but also makes it very implausible, *per accidens*, so to classify the vague commitment to design with which the *Dialogues* leaves us. (One speculative possibility that is not excluded is that Hume considers that what Philo assents to in Part XII is a remnant of religion which lingers on in those whose own personalities, or cultural environment, have been made religious by the pathological forces he describes in the *Natural History*; a remnant which subsequent exposure to philosophical reflection cannot altogether eliminate.)

The primary force to which Hume traces the origin of religion is fear in the face of unexplained phenomena. Originally this generates polytheism. It is important that Hume's account of the transition from polytheism to monotheism includes no suggestion that any sort of argument, or any recourse to philosophical principles, is involved. It is rather the attempt by a group of worshippers to win the favour of some deity by exaggerating his powers and proclaiming his supremacy. In other words, the forces that cause men to engage in worship create a practice that has a momentum of its own, which leads naturally to monotheism. This is attended with evils from which polytheism is free—hypocrisy, self-deception, and the lauding of the 'monkish virtues'. It is noteworthy that the arguments about the difference between 'true' and 'false' religion which take up more than half of Part XII of the *Dialogues* are strongly reminiscent of the *Natural History*, and make it clear that the severe limitations Philo places on his deism would prevent anyone accepting it from straying, even minutely, toward any of these evils; whereas Cleanthes does not see the practices of actual religion in his own time as reflecting them in the way that Philo does.

The precise nature of Hume's relationship to Scepticism is far too vast a theme to explore here, though I think Professor Popkin's account of it needs, at most, minor emendation and elaboration.[5] For present purposes I will confine myself to a few generalizations that bear particularly on the interpretation of Part XII. First, it is uncontroversial that Hume is deeply concerned to take the measure of the Sceptical tradition, and to define his stance towards it carefully, however we think he does in fact define it. Second, he appears

---

[5] See Popkin 1951 and Chapter 9.

to have a rather unsubtle interpretation of the explicitly Pyrrhonian form of Scepticism as we find it handed down to us by Sextus Empiricus, treating it as a more extreme, omnivorous version of the doubting and questioning found in the Academic Scepticism for which he expresses sympathy. Third, his reason for rejecting Pyrrhonism as he describes it is that the beliefs Pyrrhonian arguments undermine are not due to reasoning and cannot be dislodged by it, so that even if the Pyrrhonian were able successfully to use reason to undermine itself, this would not affect the natural beliefs we have, or interfere with the necessary commitments of common life. Fourth, when Pyrrhonian arguments do succeed in getting a foothold in the minds of the philosophically-inclined, which they can do for short periods, the result during those periods is not the relaxation and unperturbedness which the classical Sceptics said would follow, but bewilderment and anxiety. Finally, the adherent of mitigated, or Academic, Scepticism will avoid both these perturbations and those consequent on dogmatism and religion by confining himself to the 'reflections of common life, methodized and corrected', (*EU* xii. 162).

However much of a Sceptic one judges Hume to be, Philo is explicitly said to be one. Pamphilus refers to his scepticism as 'careless'. The views that Philo expresses in Part I are a repetition of the statement of mitigated scepticism offered in Section XII of the first *Enquiry*; and of course there is the recommendation of 'philosophical' scepticism to Cleanthes at the close of Part XII. However we choose to interpret the transition from the careless Philo of Parts I to XI to the intimate Philo of Part XII, it is beyond question that the criticisms of the Design Argument that he presents in Parts II to XI are manifestations of mitigated, not only of Pyrrhonian, scepticism. In particular, they do not depend in the least upon sceptical questionings of secular natural beliefs. Much of the byplay in Part I about the practical impotence of scepticism is designed to emphasize this. Yet Philo's deism is a belief which survives all these criticisms. So even if one does not wish to attribute any vestige of Pyrrhonism to Hume, and does not read him as following that tradition in denying the rationality of the natural beliefs, one has still to recognize that in the particular case now before us, Philo retains his minimal belief in God in the face of the destruction of the rational grounds offered for it—even if he acquired the belief by entertaining them.

My own reading of Hume is that he considers the Sceptical tradition to be successful in exposing the groundlessness of our natural beliefs but to fail in suggesting we can suspend them. But even if this is not what he thinks about our natural beliefs, it *is* what he seems to tell us about the minimal deism of Part XII of the *Dialogues*.

## III

At the close of Part I, Philo draws the company's attention to the fact that religious apologists have recently begun to defend theism through dogmatic or metaphysical principles, in contrast to earlier apologists who saw such principles as the source of intellectual arrogance and religious doubt. The earlier apologists, he says, thought in a context where 'education' influenced men's minds. I take 'education' here to mean habituation and tradition, as Philo contrasts it immediately with 'a more open commerce of the world'. In these remarks, Philo is contesting Cleanthes' previous equation of Scepticism and atheism, and pointing forward to his final recommendation of Scepticism as a necessary propaedeutic to sound, believing Christianity. He is also echoing the Academic protagonist, Cotta, in Cicero's *De Natura Deorum*. Cotta attacks the Stoic arguments for theism as they come from Balbus; but does so not as an atheist but as a practitioner (indeed a functionary) of traditional religion. Religion, to Cotta, is not only a matter of tradition but should remain that way.[6] This is a clear classical version of what I have called Sceptical Fideism. It is interesting to compare it with the way Sextus Empiricus expresses the Pyrrhonian stance toward religion in the *Outlines of Pyrrhonism*:

Although, following the ordinary view, we affirm undogmatically that Gods exist and reverence Gods and ascribe to them foreknowledge, yet as against the rashness of the Dogmatists we argue as follows . . .[7]

He then summarizes a number of Sceptical rebuttals to Stoic natural theology. In the much fuller theological discussions in *Against the Physicists*, Sextus ends with suspension of judgement;[8] but this of course does not preclude the ritual piety he expresses in the *Outlines*. Any difference one finds between Academic and Pyrrhonian Scepticism is at its minimum here. Both issue in undogmatic or beliefless

---

[6] Cicero, *De Natura Deorum* III. 9; page 196 of the McGregor translation 1972.
[7] Sextus Empiricus 1933 edn., vol. 1, 327.
[8] Sextus Empiricus 1933 edn., vol. 3, 97.

conformity, unsupported and unexamined participation. In spite of its absence of justification this is not the same as the simple piety of the multitude who are untouched by philosophy. For them the forms of religious life have a meaning, and are a mode of involvement with non-evident realities, in a way which makes them constantly prone to anxieties and fears. To the Sceptic, the meaning has been evaporated by the process of argument for and against the dogmas that are supposed to support it, and he is able to return to the traditional rites and practices in a detached and unanxious manner, flowing with the local stream but with his head above it. This is the classical version of Sceptical Fideism.

As Popkin has made clear,[9] Sceptical Fideism was an important force in early modern philosophy, being used particularly as a mode of defence of Catholicism against Protestantism, and of Christianity against atheism. This is, on the surface, strange: how can a tradition teaching detachment serve as a bulwark for one that teaches commitment? Part of the answer is to be found in the fact that modern Sceptical Fideism has taken two forms. Its first form is much closer to the stance of Cotta and Sextus: it represents Christian faith as a mode of the uninvolved participation that they espoused for the Sceptic. This might seem a grotesquely implausible understanding of what faith is, but it is intelligible that it should have appealed to apologists who wanted to defend a conservative conformism, or deprecated dogmatic divisions. We can accordingly find it in Erasmus, who was excoriated by Luther for it, and it is one of the positions taken up by Montaigne in the *Apology for Raimond Sebond*. I will call it *Conformist* Sceptical Fideism. In the second form, it is recognized that Sceptical detachment and Christian faith are indeed the polar opposites they seem, but Scepticism is seen as a philosophical tradition which has served the cause of faith by exposing the inability of reason to provide a source of commitment, and has thereby paved the way for grace to supply it instead. The appropriate outcome of an immersion in Sceptical argument is not beliefless observance, but *belief*—belief, nevertheless, without the pretence of philosophical credentials. I will call this *Evangelical* Sceptical Fideism. It is not a form of Scepticism, but requires the absorption of Sceptical despair about human reason. It is to be found in Pascal, and later in Kierkegaard—and, with blissful inconsistency, in Montaigne also.

[9] Popkin 1979.

These two forms of Sceptical Fideism are obviously incompatible, even though individuals may oscillate between them. They share the common premise that the Sceptic has exposed the claims of the Dogmatist, who is not the defender of faith as he thinks, but its competitor. It is worth noting that if we substitute nature for grace, what the Evangelical Fideist says about religious belief is exactly what Hume says about our secular natural beliefs: a point which would certainly not have escaped his notice.

In the remainder of the paper I want to bring out some of the ways in which Hume, in Part XII, makes ingenious use of the Sceptical Fideist tradition to reconcile his naturalism and his secularism. I shall argue that Philo's position is very close to that of Cotta and Sextus, familiar to his readers through the Conformist Fideists, and that he tries to make it palatable to Cleanthes by echoing the words, though not the sentiments, of the Evangelical Fideists.


## IV


I begin by quoting Sextus again:

Although, following the ordinary view, we affirm undogmatically that Gods exist and reverence Gods and ascribe to them foreknowledge, yet as against the rashness of the Dogmatists we argue as follows . . .

Apart from the foreknowledge, isn't this just what Philo says?

Not altogether, of course; for Sextus does not say that he affirms the existence of the Gods undogmatically because of a Dogmatist's argument. What Philo does do is repeat Sextus's position as closely as his own system allows, and this is far closer than one might suppose.

Whatever we think about Hume's estimate of Pyrrhonian attacks on common-sense beliefs, it is uncontroversial that he thinks exposure to them chastens our confidence in philosophical constructions. It is also uncontroversial that he thinks they have their own dangers: that if unchecked they generate anxiety on their own account. What checks them is our nature's built-in tendency to believe. Unlike Sextus, Hume does not see belief as a source of anxiety and distress, unless it is culturally associated with dogmas or superstitions. When these are kept at bay, as they can be by *mitigated* scepticism, the commitments our nature is programmed to make function beneficently, and wean us away from the stresses that beset the philosopher in his study or the monk in his cell. So although Hume shares Sextus's detachment from dogma, he does not aspire to a generalized Sceptical aloofness, which he rejects as impractical and dangerous.

So Philo has to strike a balance. He must reject theological constructions, but not reject benign participation in common affairs. But how can he strike this balance when he concedes the residual deism that he admits to in Part XII? Does this not open the door both to constructive theology and the demands of popular faith? It was the burden of Butler's natural theology that it does just this—Butler starts where Philo ends. But it is the burden of the *Dialogues* that even if we accept deism it does not lead to these things. Philo shows us this in two ways.

(1) The first way is by insisting that *this* belief, even if ineradicable, need have no more effects on personality or conduct than our other ineradicable beliefs would have without it: that in the single case of this belief, the man of letters can live, even though he has it, in the way Sextus said the Sceptic lives—in a stance of beliefless, conformist affirmation. (2) The second way is by showing (not saying) that although they may not realize it, this is in fact the way in which those who follow Cleanthes in espousing an empirical theology conduct themselves already: a fact which makes Philo's conformism even easier. It is in the service of this second way that Hume makes use of the forms of Evangelical Sceptical Fideism.

(1) It would be too much to expect the author of the *Natural History* to recommend conformity to the practices of *popular* religion, especially since by Hume's day these were practices of popular *monotheistic* religion, where the limitations of polytheistic worship no longer operate. Such conformity would open one too readily to the fears and anxieties against which the man of letters' reflections have only begun to armour him. So the man of letters has only found himself committed to a minimal deism. This is a theology without any content; it avoids the pitfalls of popular religion, obviously; but what is there left, then, for the man of letters to conform to?

What is left, of course, is what Cleanthes espouses already: 'true religion'. Philo and Cleanthes agree on what it is, and only disagree over how far actual religion differs from it. Cleanthes describes it thus:

The proper office of religion is to regulate the heart of men, humanise their conduct, infuse the spirit of temperance, order, and obedience; and, as its operation is silent and only enforces the motives of morality and justice, it is in danger of being overlooked and confounded with these other motives. *When it distinguishes itself, and acts as a separate principle over men, it has departed from its proper sphere and has become only a cover to faction and ambition. (D* XII. 146–7; my italics)

True religion is, in other words, featureless; its role is to act as a vague and undefined support to virtues which owe their origin and value to quite distinct sources. One supposes that actual examples of it are the non-sectarian prayer exercises that precede civic or parliamentary gatherings nowadays in some otherwise quite secular societies. Hume is quite prescient enough to see that a religious belief that offers, as its credentials, supposedly scientific arguments that he is able to discredit, will in the course of time become nothing more than a set of such wholly domesticated and formal rituals. The most exacting Sceptic can conform to this sort of behaviour with a clear conscience— indeed it is only the tiresome and abrasive unbeliever who disturbs social peace by registering objections. Philo has no problem with it.

(2) But what about Cleanthes himself? Part XII shows that he is reluctant, indeed unable, to concede that if this is what true religion is, all real religion is false. Whenever he seems to find value in it, Philo slaps him down: but he keeps on suggesting that if one finds *too* much fault with false religion, one will miss out on the true kind. This shows that it will take time for him to realize how empty secular liberal theology really is. Indeed, he never may, and it may be in the interests of social harmony for all concerned if he never does. What is important is that he be fully reconciled somehow to the pure deism to which his natural theology has been reduced, and to the dogmatic reticence it implies. That way he can always be headed off whenever he tries to draw religiously real conclusions from it. To achieve this result Philo has to commend it to Cleanthes in some way which will reinforce the humility of true religion while concealing its unreligiousness. The way is ready to hand in the thought-forms of the Evangelical Sceptical Fideist, who, persuaded of the helplessness of reason, turns to groundless faith and to revelation for help. So Philo pretends to be such a person. He tells Cleanthes that the man of letters, persuaded of reason's limits and of the simple proposition of 'the whole of natural theology', will refrain from trying to expand upon it philosophically as the haughty dogmatist does, for that is to substitute argument for revelation. Instead he will 'fly to revealed truth with the greatest avidity'.

As has been noted before, this recommendation is expressed in a way that serves to deceive only Cleanthes. It is expressed as a wish that 'Heaven would be pleased to dissipate, at least alleviate, this profound ignorance by affording some more particular revelation to mankind' (*D* XII. 227). In other words, although the man of letters will hope for special revelation, none is on hand up to now.


## V


I will commence my conclusion with a summary of my suggestions concerning Philo's position in Part XII. The minimal theism he assents to resembles our secular natural beliefs in being beyond the power of reason to dislodge, even though reason has shown it to have no better grounds than its alternatives. Unlike them, however, it is not requisite for daily life, and would even be a hindrance if it were used as a basis for involvement in popular religion. Since it has no real doctrinal content, however, there is no ground for such a link-age. In fact its more natural expression is in 'true' religion, which amounts at most to a formal set of Establishment rituals. These are, unfortunately, the historical descendants of the practices of real (i.e. 'false') religion. Because of this, the proponents of philosophical theism, such as Cleanthes, see themselves as defenders of real reli-gion, even though their methods, and above all their social and moral practice, show this not to be so. The persuasive power of the core of their theism shows the most prudent course to be the adoption of the polite accommodation that is manifested by the smoother Philo of Part XII. This will keep philosophical theists in the path of innocuous observance and creeping secularity. It will do this through co-operation with their practice, and a philosophical vigilance which steers them away from doctrinal commitment or real religious feeling.

Essentially this describes Philo's reversal in a manner which I hope is consistent with the text, but fits Hume's general view of the cor-rectness and impotence of sceptical argument and reflects his rejec-tion of the abrasive unbelief that would be the natural result of Philo's earlier attitudes.

But I must now confess that I still feel uneasy, since no account that fits the text seems able to do more than provide a set of pal-liatives for readers who are unprepared for Philo to change in the

way that he does. If I am not alone in my uneasiness, I may not be
alone in the speculation with which I will end.

Perhaps we are all wrong in being as ready to identify Philo with
Hume as we have been since Kemp Smith. Perhaps we are wrong,
in consequence, to suppose that *either* Philo does not mean any of
what he says in Part XII, *or* Hume feels himself stuck with a residual theism for which his system has no spiritual space. Perhaps Philo's
reversal is genuine, but is not Hume's own position any longer.

In making this suggestion I am to some extent in the company of
James Noxon.[10] He, however, considers that we should distinguish
Hume from Philo throughout the *Dialogues*, whereas I do not feel
able to separate them before Part XII. Hume's own intellectual excite-
ment breaks through too frequently in Philo's speeches before his
reversal for such a separation to be plausible. On the other hand, if
I now suggest that we can help explain his reversal by dissociating
Hume from Philo's later words, the apparent change *in Philo* must
still make sense on its own account. I think it can do so.

For what the reversal reflects is something that Kant, as well as
Hume, emphasized: that the Design Argument has an appeal, a seeming obviousness, that ought not, if there were philosophical justice,
to survive critical examination, yet does—through Thomas Paine and
William Paley and on to infinity. So many readers say 'No' with Philo
*against* Cleanthes in Parts II to XI, and then say 'Yes' with Philo
*to* Cleanthes in Part XII. Or at least, they would have in Hume's
day, and would have gone on doing so for a long time afterwards.
It is not so clear that they still do so, for an obvious reason: many
contemporary readers do not have any predisposition to accept even
the vaguest theism. But this has taken time, and is the result of the
progressive secularization of a whole culture, not just the impact of
counter-arguments on a few philosophers. When Hume wrote the
*Dialogues*, he would have been confronted with a near universal
consensus that some belief in God was intellectually indispensable,
and that atheism could not be seriously entertained. It is commonly
said that Hume himself was largely, if not wholly, immune to this
assumption, and did not share it. If my previous analysis of Part
XII is to stand, this view of Hume needs some qualification; but let
us for the present accept it. Then Hume becomes, what he so clearly
is in many other ways, a twentieth-century person before his time

[10] Noxon, in Chappell 1966.

in religious matters—faced, however, by an audience which he could see to be unable to draw the ultimate consequences of Philo's arguments.

Why would they be unable to do this? Because the essentially unnatural but widespread forces which he had described in the *Natural History*, and had traced in their influence right up to the generation of monotheism, were too powerful to be defeated altogether by the influences of secular society and the arguments of Sceptical philosophers. So even while accepting these arguments, men of letters were unwitting bearers of a vestigial theistic orientation. The later course of secularization might cause this vestigial trace to fall away; but the time was not yet. For the present the most that could be done was to consolidate those intellectual victories which would prevent lapses into superstition and ensure that residual theism was never a source of theoretical or moral initiatives on its own account. So Hume makes Philo inconsistently espouse the domesticated theism that he judged to be the limit the process of secularization could reach in his contemporaries. The purpose of all the ironies and Sceptical poses would then not be to *disguise* this inconsistency from those who could perceive it, but emphasize and explain it.

This is only speculation, made worse by the fact that someone who feels alone in an opinion is certain to be prey to anxiety that his own views may be unnatural rather than everyone else's, so that Hume may not have known with clarity how far he and Philo thought the same way. This is the dilemma of many honest thinkers reflecting on religion. In our own time, when Hume the secularizer is more in tune with the majority than Demea or Cleanthes, the question of what is natural to believe is even harder to answer, but its importance has not diminished.

# 11

## *Religion in the* Enquiry *and After*

THE *Enquiry Concerning Human Understanding* contains two sections devoted to religious themes. Neither has a counterpart in the *Treatise.* The first, Section X, is probably the most famous of all Hume's writings, and has generated more responses than any others; the second, Section XI, is hardly ever given separate attention, being passed by because it is seen as an early version of certain major arguments in the *Dialogues.* Antony Flew has, very reasonably, complained of the tendency not to read the *Enquiry* as a work deserving examination in its own right, commenting particularly on the fact that these two sections in it are not examined together as though they form a connected argument.[1] I am sympathetic to both complaints, especially the second. I want first to revisit these two sections, to see how much of a connected argument there is, and then to see how much the *Enquiry* reveals of Hume's detailed views on religion.

### I

There is one obvious reason why Sections X and XI would not be read as though they formed one continuous argument, and that is of course the sharp contrast in style and presentation between them. The first is direct, aggressive, and laced with sarcasm. The second is noteworthy for its indirection, its quasi-fictional presentation, and for its use of devices that would deflect an inattentive reader. How *can* they be all of a piece? A partial answer is easy. One of Hume's purposes in the *Enquiry* was to present his views in ways that made them more accessible to a wider reading public, and that

---

[1] Flew 1961, 215.

public was very familiar by the time of its publication with what Burns calls the Great Debate on Miracles, in which there had been plenty of hard-hitting contributions before, and which might even be thought to have been played out.[2] Nothing more restrained would have been in place. Section XI, in contrast, opens to the deepest question some assumptions of the intellectual culture within which the miracle debate had gone on: assumptions about the human capacity to learn about God through reason, the practical relevance of this knowledge, and the corresponding moral dangers (or alleged moral dangers) of atheism. For someone who had so recently been deemed, like Socrates, unfit to teach the young, the questioning of such assumptions demanded circumspection.[3]

This partial answer suffices to make clear why the two sections differ so markedly in style; and once that is put on one side, it is possible to see the wisdom of connecting their contents and not following the standard practice of reading Section X as though it had no sequel.

One person who was guilty of reading it in this way was William Paley. In the 'Preparatory Considerations' that open his *Evidences of Christianity*, we find the classic statement of a concern that has exercised many readers of Hume's argument in Section X. Although Hume says that 'a miracle may be accurately defined, *a transgression of a law of nature by a particular volition of the Deity, or by the interposition of some invisible agent*' (*EU* x. 115), the argument of the Section depends only upon the fact that a miracle would contravene a law of nature, not upon the fact that it would be an act of God. Surely, says Paley, the likelihood of the testimony to a miracle being credible cannot be fairly assessed without taking account of the fact, if it is one, that the world we live in has a Creator who is concerned for his creatures' happiness, intends for rational creatures a 'second state of existence in which their situation will be regulated by their behaviour in the first state', and is therefore quite likely to vouchsafe a revelation so that these creatures can learn of his intentions for them? In such a situation miracles do not have the extreme degree of improbability that Hume argues they have, and testimony to them must appear in a different light. Paley continues:

We do not assume the attributes of the Deity, or the existence of a future state, in order to *prove* the reality of miracles. That reality must always be

---

[2] Burns 1981.          [3] See Emerson 1994 and Stewart 1995.

proved by evidence. We assert only, that in miracles adduced in support of revelation there is not any such antecedent improbability as no testimony can surmount.[4]

Paley proceeds in the *Evidences*, to defend the testimony of the first Christians to the crucial New Testament miracles, and later, in his *Natural Theology*, to produce what is still the best-known presentation of the Argument from Design.

It has been noted more than once that although Paley responds to Hume's attack on miracles, he never responds to the *Dialogues Concerning Natural Religion*, where the Design Argument is undermined.[5] While this is true, it is surely more noteworthy that he does not respond to Section XI of the *Enquiry*, where Hume argues (in the person of Epicurus) that even if natural theology of the kind Paley was to practise is successful, it cannot teach us the things about God's intentions that its practitioners think it can, and then argues (in his own person) that it rests upon an untenable form of causal reasoning.

I do not suggest that Paley's criticism lacks substance. I am merely indicating the obvious truth that it is anticipated by Hume in the very work where he attacks belief in miracles. This suggests that the devices of partial concealment that Hume uses in Section XI are only too successful.

## II

I will now consider the nature of the debate that Hume joined in Section X. It was a lengthy one, and took place between two main groups who shared presuppositions that Hume does not address until Section XI. I shall follow Burns in calling the two groups the deists and the orthodox.[6]

I should note before examining it that David Wootton has argued persuasively that the material on miracles which was excised from the *Treatise* before its publication, in order to make that work inoffensive to Butler, and which must have been at least closely similar to the content of the Section X of the *Enquiry*, was mostly

---

[4] Paley 1838, vol. II, 2. Paley's comments on Hume are reproduced in Swinburne (ed.) 1989, 41–7.

[5] See, for example, Sprague 1967 and ch. 2 of LeMahieu 1976.

[6] My indebtedness to Burns' work cited above will be obvious in what follows.

composed by Hume while he was at La Flèche, and was not originally written in response to English debates but to French controversies originating with Arnauld. He argues that changes made by Hume in the second version of the *Enquiry* are evidence of this, and constitute signs of a more informed attempt on his part to take account of the English disputes. I think this is fully compatible with Hume's believing that this material, even in its first form, would constitute a decisive contribution to the English discussion.[7] I turn now to that debate.

Ever since Aquinas, Christian apologists had tended to follow argumentative procedures that depended on the distinction between natural and revealed theology. Natural theology was thought to be that part of philosophy that showed by reason that it is certain or highly probable that God created our world and guides it providentially. Revelation, in the form of scripture and tradition, also teaches us these truths, since otherwise only the philosophically competent could know them; but it also teaches us other truths, such as the divinity of Christ and the doctrine of the Trinity, that human reason cannot grasp of itself, but which are necessary for salvation. But although our unaided reason cannot discover these truths, they are still commendable to reason, since there are clear evidences of the reliability of revelation. Prominent among these evidences are the miracles that accompanied the teachings of Jesus, the miracle of his resurrection, and those miracles that have occurred in the history (especially the early history) of the Christian community since. Roughly, while the demonstrations of natural theology show that it is irrational *not* to believe in God and his providence, these evidences show that it is also rational to go further and accept the claims to revelation that the church makes in addition.

There were those, even among Christian apologists, who dissented from this apologetic tradition, namely the fideistic thinkers whose most prominent representative is Pascal; and Hume is aware of their views and occasionally copies (or parodies) them.[8] (See the concluding paragraph of Section X.) But their position, which leaned heavily on Pyrrhonistic arguments, was a minority view not much reflected in the English debate.

The mainline debate was about the connection between these two stages of the traditional apologetic. The deists wished to separate

---

[7] Wootton 1990. On the excisions from the *Treatise*, see Mossner 1970, 110–12.
[8] See Popkin 1979 and Penelhum 1983.

them, and argued that once we have recognized that our world is created by God, we can also recognize, not that we need further revelatory truths, but that God would so have planned his creation that his creatures would have no need of such intervention to achieve happiness and to live as he wished them to live. Natural religion is enough, and revealed religion is unnecessary and divisive.

The concept of natural religion is not a well-defined one, but in its minimal form it was thought to consist simply of an acknowledgment of the existence and goodness of God and an acceptance of the moral law, the latter being conceived of as the sum of the deliverances of the ordinary conscience.[9] That natural religion in this sense is incontestable was assumed by the orthodox as well as by the deists. The orthodox claimed that the additional doctrines and duties of revealed religion had credentials that should commend them to all those whose reason had already led them to espouse the natural variety. One reason they gave for this judgement was that the pronouncements of revealed religion were in part (though not of course in total) mere republications of what natural religion already contained.[10]

Ironically the deists, who proclaimed less doctrine, were more confident than the orthodox in pronouncing what God would or would not do. God would not require assent or obedience from us on matters where our beliefs or practices depended on a revelation that is only given to some and not to others. Everything he required of us would be clear and obvious and accessible to our reason without the need of special intimations that only one nation or one religious community were privileged to receive. Thus Matthew Tindal, the deists' most famous representative:

As far as divine wisdom exceeds human, so far the divine laws must excel human laws in clearness and perspicuity; as well as other perfections. Whatever is confused and perplexed, can never come from the clear fountain of all knowledge; nor that which is obscure from the father of inexhaustible light; and as far as you suppose God's laws are not plain to any part of mankind, so far you derogate from the perfection of those laws, and the wisdom and the goodness of the divine legislator.[11]

---

[9] The best treatment of these matters is to be found in Byrne 1989.

[10] See, for example, Tillotson's sermon 'Instituted Religion not Intended to Undermine Natural' in Tillotson 1735, vol. 2; also Butler 1900, Part II, ch. 1.

[11] Tindal 1978, 105 f.

On the orthodox side, it was Joseph Butler's primary concern in the *Analogy of Religion* to argue that the reality of natural knowledge of God does not preclude deep and extensive ignorance of God's detailed purposes, and is certainly not so extensive as to justify such shallow confidence in judging what God would or would not do. Hence there might well be need for revelation, and consequently a need for miracles and prophecies to 'attest' it.[12] Butler comes close to Hume's definition of what a miracle is when he says that 'a miracle, in its very notion, is relative to a course of nature; and implies somewhat different from it, considered as being so'.[13] This seems to imply that a miracle cannot even be identified as such unless we are aware of a law or laws of nature that it violates—although it cannot imply that we would be able to state the relevant laws accurately. Butler distinguishes between visible and invisible miracles; the latter (most importantly the Incarnation) are 'attested' by the visible ones. His most interesting arguments are those directed to showing there is no proper presumption against the miraculous. The argument that has occasioned the most comment is that there are many ordinary facts (his example is the story of Caesar) against which there is a 'presumption of millions to one', so that the 'small presumption, additional to this' that is involved in the case of miracle 'is as nothing'. Butler is normally judicious in his use of the notion of probability, which is central to many of his arguments, but this is not his happiest use of it.[14] A more attractive argument suggests that even though a miracle may contravene a *natural* law, God's miraculous interventions 'may have been all along . . . by *general* laws of wisdom'.[15] Providence, in other words, may function in a lawlike manner even though this may entail the violation of laws of *nature.* This is a reasonable defence against those like Tindal who had insisted that God's laws must always be clear to our understanding. Butler says in response that the truths of natural religion have to be interpreted in such a way that they allow for what are mysteries to us but are likely to be rational principles known to God. We may not

---

[12] The whole of Part II of the *Analogy* is devoted to showing this. I have attempted an appraisal of its main arguments and an assessment of how far they are vitiated by the context in which they were written, in Penelhum 1985, pt. 2.

[13] Butler 1900, Part II, ch. 2, 158.

[14] Butler 1900, Part II, ch. 2, 159–60. The argument has been defended by Burns 127 f.

[15] Butler 1900, Part II, ch. 4, 181.

know these principles well enough to predict miracles in advance, but they might be dimly discernible to us retrospectively in the light of miracles once these have happened. But while this suggestion is forceful enough against Tindal, it does not help us in determining how we are to know when a miracle has actually occurred. So while Butler argues with some power against the deists' claims that all evidence for miracles should be rejected *a priori*, his particular defences of the Christian miracle stories are less persuasive.

The *Analogy of Religion* was published in 1736, and it is doubtful that Hume could have read it before the completion of the *Treatise*. It is well known, however, that Hume excised some material on miracles from it before it saw publication, as he hoped to gain Butler's approval of his work.[16] This certainly suggests some acquaintance with the *Analogy* between 1736 and 1739, and it is unlikely that Hume would not have studied it before he composed the first *Enquiry*. He would have wished to respond to it in some manner, especially in the light of his own intellectual discoveries about its key concept of probability.

## III

I think this background information gives us reasons for taking sides on some of the controversies that have developed about the intent of Section X.

I take the most obvious point first. The Great Debate on miracles took place between two main parties both of whom assumed the cogency of the Design Argument and the rational certainty of belief in God. Section X does not address the assumption they share, only the issue that divides them; and, with major qualifications to be added later, it clearly sides, on this issue, with the deists.

But this prompts a question. It is striking that Hume proceeds in an order that reverses the traditional apologetic sequence. He addresses a core apologetic argument for revealed religion first, and turns to the core argument for natural religion later. Part of the reason is the advantage of joining a familiar debate before delving into its presuppositions. But in view of the fundamental importance of the deeper question, this cannot be the whole story. I think that Burns

---

[16] See Mossner 1970, 109–12.

must be right in maintaining, at the close of his detailed criticisms of Section X, that Hume believed the argument of that Section could stand on its own, and was decisive against basing a system of religion on miracles even if one accepted an open form of natural religion like Butler's rather than a closed one like Tindal's. Even if we could learn through the Design Argument that the world is the creation of a benign deity who for all we know might intervene in it for our instruction, there is still decisive reason to reject testimony to his having done so on any particular occasion.

If this is right, it tells in favour of reading Section X as primarily about the evidence for miracles (that is, testimony), rather than about the possibility (logical, or physical or theological) of miracles themselves. The difficulty in taking sides on this question derives from the fact that Hume makes no effort to hide his contempt for belief in miracles or his conviction that there are none. But I think the wider setting of his arguments, and their sequence, points rather toward Flew's reading of Section X than Fogelin's.[17] That is, it suggests that Hume thinks the arguments of Section X show not that miracles are impossible (though he clearly believes this) but that (a) in face of the uniform experience in support of the law the alleged miracle would have violated, even abundant and impeccable testimony can do no more, even in theory, than lead to a 'mutual destruction of arguments', and that (b) since the actual testimonial evidence in favour of miracles has never been impeccable, even though it has often been abundant, no miracle can be proved by testimony to establish a system of religion. In sum, the evidence in favour of the law allegedly violated must always overwhelm the weight of testimony available for the miracle.

If *this* is correct, then since (b) is the burden of Part II of the Section, I think Burns is wrong to suggest that Part II consists only of a series of afterthoughts that Hume included to adjust the over-confident claims of Part I to the parameters of the earlier English debate.[18] I think Part II has the real and necessary function of showing that there is no possibility of resting in the 'counterpoize, and mutual destruction of belief and authority' that could theoretically be the outcome of a confrontation between scientific and testimonial evidence as described in Part I.

---

[17] For Flew's view see ch. 8 of Flew 1961. See also Fogelin 1990 and Flew 1990.
[18] Burns 1981, 154.

## IV

I turn now to a related but somewhat different disagreement about how Section X should be read. In a perceptive recent essay, Alasdair MacIntyre has suggested that there are in fact two arguments against miracles in Part I of the Section.[19] The first, which he calls the empiricist argument, leans on the actual or supposed fact that the credibility of testimony depends on the prior experience of the hearer of it. It is summed up in (a) above.[20]

[19] MacIntyre 1994.
[20] I offer my own detailed paraphrase of this argument. A wise man proportions his belief to the evidence. 'Infallible experience' leads him to form expectations 'with the last degree of assurance' and to treat his past experience as a 'full *proof*' of the future existence of that event'. Less uniform experience leads him to balance positive and negative cases and to think only of *probability*. This contrast extends to his judgement of testimony. As there is no necessary connection between events and the testimony to them, whether testimony yields proof or probability depends on how our past experience causes us to estimate the quality of the testimony available to us. One factor that diminishes the strength of the testimony is the extent to which the event reported 'partakes of the extraordinary and the marvellous'. While the case of the Indian prince should make us aware that our experience may come to be enlarged to admit events that have hitherto been no part of it, no such reservation is relevant in the case of miracles. For if witnesses testify to a miracle, they are testifying to a violation of a law of nature. Here their testimony, even if it is enough to constitute proof as Hume has defined it, is faced by a contrary proof 'from the very nature of the fact'. For laws are established by a 'firm and unalterable experience'. Since such an experience amounts to a proof, there is 'a direct and full *proof*, from the nature of the fact, against the existence of any miracle'. Such a proof cannot be destroyed, except by 'an opposite proof' which is superior. Hence no testimony can establish a miracle unless its falsehood would be more miraculous than the fact which it endeavours to establish.
    Some brief comments: (1) I think it is possible to answer a common criticism, articulated forcefully by Taylor (1927: 4). 'On the face of it, there would seem to be something amiss with reasoning which proceeds from the principle that "a wise man proportions his belief to the evidence" to the conclusion that in a vast, if none too well defined, field, the "wise man" will simply refuse to consider "the evidence" at all.' I leave aside the fact that Hume's comment about competing proofs seems to imply that the wise man will reach 'counterpoize' *after* considering the evidence, and stress something more fundamental to Hume's argument: that 'the evidence' for a miracle does not only include the testimony to the particular sequence of which it is a part, but also all the previous experience establishing the natural law to which it would be an exception. I see this as the core of Hume's case, at least in this empiricist argument. (2) Hume's famous remark that no testimony can prove a miracle unless its falsehood would be more miraculous than the event it is supposed to establish makes use of a notion of degrees of miraculousness; and this is not something for which Hume has given us any intellectual room. (See here, however, the ingenious suggestion of Stewart 1994.) (3) Taylor says that the notion of contrary proofs is unintelligible (Taylor 1927: 15). I do not think this is so, if one recalls that in Hume's semi-technical use of the term here, it is logically possible to have a proof of a proposition that is in fact false.

In addition to this argument, MacIntyre finds another, metaphysical one, which he calls the naturalist argument. He agrees here with Fred Wilson, whose recent major study of Hume's analysis of causal reasoning includes an extensive reading of Section X that interprets it in these terms.[21] The naturalist argument maintains, as a *premiss*, that there is a law of nature that explains every event, and proceeds from this, via the intermediate conclusion that there are, therefore, no miracles, to the final conclusion that no testimony can ever establish one.[22]

I do not find this second argument in the text of Part I. But I must admit two things. First, there is no doubt that Hume *believes* that there is, for every event, a law that explains it. Sections IV to VII of the *Enquiry*, and of course Part III of Book I of the *Treatise*, contain his account of how causal reasoning comes to be established in the understanding, and there is no doubt that he thinks, correctly or not, that this account includes such justification as his system admits of for our reliance on the principle that every event has a cause, as well as the principle that the same cause will always lead to the same effect. It is also true that in Section VIII he has appealed to the universality of causation openly (and dogmatically) in attacking the libertarian understanding of free will. It is further true that one can see the first *Enquiry* as a whole as having, as one of its dominant themes, the emphasis on the confrontation between his understanding of causal reasoning and the claims of religion. But although all this would make it natural enough for him to appeal to the causal principle to dismiss the evidence for miracles, he does not in fact bypass purely historical considerations in this way. Instead he confines himself to one aspect of historical methodology that his analysis of causal thinking has led him to emphasize, deferring the appeal to other parts of this analysis to Section XI. By doing this he has made a more effective and long-lasting contribution to historical method than would have been possible had he brought the full battery of his theses about causality to bear on this one question.[23]

[21] Wilson 1997, 283–307. MacIntyre's reference is to an earlier essay by Wilson.

[22] Wilson 1997, 305: 'The argument is that the claim that a miracle has occurred is repugnant to the principle that every event has a (natural) cause'.

[23] If I am right, this is one place where Hume has not followed Ciceronian precedent. Consider the following from *De Divinatione* II. xxviii: '(W)hatever comes into existence of whatever kind, must needs find its cause in nature; and hence, even though it may be contrary to experience, it cannot be contrary to nature. Therefore, explore the cause, if you can, of every strange thing that excites your astonishment . . . and employ the principles of natural philosophy to banish the fear which the novelty of

He has thus made it standard for historians to assume that the weight of testimony can never be greater than that of the evidence for the relevant natural laws.

A second point I must concede is that the nerve of Hume's argument in Part I is to be found in the implications of his definition of miracle. If a miracle is a violation of natural law, then the event to which the testimony being evaluated is relevant is an event that both sides already agree to be one that is subsumed under some such law. One cannot hold this without holding that there are laws covering events of this type; though one could of course accept *that* without claiming to know very exactly what the laws in question are and without being committed to the view that every event *whatever* is subsumable under natural law. (Not that this latter thought is comforting to anyone who believes in miracles, since any event that was not subsumable under natural law would not be miraculous, whatever else could be said about it.)

But having conceded these two things, I repeat that as I read Part I of the Section, Hume merely argues there that it is always erroneous to assent to miracle testimony because the law of nature that the testimony tells us has been violated is established by 'a firm and unalterable experience'. Unless we take him to be embodying his own disbelief in miracle in the use of the word 'unalterable', we must take this to mean 'a uniform past experience'.

All I find here, then, is what MacIntyre calls the empiricist argument, not the naturalist one. Many would think that the naturalist argument would be a stronger argument than the empiricist argument. Others would think, as MacIntyre does, that whatever its strength, the naturalist argument is needed to prop up the empiricist argument, which lacks power without it. I do not comment on this, but would emphasize again that the naturalist argument would rule out miracles *a priori*, without needing to invoke any opinion about the evidence for them; and that what Hume seems to me to have done in Part I is rather to tell us that what establishes natural laws is a body of evidence that also weighs overwhelmingly against any miracle testimony there may be. So it is misleading to describe Part I of the Section as an *a priori* argument in the way Burns and many others do.

the apparition may have occasioned' (Cicero 1953 edn.: 439). This passage is noted at the beginning of the valuable chapter on miracles in Sanders 1993.

V

I have argued that Hume thinks his case against miracle testimony in Section X is decisive even if one accepts the presuppositions shared by the deists and the orthodox in earlier debate. Section XI takes the argument to a much profounder level by undermining those presuppositions.

I have said that Hume has come out in Section X on the side of the deists. But this is only a partial truth.[24] We can better appreciate his argument in Section XI by recognizing that he has appropriated some of Butler's arguments against the deists and carried them further in a manner that undermines both.[25]

Butler assumed, with his opponents, that it is unthinkable that our world could exist without a designing intelligence: that there is 'an intelligent Author of Nature, and natural Governor of the world'. He then argues, with considerable ingenuity, that our knowledge of the nature of God's governance is limited, since the world contains obscurities and evils that the deists' sunny optimism leads them to ignore, and which, in his view, are better accounted for by invoking the Christian revelation than by denying it.[26] This argument gives Hume the opportunity of pointing out a far simpler resolution of the debate: if we continue to assume a designing intelligence behind the world, the evidence only justifies our holding that the purposes of that intelligence are fulfilled by the world as it is, not that there are additional purposes that natural or revealed religion are needed to make clear to us. Hence the natural theology that leads us to postulate this governing intelligence can have no practical bearing on human choice, since a calculation of policy based on observation of the world, and a calculation based on our actual knowledge of divine purposes turn out now to be identical. This is the burden of the speech of Epicurus and of the first part of the subsequent exchange between Hume and his friend after Epicurus concludes. It undercuts the debate between the deists and the orthodox, both of whom had assumed that in natural religion we have access to significantly more information

---

[24] For a valuable comparison between Hume and the deists, see Byrne 1989, 113–28.

[25] I draw here on Penelhum 1985, Part Two.

[26] It is notable in this connection that belief in a future life, which is crucial for many of Butler's detailed arguments, is not a belief that he supports by invoking our knowledge of God, but is one that he claims to be probable on purely natural grounds. See the *Analogy*'s first chapter.

about the purposes of the designing intelligence than its power to cause the world we see before us, and merely differed about what additional information we have.

To make this point Hume has to draw on more of his account of causation than he has needed to draw upon in his attack on the testimony to miracles. This time he needs to appeal to the 'maxim, that where any cause is known only by its particular effects, it must be impossible to infer any new effects from that cause' (*EU* XI. 145n). Hume clearly believes that the account of causal thinking that he has given us in Sections IV to VII of the *Enquiry* has established this maxim.[27] But he still confines himself to invoking only that part of his theoretical arsenal that he needs to use.

The Section concludes with his bringing out his most destructive weapon. He has just argued that if we attend carefully to the rules of 'analogy' to which Butler appealed, we can see that Butler was more right than even he realized when he emphasized our ignorance of divine purposes. What he suggests in the Section's final paragraph is that the analogical reasoning on which natural religion depends to assure us of the very reality of the divine mind violates the principles of causal reasoning of which it is supposed to be a compelling example. 'It is only when two *species* of objects are found to be constantly conjoined, that we can infer the one from the other; and were an effect presented, which was entirely singular, and could not be comprehended under any known *species*, I do not see, that we could form any conjecture or inference at all concerning its cause' (*EU* X. 148). Both the universe (the alleged effect) and the deity (the alleged cause) are, in contrast, 'singular and unparalleled'. While Hume leaves his friend to 'pursue the consequences of this principle', it is clear what they are. Just as revealed religion has been argued in Section X to lack the compelling support that testimony to miracles was alleged by the orthodox to provide, and natural religion has been argued in Section XI to lack the practical consequences that both deists and orthodox believed it to have, natural religion is now shown not merely to be devoid of practical content but to be devoid of theoretical basis (or so Hume thinks).

---

[27] It is not as easy as one might suppose to find which part of the arguments of Sections IV to VII do establish it. If we look back for help to the *Treatise*, some might find it established by the *Rules by which to judge of causes and effects* in I. iii. 15; though the clearest anticipation of it is in the previous section where Hume tells us that the 'distinction, which we often make betwixt *power* and the *exercise* of it, is equally without foundation' (*T* I. iii. 14. 171).

## VI

Even though the theory of causal reasoning on which Hume draws
in these arguments was developed in the *Treatise*, and the argument
against miracles was to have been part of that work originally, it is
obvious that what Flew has called the 'hard, exasperated, secularizing
notes' of Hume's introductory passages in Section I are indicative
of a strong sense of mission that is far more prominent in the *Enquiry*.
The mission is the assault on superstition, of which Hume felt himself
to be the victim in his loss of the Edinburgh professorship. While
Hume had been anxious to defend the *Treatise* against charges of
atheism in the *Letter from a Gentleman*,[28] even to the extent of
suggesting that his theory of causation did not impugn the inference
to design, the *Enquiry* is aggressively anti-religious throughout, in
spite of the indirections of Section XI. It is clearly Sections X and
XI that are intended to justify the decision so to describe the policy
of mitigated scepticism in Section XII that it entails the restriction
of intellectual activity to abstract reasoning concerning quantity or
number and experimental reasoning concerning matter of fact and
existence: a restriction of subject-matter rather than a rationing of
time and energy as recommended in the *Treatise*.[29] This culminates,
as we all know, in the bookburning positivism of the final paragraph.

But a question of intention remains. Mitigated scepticism teaches
us that 'philosophical decisions are nothing but the reflections of
common life, methodized and corrected' (*EU* XII. 162). Where does
this leave the duly mitigated sceptic with regard to religion? Hume
has rejected philosophical arguments for the authority of revelation,
the moral significance of natural religion, and the very existence of
a divine mind that arranges the order in the world. Are we to take
it that he rejects the conclusions of these arguments as well as the
arguments? Does he even reject natural religion as well as the arguments used to support it?

It is very natural to suppose that he does. How else are we to interpret the mockery in Section X and the sarcasm of the short paragraph on 'Divinity or Theology' on the final page of Section XII?
But we must pause and acknowledge the clear message of Section XII
as a whole that common life has an authority that is prior to any
contribution of philosophy, which can only methodize and correct

[28] Hume 1967, esp. 19–26.    [29] On this contrast, see Chapter 9.

what it learns from it. For common life, after all, is full of religion, or it was then. Does that mean that Hume's deference to common life ceases here?

There is a great divide among Hume's interpreters on this matter, although argument about it tends to concentrate, naturally enough, on the reading of the *Dialogues* rather than that of the *Enquiry*. Some scholars are firm in their conviction that in spite of his negativity about natural and revealed theology, Hume is still a theist, or a deist. Some of his most informed interpreters hold this opinion.[30] I cannot bring myself to read him in this way, although I did manage it briefly at one time. I want to approach this fundamental matter now through some further reflections on the *Enquiry* and its relation to Hume's other writings on religion.

The overall effect of the *Enquiry*'s treatment of religion is clearly negative. When Hume methodizes and corrects the arguments that believers offer for miracles, the moral significance of natural religion, and the very belief in a divine mind, these arguments do not re-emerge in a more sober and tenable form, but vanish completely. Is there, in the first place, anything remaining in the *Enquiry* itself to support the suggestion that the traditions and customs of common life might leave some form of religion with a residual authority in which the Humean sceptic, as defined in this work, must acquiesce?

I think there are two places where one just might think such a suggestion could get support, but they are slim pickings. One is the remark in Section V that there is 'a kind of pre-established harmony between the course of nature and the succession of our ideas' and that those 'who delight in the discovery and contemplation of final causes, have here ample subject to employ their wonder and admiration' (*EU* v. 54). To me the irony here is obvious, though of course the ironic language can still express a recognition that this coincidence is *remarkable*. The other place is the speech of Epicurus, in which he begins by telling the Athenians that he willingly acquiesces in the tradition of their forefathers and the doctrine of their priests, and only has a quarrel with their philosophers. I do not think that much can be made of this third-hand acquiescence, which is not even ascribed here to Pyrrho or Carneades but to Epicurus, who is said

---

[30] See ch. 9 of Capaldi 1975; chs. 6 and 7 of Gaskin 1988; Logan 1993 *passim*. Donald Livingston, in Livingston 1998 (esp. chs. 3 and 7) has said again that Hume is a theist; while I admire this work greatly, I am unable to follow him in this. I am also unpersuaded by the eloquence of ch. 8 of Mounce 1999, which argues similarly.

here (unhistorically) to deny divine existence. The most that could be squeezed from this is the concession that the rituals and socially cohesive myths of a traditional society could be beneficial and serve to reinforce the virtue that Epicurus is at pains to point out must have a purely secular source.

I read the first *Enquiry* as telling us forcefully that common life should be freed by the true philosopher's exertions from the anxieties and supposed supports offered by religion as Hume saw it around him. But Hume wrote a good deal more about religion than we find here. Does the *Enquiry* perhaps give us a one-sided picture of his views about it? Does he modify these views elsewhere?

## VII

Let us turn first to the *Natural History of Religion*. Here I must be far too brief, but would say three things about what Hume tells us there. (1) Theism has a far closer (and more corrupting) connection with philosophy than the polytheistic religions of classical antiquity with which Epicureans and Sceptics could so easily co-exist, even now and then as functionaries. (2) In spite of this, theism develops from primitive polytheism, which originates in fearful responses to extraordinary events and calamities, not from any recognition or awareness of natural order. (3) Hence the lip-service that Hume pays in the *Natural History* to the rational status of theism has to be balanced against the fact that the main argument of the work is an account of the origins of theism in which rational argument has no place. It is a great merit of Keith Yandell's work on Hume's philosophy of religion that he recognizes the importance of the *Natural History* and brings out the similarities between its accounts of the origins of religious beliefs and Hume's theories about the origins of our natural beliefs in the *Treatise*.[31] Rational factors have no role in any of them. Hence the praise that rational argument for belief in God receives in the *Natural History* cannot be taken at face value.

So I do not think the *Natural History of Religion* is the place to look if one is trying to find signs of a Humean acceptance of any form of natural religion. If we are to find it anywhere, it must be in the *Dialogues concerning Natural Religion*.

[31] Yandell 1990, Part One.

Section XI of the *Enquiry* is often said to be an embryonic version of the *Dialogues*. It is perhaps instructive to see how the arguments that make their first appearance in that Section reappear in the later work. The first point to notice is that the arguments in Section XI that establish the practical emptiness of natural religion are expressed by Epicurus or by Hume's fictional friend, and the concluding argument that the uniqueness of the universe prevents causal explanation of it is in Hume's own person; in the *Dialogues*, however, all of them are given to Philo. Since Hume does not appear in his own person, this might not seem interesting, but I think some significance can be found in it for the way we are to interpret Philo's contributions. It emerges, I think, when we notice also that in the *Dialogues* the order of these arguments is different. The radical suggestion that no causal reasoning is appropriate when the subject is the origin of the universe comes very early, and the emphasis on the practical emptiness of natural theology comes very late. (To be more exact, the argument that causal inferences require us to have experienced repeated examples of phenomena resembling the cause being followed by phenomena resembling the effect is one of the first to be given to Philo once Cleanthes has stated the Design Argument, and appears in Part II (*D* II. 149); the argument of Epicurus, that we are only entitled to ascribe those powers to a cause that suffice to produce the observed effects, appears in Part V (*D* v. 166), where its awkward consequences for the belief in creation are then much dwelt upon, and is also used, in effect, in the discussion of evil in Part XI, although what is stressed in both cases is not the irrelevance of its conclusion for ethical decision, as in Section XI of the *Enquiry*, but its unorthodox implications for the understanding of the divine nature; the practical emptiness of a duly chastened natural theology is a theme that Philo stresses at the very conclusion of Part XII.) I venture to interpret this as showing us that Hume's own position may appear in the *Dialogues* early, and that the puzzling stance taken by Philo in the concluding Part is to be distinguished from it. I suggest, that is, that the *Enquiry* is the key to interpreting the apparent ambiguity of the *Dialogues*.

The exegetical puzzle about the *Dialogues*, as all its readers know, is the apparent change in Philo's position in Part XII. He presents himself there as one who accepts the conclusion of the argument Cleanthes has put forward, which he has, throughout, subjected to devastating criticisms. And he does this without giving any sign that he is changing his mind. One solution, argued by Kemp Smith, is that Philo does not mean a word of what he says in Part XII, and that Hume is expressing himself through heavy irony 'in keeping with his general policy of stating his sceptical positions with the least possible emphasis compatible with definiteness' (*D* 73). When the work has reached us by deliberately posthumous publication, I think this needs emendation. Another solution is the opposite one: to ignore all the signs of irony Kemp Smith finds and explain the change as a genuine one brought on by Demea's departure at the end of Part XI. On this line of reasoning, Philo has been showing off his careless scepticism in front of Demea, but speaks sincerely to Cleanthes now that they are on their own. I think this is inadequate too: if one thinks of the *Dialogues* as a philosophical drama, which of course it is, it would surely be naive of its audience to take at face value the protestations of sincerity that one of two characters makes to the other when a third character has left. The change may merely mark an alteration in the role the first character is now about to play, not a transition from play-acting to truth. But just as there are indeed signs of irony, in abundance, in Philo's last speeches, so it is correct to take seriously the fact that they are addressed to Cleanthes alone. I will develop this a little.

One of the main themes of the first Part of the *Dialogues* is the limited power of scepticism. This is a theme that Philo himself takes up at the close of Part X, where he claims to 'triumph' over Cleanthes in their dispute about the moral attributes of God. On the natural attributes of intelligence and design Philo concedes there that he has needed all his 'sceptical and metaphysical subtilty' to elude Cleanthes' grasp, and that he is unable to deny the 'irresistible force' of beauty and final causes. This passage is placed where it is to prepare us for Philo's stance in Part XII. Some are tempted to read Part XII in the light of this as implying that the belief in intelligent design is a natural belief—one that sceptical argument may show to be without philosophical foundation, but which cannot be abandoned any more than our belief in the distinct and continued existence of external objects can be. I yielded to this temptation once (see Chapter 9) but have seen the error of it since (see Chapter 10). The main argument against it is that not only does the *Natural History* teach us that religion is not universal, but both the *Enquiry* and Part XII of the *Dialogues* emphasize the irrelevance of the belief in design, however arrived at, to daily life. I think, though, that

something can indeed be made of the careful placing of Philo's concession in his statement of triumph at the end of Part X. It serves
to render Philo's overall stance in the work a reasonably consistent
one—if one does not pick up the ironies in his protestations of
theism in the final Part.

That overall stance is one that makes Philo sincere in saying, in
Part I, that the dispute is only about the nature and not about the
being of God, and also makes him sincere in conceding in Part X
that his arguments against Cleanthes hitherto have been mere sceptical cavils. It is also a stance that leads to the religiously minimal
conclusion of Philo's final speech. If we then identify Philo with Hume,
we will conclude that the natural religion that results from the discussions in the *Dialogues* is a bare philosophical theism, or deism,
that permits moral choice to be based on purely secular considerations, and admits no popular pieties, and we will also conclude that
the main purpose of the work is to establish this. This will identify
its purpose with that of Part XI of the *Enquiry, minus its last paragraph*. It has to be admitted that this interpretation is indeed a
consistent one, and that if it were correct, nothing in Philo's position
in Part XII should surprise us.

But of course it *does* surprise us, or most of us. It does so for two
main reasons. The first is that in spite of the disclaimers we have
listed, Philo has not talked earlier on as though he is merely trying
to refine and circumscribe the theism Cleanthes is arguing for,
rather than to refute it. The second, which I can only state here and
not elaborate, is that Philo's protestations in Part XII are indeed
shot through with hints of insincerity as Kemp Smith says, and only
someone as obtuse as Cleanthes could miss all of them. (Think, for
example, of the sign of order and design in the rotting of the turnip;
or of the six thousand views and intentions that nature has executed
to construct the musculature Galen discerns in the human body; or of
the impossibility of having 'no system at all' in the face of a theory
supported by reason, natural propensity, and 'early education'.)

There are now two possibilities. One is to ascribe insincerity to
Philo as Kemp Smith does. I repeat that it is hard to see why this
would be necessary for Hume in a posthumous work; and it also
ignores the fact that Philo's positive protestations about design are
directed to the very *argument* against which he has raised all his
sceptical difficulties throughout, and genuinely seem to reverse their
impact. The elaborate device seems to lack a purpose.

I suggest an alternative.[32] It is that Hume is ascribing a minimal, though still positive, position *to Philo*, but is hinting at a more negative position on his own part. The ironies are his rather than Philo's. I would suggest that Philo represents the limit to which Hume, as a sceptic, can go within the confines of the debates on natural theology of which the *Dialogues* is the supreme example. These are debates in which, as Philo is made to say, atheism is an unthinkable position whose proponents could not possibly be serious. These were debates between theists and deists: between those who did not think God would intrude into the realm of nature, and those who believed he had already done so.

Philo's final position is that the arguments give us no basis for saying whether God would or would not do such things, or even whether the sources of order in the world are singular or plural. I suggest that by appearing to distance himself from what Philo says, Hume reveals, or hints at, the private view that even this religiously empty position, closer to that of the deists than to that of the orthodox, goes further than the facts warrant. For it still entails that the order and system we find in nature demands an external, causal explanation. This is assumed as self-evident by both sides in the debate Philo concludes, but on Hume's principles it is something we cannot concede.

In Part XII Philo seems to forget that he has said this much in Part II, and that in Part VIII he has offered a proto-Darwinian (or 'Epicurean') explanation of the appearance of design in nature: that accidental concatenations of matter have survived in ways that make it seem, contrary to fact, that there is such design. Given Hume's sceptical opinions, this explanation of that appearance is at least as good as any other. Of course it is no better either—unless one resorts to some metaphysical principle like Occam's Razor, which Hume is in no position to flourish. But the very fact that it is no worse is a ground for supposing that Hume could see in it a reason for opting out of the assumption, nominally held in common by Philo and Cleanthes, that God's being cannot be at issue. Since Philo seems to say in his last speech that the order in nature might have plural causes, it is not quite clear that he (Philo) really holds to this; but he does, nominally, most of the time. I suggest, however, that we need not suppose that Hume himself does. We should recall again

[32] See the conclusion of Chapter 10.

that Hume has given us an account of the actual origins of theism in the *Natural History of Religion.* He tells us there how it has developed out of more primitive religious forms—a process involving no wonder at nature's order, but rather fear-laden responses to calamities that we do not think of subsuming under that order, and an abasement before deities that we invent in order to control them. If his story there is true, it provides an explanation of why it is that when thinkers do come to be struck by the order of the cosmos, they already have, in the culture, the belief in a deity who can then be invoked to explain it. We are to infer, I think, that this is Hume's account of how the God of orthodox religion is thought by so many to be the self-evident answer to the question of how that order comes to be. For it is surely the burden of the *Dialogues,* throughout, that without the predispositions to belief and worship whose sources the *Natural History* describes, the God of monotheism is not the most natural answer at all.

Is Hume, then, a closet atheist? I think this is the likeliest possibility if we are trying to guess at his probable private opinions. But it is alien to his sceptical mind to think we can have sound reasons to accept a view that tells us so definitely what the universe does not contain. One recalls the famous story of Hume's being surprised by the room full of atheists at Baron d'Holbach's dinner party.[33] There is no reason to think that Hume's comments there were a pose; but that does not mean Philo represents him when he says that atheists cannot be serious. What Philo represents is Hume's considered opinion on how far reason can take us in these matters, and also how anyone who recognizes its radical limitations should accommodate himself or herself to their more religious associates. Hume could and did live in harmony with the secularized Moderates of his day, and he has Philo express platitudinous sentiments about God while making it clear to those who, unlike Cleanthes, are prepared to look, how devoid of theological content secularized faith is. While his personal convictions were probably far more negative, he has no reason to adopt the abrasive negativity of the *philosophes* when he is welcomed into the environment of secularized religiosity typical of his Moderate friends. The stance Philo takes toward Cleanthes, who represents them, embodies the position Hume is content to have them ascribe to him. But (and let us recall again that

[33] Mossner 1970, 483.

the *Dialogues* is a posthumous publication) it is not the one he leaves for *us* to ascribe to him.

Does Hume share Philo's stated wonder at the orderliness of nature, and his stated conviction that it has to have a cause or causes that resemble the human mind? The answer to the first seems to be Yes: at least, Hume is willing, when it suits him, to insist upon the systematic uniformity of our world. I suggest that the answer to the second is probably No. But although this seems to me to be the burden of the discussions of religion in the *Enquiry*, and to be the probable import of the *Dialogues*, Hume would have recognized that the readers of his day could not be carried further than the half-way house of a minimal deism. He would also have seen that the doctrinal emptiness of this would lead to the widespread godlessness of our own time eventually. It is this perception of what the future held that has helped make the *Dialogues* a contemporary document for us. But it also shows, I think, that it does not incorporate any real change from the positions of the *Enquiry*.

# 12

## Butler and Hume

THERE is not much direct evidence of connections between Hume's thought and that of Joseph Butler. We do know that Hume wanted to interest Butler in the *Treatise of Human Nature* at the time of its first publication, and took out material about miracles in order to assist in this.[1] Although this attempt came to nothing, we also know that in 1742 Butler was recommending Hume's *Essays Moral and Political* 'everywhere'.[2] There is no reason to doubt that Hume's wish to gain Butler's approbation was based in part on genuine respect; and he includes Butler's name in the Introduction to the *Treatise* when listing those students of human nature whose work has preceded his own. The late Professor Mossner argued that Cleanthes in the *Dialogues* is intended to represent Butler,[3] and it would certainly be unreasonable to doubt that Butler was much in his mind as that work was composed over the years.

### I

If one assumes that Hume thought it important to include answers to Butler in his own theories, even as a secondary objective, one can, I think, see a little more deeply into the thought of both philosophers. I shall try to do this by making some comparisons between their ethical views, and then by pursuing some suggestions these comparisons generate about the way Hume tries to respond to Butler in the realm of natural theology.

---

[1] See Letter 1, to Henry Home, 1737, in *NLDH*, 1–3.
[2] See Letter 5, also to Home, 1742, in *NLDH*, 10.
[3] Mossner 1936. In addition to his well-known Hume scholarship, Mossner's contributions to the understanding and recognition of Butler are considerable. See Mossner 1971.

To begin, some dates are in order. Butler's *Fifteen Sermons Preached at the Rolls Chapel* was first published in 1726, and went into a second edition in 1729. It will almost certainly have been the source of Hume's reference to Butler in the Introduction to the *Treatise*. Butler's *Analogy of Religion* appeared in 1736, and went into a second edition in the same year. Hume returned to England from France in 1737, and published the first two Books of the *Treatise* in 1739. Book III appeared in 1740. While it is possible that the excisions from the *Treatise* were due to an actual study of the *Analogy* (where there is considerable discussion of miracles), Butler's ecclesiastical status would have been enough reason for Hume to suppose his own reflections (at least as we know them now) to be unattractive to him without this. On the other hand, Hume would certainly have been able to absorb the *Analogy* by the time the first *Enquiry* appeared in 1748. In addition to this, by the time the ethical portions of the *Treatise* came out in 1740, Hume would have read the Dissertation 'Of the Nature of Virtue', which was an appendix to the *Analogy*, as well as the Rolls *Sermons*, and would therefore have had all Butler's ethical teachings before him.

Hume is the greatest and most systematic philosopher to have written in English, and because he is systematic in a way that Butler was not, he responds to a wide range of influences of which many are only now coming to be recognized. But there are two reasons for thinking it worthwhile to examine, and to speculate about, the effects Butler's work may have had on him. The first is that in English at least, Hume is our best, and Butler is our second best, philosopher of religion. The other is that in English, Butler is our best, and Hume is our second best, moral philosopher.

Most of us are inclined to contrast Hume and Butler in moral theory, not to assimilate them. According to the received wisdom, Butler teaches that doing one's duty is natural, whereas Hume says it is primarily artificial. Butler emphasizes the supremacy of conscience in human nature, whereas Hume's account of obligation seems to make the motive of duty derivative and secondary. Butler's ethics seems to be primarily an ethic of actions, whereas Hume's is a theory of the virtues. In general, C. D. Broad and others have won us over to the opinion that Butler is the plain man's Immanuel Kant; Hume is seen by contrast as an ancestor of Utilitarianism.

There indeed are fundamental differences in their orientation as moralists, but most of the above contrasts will not do at all. Butler is one of the five thinkers named by Hume in the Introduction to the *Treatise* as having 'begun to put the science of man on a new footing' and extend 'the application of experimental philosophy to moral subjects'. There are many ways, in fact, in which his moral theories do not merely stand in the tradition that includes Butler, but parallel Butler's in their details. I shall confine myself to their views on conscience and obligation, and their opinions on benevolence and its relation to justice.

Butler does indeed hold, as the central doctrine of his ethics, that conscience has supreme authority in human nature. So when we act in violation of what conscience dictates, our actions are contrary to our natures. This can happen because we allow a passion or affection, or another principle like self-love, to determine our choices when conscience should override it by natural right. Not only does Butler say this, but he also emphasizes what we may call the intrusiveness of conscience—he says that it is a principle which, 'without being consulted, without being advised with, magisterially exerts itself'.[4] Whatever our prior inclinations, or even prior judgements, if we are about to do something it is against, conscience functions in our natures by inserting its claim to superiority, unasked. Taken alone, this encourages a picture of Butler as holding that virtue consists in acting from what Kant called the good will—that is, acting only for the sake of duty, or from conscientiousness. It is very obvious indeed that this is not *Hume's* view of virtue. He does, it is true, recognize that we act from time to time from a sense of duty alone, but he sees this as a fact requiring special explanation. The special explanation, in brief, has two parts to it. The lesser part (lesser, that is, in terms of the space Hume gives to it) consists in an account of how the sense of duty arises: we get this account in Section I of Part II of Book III of the *Treatise*. Hume offers it in response to an imagined objection to his claim that 'no action can be virtuous, or morally good, unless there be in human nature some motive to produce it distinct from the sense of its morality' (*T* III. ii. 1. 479). He says that someone who 'feels his heart devoid' of a motive that he and we approve of, will disapprove of its absence in himself—he will, as he puts it, 'hate himself upon that account'. He will then do the appropriate action without the motive, 'from a certain sense of duty, in order to acquire, by practice, that virtuous principle, or at least to disguise to

---

[4] Butler 1990, vol. ii, Sermon 2, para. 8.

himself, as much as possible, his want of it'. So conscientiousness is an interim substitute, even a conscious substitute, for the natural motive that most people have for certain approved actions, like the care of children, but which the self-disapproving agent does not have, and wishes to cultivate. The phrasing leaves Hume's exact intentions unclear, but he is certainly attempting to treat as special exceptions to natural behaviour, actions which Butler would offer as paradigms of our true nature asserting itself.

This is the lesser part of Hume's account of conscientiousness. The larger part of his theory is developed in relation to those occasions when we do things from duty, but there is no motive normally present in our natures for which it is a substitute. These are actions done from respect for justice. Hume makes much of the fact that such actions often run counter to our natural motives; although he follows Butler in rejecting psychological egoism, he insists that the benevolence we find in human nature is too partial, or 'interested', to motivate the actions that justice requires. He denies that impartial benevolence is naturally available to us. So the sense of duty we undoubtedly have towards the requirements of justice has to be explained through human artifice. The institutions to which we adhere in just behaviour are said by Hume to arise from interest, not from duty or benevolence. The moral status which they acquire, and which finds expression in our sense of obligation towards their observance and preservation, comes about through direct or sympathetic participation in the displeasingness of violations of them, which generates disapproval. Our sense of obligation to just action, even when it is against our perceived interests, is a psychological consequence of our disapproval of the unpleasant consequences of *un*just actions. This account neatly catches the unlovableness of justice, and also the sense of intrusiveness that goes with the recognition of an unwelcome obligation.

I cannot think it doubtful that Butler was one of those Hume had in mind in his theory of justice; and it is certainly true that his account of conscientious action makes it something largely artificial, rather than natural, in its origin. But let us look at some details.

## II

What does Butler's doctrine of the supremacy of conscience in human nature amount to? In the first place, the notion of conscience that he uses is rather wider than the common-sense notion of the independent voice that interrupts us when we are about to transgress. Butler's conscience does that, but also has wider functions. If we combine what he says in the *Sermons* with what he says about conscience in the 'Dissertation on Virtue', conscience becomes our general faculty of moral reflection, and makes judgements about both actions and characters, our own and other people's; its judgements are said to express approval and disapproval. So Butler's official and considered view is that conscience is our power of moral judgement, though he often relapses into the common-sense usage according to which it is our power of making judgements about our own actions exclusively. By contrast, Hume insists that approval and disapproval are directed not to actions, but to characters, both our own and others', but he is not (in my view) any more carefully observant of his official view than Butler is of his, using forms of words frequently which suggest we approve and disapprove of individual acts. The most common terms that Hume offers as the expression of moral approval and disapproval are the terms 'virtuous' and 'vicious', as we would expect; but these are also offered by Butler, along with the more natural 'right' and 'wrong'.[5] This parallel inconstancy about the objects of approval and disapproval is matched by something else that Butler's readers overlook: that he has the same view as Hume about the desirability of non-moral motives for those actions of which conscience approves. He does not hold the Kantian view that conscientiousness is the motive which uniquely guarantees moral goodness. His view is that conscience normally functions by approving or disapproving the performance of actions which are for the most part already prompted by other motives, such as desires or fears; but that, on those occasions when conscience vetoes actions that other principles or affections incline us to do, or indicates the rightness of actions which those other principles incline us to avoid, it both can, and in the proper course of nature will, supply an independent motive of its own that overrides these principles and inclinations. That does not mean that he judges it to be best that we do the right thing from conscience alone without other inclinations. It does not even clearly mean that it is better to do the right thing from conscience alone than from desire alone. He clearly believes that it is best

[5] See Dissertation II, 'Of the Nature of Virtue' appended to the *Analogy of Religion*; Butler 1900, vol. i.

to have *both* motives—something Hume's view suggests is impossible. Butler identifies virtue with doing what conscience dictates, but this is not the same as identifying virtue with conscientiousness.[6]

What Butler does not do, of course, is suggest that the occurrence of actions done from duty alone is a puzzle that needs explanation: to urge that such behaviour is natural is to insist that there is nothing puzzling about it, and that any puzzles philosophers may feel about such actions are theoretical obfuscations of what we all know perfectly well. No doubt he would have thought Hume's reason for puzzlement to be obfuscatory in this way. Hume's reason, it will be recalled, is that since moral approval and disapproval are passions that follow on our discernment of the character behind actions, they presuppose non-moral motives already to be present, so actions that seem to have morality alone as their motives are anomalous. With his usual concern to confine himself wholly to the practical, Butler sidesteps the question of whether conscience is a matter of reason or sentiment, but there can be no doubt that he believed it at least to include the former, and that its approval and disapproval of actions is due to an independent discernment of their being right or wrong; he insists, indeed, that it discerns them to be right or wrong in themselves, without regard to their consequences.[7]

This even leads him to emphasize that conscience must win out over benevolence. Here he says things that once again have unexpected resemblances to Hume's views. Hume agrees with Butler that we are not wholly selfish (*T* III. ii. 2. 486–7), and that we are often benevolent. But he insists that our benevolence is always interested—directed, that is, towards our families or friends or fellow-citizens. He rejects the belief in the love of mankind in general:

In general, it may be affirm'd, that there is no such passion in human minds, as the love of mankind, merely as such, independent of personal qualities, of services, or of relation to ourself. (*T* III. ii. 1. 481)

I incline to think his doctrine of extensive sympathy compromises this rejection, but he never formally retracts it. This puts him at odds with Butler, who believed that his defence of benevolence served to establish not only that we have impulses that are good for others, but also that we have a general wish for the good of mankind. Butler

[6] Sermon 1, para. 8.　　[7] 'Dissertation' paras. 2 and 6.

calls it the love of one's neighbour. His account of it makes it more
like what Hume says about extensive sympathy: for Butler, the limited scope of human emotions means that the love of mankind must
express itself in a wish to benefit those with whom we have to do—
our *neighbours*. This gives benevolence what he calls a 'less general
and nearer object' than mankind as a whole.[8] But he retains the core
concept of a benevolence that is *impartial*, which Hume insists
actual benevolence never is. Butler thinks that we do, sometimes,
show benevolence towards people with whom we have to do, just
because they are people, not because of some other relationship that
binds us to them.

But whichever of them is right about this, they still agree that we
need conscientious action because of the shortcomings of benevolence. Hume holds that because benevolence is partial, and therefore confined, a different motive is needed to make us act in the
impartial way that justice requires. He says this special motive to
justice would not be necessary if impartial benevolence were universal.
It is strange and striking to see that Butler denies this, with passion,
in the famous concluding section of the Dissertation. Here he insists
that we need conscience because no mistake could be more terrible
than to suppose that virtue could consist in unrestrained benevolence. His reason is that we do not know enough to tell the
consequences of our actions, even our wholly benevolent actions.

Hume says we need the sense of duty because the acts that a sense
of duty dictates are the acts impartial benevolence would dictate,
if we ever felt it. Dutifulness is a substitute for benevolence where
the confinedness of the latter prevents it from operating. Butler does
not think benevolence is always confined in this manner, but firmly
rejects the suggestion that conscience is a mere substitute for it. What
conscience provides is the identification of those right acts which
benevolence itself is not able to determine with assurance, even when
we seek the good of others.

So far, then, there are more similarities than traditional readings
might lead us to expect, between what Butler and Hume say about
conscientiousness and its relation to other motives, and about the
limits of benevolence, even though the wider claims of their respect-
ive ethical teachings are very different. It is tempting to say that the
detailed likenesses are due to a shared power of moral observation,

---

[8] Sermon 12, para. 3.

and the differences are due to the fact that Butler was a Christian thinker and Hume was not. While this is obviously true, it is worth a deeper exploration.

## III

I return first to the fact that Hume denies the reality of impartial benevolence and Butler asserts it, and to the fact that Hume's account of duty derives it from interest and Butler's does not. In spite of these things, it is Butler who is commonly criticized for his steady concern to prove that following conscience is to the agent's own advantage—that conscience and self-love point the same way.

There are two reasons for this. The first is that Butler is entirely a practical thinker. His aim in moral philosophy is to encourage the *practice* of virtue. He attacks psychological egoism because he sees it as a theory which has gained fashionable currency among his audience, and has thereby persuaded some of them not to practise the virtue which they know very well they should practise. As a Christian priest, he sees this self-deceiving confusion as a great spiritual danger, and wants to argue them out of it. But, for the same reason, he is quite willing to reinforce the supremacy of conscience by appealing, at the same time, to the very self-interest he has just shown not to be the only possible motive. He is not naïve enough to think that by refuting a trendy excuse for not following the promptings of conscience and benevolence, he has necessarily strengthened them; and he believes that by doing what virtue would make us do, even for another reason, we are going some distance towards acquiring it. So he has no reason to refrain from arguing that doing our duty is to our advantage.

But his doing this has left his readers uncomfortable, because he seems so resolute about it. If following conscience were indeed so *natural*, would showing its coincidence with self-love be as important to him as this? This brings us to his second, and deeper, reason for pressing this point: as a Christian theologian, anxious not only to persuade the readers of the ethical sermons to practise virtue, but to persuade the readers of the *Analogy of Religion* to practise the Christian religion, he believes that the justice and benevolence of God would not permit virtue to be against the interests of those who practise it. This is both the explanation of his apparent appeal to the advantageousness of benevolence and conscience, and the explanation of his anxiety to deny the adequacy of benevolence alone as a guide in the moral life. Benevolence and conscience must be ultimately advantageous, because the goodness of God's purposes must ensure this, even if we cannot see how; but the fact that our knowledge of God's purposes is limited is the reason it is right to follow the law he has laid down in our conscience, even when it might *appear* better for mankind in general for us to do something else. The same Christian theology that leads him to hold that impartial benevolence is a possible motive, leads him to warn us of the risks of using it as the sole criterion of right choice. Butler's account of human nature is theological. I need hardly say that Hume's account is not.

## IV

Hume likens his philosophical enquiries to those of a group of philosophers that includes Butler. Both he and Butler contrast their ethical enquiries with the a priori moral theorizing into the eternal fitness of things that was propounded by Samuel Clarke. But the latter contrast is quite different in the two cases. Hume attacks Clarke's moral philosophy as an empty form of metaphysics that can do nothing to explain or justify moral choice. Butler does not only refrain from attacking it when he distinguishes his own exercises in moral psychology from it; he says that these two ways of treating the subject of morals 'exceedingly strengthen and enforce each other'.[9] In other words, he *approves* of Clarke's supposed demonstrations that 'vice is contrary to the nature and reason of things', and is merely seeking a complementary method of combating vice by showing it violates human nature. If we needed confirmation of this, we could find it in an important methodological passage near the close of the *Analogy*, where he emphasizes that he has omitted a thing of the utmost importance in which he believes, namely 'the moral fitness and unfitness of actions, prior to all will whatever'—something which Clarke makes central, but Hume scornfully rejects (*T* III. iii. 1. *Analogy* II viii). So when he offers an account of the place of conscience, benevolence, and self-love in human nature the conception of human nature with which he is working

---

[9] Preface to Sermons, para. 12.

reflects the theistic metaphysic that he shares with Clarke, as well as containing the empirical elements that enabled Hume to claim philosophical kinship with him.

Butler always argues from positions that he shares with his audience, or from positions he thinks they hold, even if he does not. In the moral sermons, he assumes a common knowledge of what conscience commands, and goes on from there to argue with his audience that they have no good reason to suppose that the blandishments of temptation, or the cynical muddles of psychological egoism, can supply overriding grounds to neglect these commands. In the course of his arguments, he assumes a view of human nature that he considers his audience to share with him. It is easier to see this in the *Analogy* than in the *Sermons*, but the same view of our nature is present in both. It is a view that he holds in common with the Deists who were his primary opponents in the later work. It is a *teleological* view. He does not appeal, in either work, to explicitly *Christian* doctrines. He does, however, take it for granted that his audience would share with him the conviction that our natures are created by God, and that, although we may not know as much as we would like about the functions of the various principles within them, we can assume that they are there for a purpose. As free agents, we can act against that purpose, but it will exist, and the nature that we have will, accordingly, be attuned to it, so that such action will not be *natural*. It will be contrary to our *real nature*, that is, to the purposes for which we have the endowments we have, rather than to the purposes we may choose to follow instead. Our real nature is a nature we actually *have*, even if we often violate it: Broad is not quite right to say Butler is talking of *ideal* human nature.[10] But he is not just giving an empirical description of the elements we find in ourselves either. He is giving a teleological description of them. This description enables him to say that if conscience makes us uneasy about following an inclination on some occasion, when it does not make us uneasy about following that same inclination at other times, this fact has a purpose—that is, it is somehow for our good, however strong the competition might be. It is this teleological metaphysic that makes him worry about the dictates of conscience being in our interest when they may not appear to be. It is not that conscience has to be subordinated to self-love, which he denies: it

[10] Broad 1930, 57–60.

is that when conscience wins out over self-love (or, for that matter, benevolence) it *must* be better for us, because the authoritativeness we can discern in the functioning of conscience, has to be there for a purpose. It follows from all this, of course, that self-love can make mistakes, and that benevolence can too. (Perhaps even conscience can make some, but it cannot make many.) For all this to come out right, God must see to it that it ultimately does. In such circumstances we can expect to be able to see quite frequently that duty is advantageous, but not to see it every time. Butler is, as Schneewind has said, the classical exponent of the 'Divine Corporation' view of ethics: that each of us ultimately benefits from the prosperity of the moral community, whose Manager alone sees the purpose of each order.[11]

Lacking any belief in the Divine Corporation, Hume has to give a quite different account of how duty has apparent authority over us, when it seems to conflict with self-interest and benevolence. It cannot be one in which it is the supreme moral motive, and it has to be one in which it serves to reinforce the practices put in place by other motives. His account is primarily an empirical description of how it comes to have the place in our conduct that it does, and it takes the form, as it must, of showing how the approval and disapproval we exhibit attach themselves to those characteristics which we find to have useful or agreeable consequences. It must take this form, because Hume discerns no creator's purposes in the nature he describes. The result is a much more detailed moral psychology than Butler's. It is also a moral psychology which I find more difficult to view as a plausible *justification* of moral choices, as distinct from an explanation of the fact that we attach approval to them. I shall return to this, briefly, in conclusion. It is not only *Butler's* teleology Hume is trying to avoid, but it will certainly have been one of his objectives to provide an alternative to it.


V


All this would seem to add weight to the common view that Hume has Butler in his sights in his philosophy of religion. Butler has even been identified by no less a scholar than Mossner, as the prototype of Cleanthes in the *Dialogues*. This view has been questioned—by

---

[11] Schneewind 1984.

Nelson Pike, and in detail by Anders Jeffner.[12] The rather complicated relationship between the ethics of the two thinkers suggests that
the relationship will be complex in this case also.

I think a straightforward identification, of the sort suggested by
Mossner, is impossible. If we look at Butler's position in *The Analogy
of Religion*, the first thing that strikes one, because it is one of the first
things Butler says, is that he is going to assume the existence of God
to be common ground between himself and the Deists with whom
he is debating.[13] He makes it clear that he regards God's existence
as having been proved both by a priori arguments and a posteriori
arguments—that is, both by the sort of Design argument Hume puts
into the mouth of Cleanthes, and by the kind of Cosmological argument used by Samuel Clarke. Mossner identifies Clarke with Demea,
who reproduces this argument in Part IX of the *Dialogues*.[14]

Here, then, are two major differences: unlike Cleanthes, Butler does
not *use* any argument to prove God's existence, since he assumes it
beforehand, and unlike Cleanthes, he accepts the cogency of arguments
of both kinds, as he had accepted abstract arguments in favour of moral
virtue as well as empirical ones, while only using the latter himself.

These differences are the result of the purpose of the *Analogy*. Butler
wants, in that work, to take the natural theology he shares with the
Deists and then to show that there is no good reason for anyone
who concedes this much to reject the special claims of the Christian
Church which the Deists rejected. His argument proceeds by *analogy*:
an analogy between certain observed features of the natural world
we see around us, and the divine creation as a whole—that is, this
world and the Next taken together. I shall call this *religious analogy*,
though Butler does not call it this, in order to distinguish it from
the other sort of analogical argument to which he assmilates it, which
is what we now call induction. In proceeding this way, Butler is doing
what he always does, namely arguing with his target audience where
they are. They think they have proved God's existence, but they
also think that the God whose existence they have proved cannot
be the self-revealing interventionist deity of the Christian tradition.
Butler wants to refute this negative inference.

The analogical argument he uses to refute it leans heavily on what
he and the Deists share in common, namely the supposed fact that

---

[12] See Pike's edition of the *Dialogues*, 1970, and Jeffner 1966.
[13] *Analogy*, Preface para. 6.
[14] *Analogy*, Preface para. 8 and I, vi, para. 3.

the world is created by a rational and purposive Mind. From this common premiss, Butler is able to argue, with effectiveness, that the whole creation, seen and unseen, is quite likely to be a system, and that we will be able to discern some of the laws and character of that system, though only in a fragmentary way. Our ignorance of many of the details is enough to undermine the Deists' confidence in claiming what God would *not* do, yet our limited powers of discernment enable us to detect observable signs of the moral intent of what God *has* done, and to see that it might well embrace the specific intentions of which the Christian revelation speaks. The contextual effectiveness of this analogical argument depends on the common Deistic premiss in two ways. First, only if this world and the next are both the handiwork of one consistent and rational Mind is there any reason to suppose the purposes at work in the one will be integrated with those ascribed to the other. Second, only if the world is the handiwork of such a Mind have we any reason to ascribe purposes to those regularities in it which we find remarkable, such as the (alleged) usefulness of acting virtuously, or the (allegedly) educative value of enduring evil. The argument Butler is engaged in here, like the one he uses for the advantageousness of following conscience, depends on the *assumption* of a systematic teleology. He makes no secret of this, but reminds his opponents (who are supposed to concede it) that he and they both believe it.

There is a further feature of Butler's argument that is of great importance, both in itself and in relation to Hume. Butler's critics on the theological right often feel he concedes too much to the Deists. They think that in order to refute their attacks on revelation, he ascribes too much power to our natural cognitive faculties. One place where this is noticeable is in his insistence on the continuity between natural and revealed religion, and between natural and revealed morality. In defending the credentials of Christian revelation, Butler maintains stoutly that much of it merely repeats the content of natural religion —that is, it tells us over again truths about God that human reason can discover for itself, and has. This continuity extends to the ethical sphere. Butler believes, of course, that conscience is implanted in our natures by God. But in implanting it, God has given us *natural* knowledge of right and wrong. We do not need *revelation* to make our daily moral decisions; and Butler has no trace of a Divine Command theory of morality.[15] What revelation does do, however,

---

[15] *Analogy* II, viii, para. 11; also Penelhum 1985, 77–8.

besides repeating what conscience can tell us without it, is to tell us some further facts about our relation to God, from which our consciences can infer additional moral duties that would otherwise escape us—namely those of worship, piety, and sacramental participation. But these are duties which we can discern once the theological truths on which they are based are available to us. There is no neo-orthodox nonsense about Christian faith demolishing secular morality: to Butler one is continuous with the other.

I have now said enough to offer some speculations about Butler's relationship to Cleanthes. I assume that in the *Dialogues*, Hume is, for the most part, to be identified with Philo, and also that Philo undergoes at least the appearance of a change of opinion in Part XII.

I begin with the fact that Butler seems to have accepted both a priori and a posteriori arguments for God's existence, but to have used neither. At the outset of Part II Demea says the forthcoming argument can only be about the nature of God, not his being, and Philo agrees, even mouthing some bits of the Cosmological Proof in support. Cleanthes, ignoring these 'circumlocutions', immediately plunges into his opening statement of the Design argument, saying that it proves God's being and his nature at once. When the a priori argument is examined, and brusquely rejected, in Part X, it is Demea who offers it, and Cleanthes who refutes it. What are we to make of all this? Partly, I think, this: Mossner is probably right that one of Demea's roles is to represent Clarke (though it is only fair to say that Clarke was cleverer). Hume is happy to dismiss Clarke's natural theology with general considerations from his own system about the impossibility of proving matters of fact a priori. What Cleanthes represents will then be Butler, *minus* the covert appeal to Clarke's a priori arguments for God. For Hume would say that if the apparently empirical appeals to observation that Butler makes against the Deists have no a priori proofs of God behind them, then the same method of observation that we make to discern the signs of the purposes of the God we presuppose have also to serve to prove his very being. This has many consequences, and I cannot explore the details here; but one obvious consequence is that the evils and obscurities which Butler was able to use against the Deists and in favour of Christianity, now have to be confronted before the being of God is admitted, so that Cleanthes emerges as the sort of facile optimist that the historical Butler was not. Even more importantly, religious analogy collapses. As Philo argues immediately Cleanthes concludes his first statement, analogies between phenomena we detect *in* the world and alleged features of the world as a whole are very shaky ones—if, that is, the existence of the divine creative mind is not already taken for granted, but has itself to be established by a posteriori methods. If Hume intends to make any comment on Butler in creating the *persona* of Cleanthes, the comment would be that without the a priori case for God's being that Butler assumed, his a posteriori arguments about God's nature and purposes have to presuppose that His existence is established by natural, *non-religious* analogy. It is, of course, the burden of the *Dialogues* as a whole that this cannot be done.

At least, this is the burden of the first eleven Parts of the *Dialogues*. One returns, as always, to Part XII. I have long ago decided that I have no settled view about it, but I now offer two suggestions on the limited question of what it shows us about Hume and Butler.

My first suggestion is this. Whether or not Hume follows him in this, *Philo* in Part XII seems to me to accept what John Gaskin has called attenuated Deism.[16] He seems to accept, that is, that 'the cause or causes of order in the universe probably bear some remote analogy to human intelligence'. It is part of the minimal Deism that Philo seems to accept that we have no reason to believe that this cause, or these causes, of order in the universe bear any resemblance to other qualities of the human mind. So no evidence exists to justify ascribing *moral* qualities to the deity. Hence the end result of the Design argument is that there is probably a God or gods, but we cannot ascribe any qualities to him, or to them, that can connect his nature, or theirs, with our moral choices. This is the position from which Butler *starts* in the *Analogy*. Hume's verdict is that if one does not presuppose a priori arguments for God, this is also where one ends. I am not sure whether Hume really wants to concede even this much, but I am sure he wants to concede no more. Here Butler *is* represented in Cleanthes, and Philo has defeated him.

But the defeat is concealed within all those ambiguous remarks that suggest that Philo has just been playing Sceptical games until now, and is conceding victory to Cleanthes now that Demea is out of the way.[17] What are we to make of *this*? Here I think we have to place Cleanthes in the context of the lengthy and highly coded argument about 'true religion'. As we all know, Hume thought revealed religion, as he perceived it in the churches around him, was a negative and not a positive moral force. In particular, it encouraged the

[16] Gaskin 1978, 166–78.        [17] See Chapters 10 and 11.

'monkish virtues' of piety and mortification, which are useful and agreeable to no one. For all his orthodoxy, no one could cast the historical Joseph Butler, who was as much of an enemy of 'enthusiasm', in his own quiet way, as Hume was, in this role of moral spoiler.[18] But unfortunately, Butler's arguments were designed to defend the very revealed traditions that Hume saw in this way. His solution is to have Cleanthes, who, cruelly, does represent Butler here, offer a notorious account of true religion:

> The proper office of religion is to regulate the heart of men, humanize their conduct, infuse the spirit of temperance, order, and obedience; and as its operation is silent, and only enforces the motives of morality and justice, it is in danger of being overlooked, and confounded with these other motives. When it distinguishes itself, and acts as a separate principle over men, it has departed from its proper sphere, and has become only a cover to faction and ambition. (*D* XII. 220)

Hume has taken conscience, our natural principle of moral discernment, and ensured its theological emptiness by destroying the theological bases on which, in Butler's view, its discernment of special religious duties would have to depend. He has made Cleanthes identify true religious morality with secular ethics. Butler is open to this treatment; but it is concealed from him, and from Cleanthes, by their belief in the continuity of natural and revealed religion. Hume leaves it to Philo to rail, in the face of Cleanthes' warnings, against the moral dangers of real (or 'false') religious morality. Put more simply, Hume is prepared to live with minimal Deism, and pay lip-service to the reality of God, if the moral consequences of so doing are admitted by those who believe in God, to be zero.

So Cleanthes is not a literary reproduction of the historical Bishop Butler. But he represents Hume's judgement of the theological emptiness of rational theism, and Hume's willingness to live with rational theism if it remains morally unproductive in practice.

## VI

I conclude with a further speculation. It is that Hume tacitly admits to a motive for *welcoming* 'true religion' rather than merely *tolerating*

---

[18] The most famous item of evidence is Butler's conversation with Wesley. It is reproduced from Wesley's *Journal* by Gladstone in his edition of Butler, vol. 2, 366 f.

it. In his account of its function he says it enforces the motives of morality and justice. 'Enforces' here has to mean 'reinforces,' for Cleanthes' point is that true religion does not add extra duties, but helps us to perform those we learn about without it. If that is right, then true religion will help to do something that Hume's ethics needs; namely, to provide a practical, if not a theoretical, response, to the 'sensible knave' of Section IX of the moral *Enquiry*. The sensible knave is one who understands the sources of justice, but then decides that there are some occasions when he can follow his own interests by violating its requirements. If its conventions owe their very being to our interests, how is he to be answered? Hume concedes that if the knave is determined as well as sensible, he cannot be. The best we can do is to lecture him about the value of universality. But he knows that already. *Butler* could tell him that if his conscience says the action he proposes is wrong, he knows very well what he should do. Hume's knave has already rejected this appeal, even if it is a sound one. In this situation, which is far from a mere theoretical fancy, there would be something to be said for 'true religion', and therefore something to be said for the Cleanthes of this world who propound it.

For they represent an institution that, in the right hands, reinforces the conventions the sensible knave is preparing to flout. So Hume has a motive, quite near the surface, for leaving true religion alone, even if he does not believe in it himself. I do not suggest that Hume is one of those who think that if God did not exist, everything would be permitted. Most of his ethics is designed to prove just the opposite. But he may very well believe that the price of the death of God would be the birth of more sensible knaves. And how right he is![19]

[19] That this thought is not wholly alien to Hume's thinking may be inferred from a remark in *EU* xi. 147. Speaking in his own person to the friend who has invoked Epicurus to propound arguments against the practical relevance of natural theology, he says, 'You conclude, that religious doctrines and reasonings *can* have no influence upon life, because they *ought* to have no influence; never considering, that men reason not in the manner that you do, but draw many consequences from the belief of a divine Existence, and suppose that the Deity will inflict punishments on vice, and bestow rewards on virtue, beyond what appear in the ordinary course of nature. Whether this reasoning of theirs be just or not, is no matter. Its influence on their life and conduct must still be the same. And, those, who attempt to disabuse them of such prejudices, may, for aught I know, be good reasoners, but I cannot allow them to be good citizens and politicians; since they free men from one restraint upon their passions, and make the infringement of the laws of society, in one respect, more easy and secure.'

# 13

# Human Nature and Truth:
# Hume and Pascal

IT may seem strange for anyone to combine in one title the names of two such radically opposite thinkers as Blaise Pascal and David Hume. This may seem to be a combination that takes us well beyond the limits of profitable comparison. But I shall suggest that when we juxtapose some of the fundamental aspects of their thought, the result is instructive in several ways. First, though least in real importance, I think it becomes possible to make some conjectures about direct influence from Pascal in the seventeenth century to Hume in the eighteenth. I say 'conjectures' for several reasons. One of them is that Hume is a master of non-citation when it suits him, and the overt references to Pascal that we find in his writings do not suggest direct influences. Second, since we are dealing here with two figures of the very highest genius, the one the greatest of all Christian apologists, and the other the most considerable of all the philosophical secularizers of modern times, it is instructive to find them offering totally opposed inferences and value-judgements, indeed totally opposed life choices, on the basis of remarkably similar understandings of the inner workings of the human spirit. There is no doubt at all that they would have disliked one another extremely had they been contemporaries; but it is equally beyond reasonable doubt that they share many perceptions of the human condition, even though they offer wholly contrary prescriptions for human ills. Between them they represent two poles in the debate over the nature of humankind in modern times. Between them they define modernity.

The third way in which I think we can derive instruction from the juxtaposition of the thought of these two men follows from the second. Although each is of the greatest importance in the historical understanding of the seventeenth and eighteenth centuries, each has a stature that obviously transcends this. The debate between them is one that still continues; and I shall suggest that, whichever side of the debate one is inclined to favour, the comparison between them prompts disturbing reflections about the nature of this debate itself. I shall conclude by airing a few of these.

A few brief personal comments. I come to this theme as a philosopher who read Hume in his very first year as a student of the subject, as most philosophy students do, and who came in later years to have occasion to study his system in some detail, and to take a small part in the very vital debates about the nature of that system that are still in progress now. I claim no parallel specialist knowledge of Pascal. I came to study him in the course of my reflections on questions in the philosophy of religion, and also in personal reflections on religious issues; and any assertions I may make in what follows about what he says are merely those of an uninformed enquirer confronted by someone of unique psychological and literary power, who has been stimulated by this to try to learn something about his times and his objectives from the works of other scholars.

In summary: I shall suggest that Hume's philosophical system contains within it careful and elaborate responses to many of Pascal's fundamental claims, which are only possible because the two men hold many detailed theses in common. Before arguing this, I should first look at Hume's direct references to Pascal, such as they are; and I should say something about the important historical matter of how far Pascal's thought was available to the world of letters in Hume's day.


I


Hume comments on Pascal in only two places. The first is in a lengthy footnote to his famous Section 'Of Miracles' in the *Enquiry Concerning Human Understanding*. While the primary target of Hume's argument in that Section is the belief in the miracle-stories of the New Testament, especially the Resurrection narratives, he also takes time to comment, adversely of course, on alleged miracles of his own time. The note is mostly concerned with miracles associated with the tomb of the Abbé Paris; but the concluding paragraph is about 'a miracle, wrought on the niece of the famous Pascal, whose sanctity of life, as well as extraordinary capacity, is well known' (*EU* x. n.346). This event, dated 1656, was the miracle of the Holy Thorn, in which Pascal's niece, Marguerite Périer, appeared to have been cured of a lachrymal tumour when it was touched by a relic said to be a fragment of the original Crown of Thorns. This cure helped to cement Pascal's loyalty to the Jansenists of Port-Royal, where it took place. As we would expect, the story is treated by Hume with derision.[1] He probably singles out this story in order to strike a blow against the views about miracle testimony found in the Port-Royal *Logic*.[2] Pascal figures in his comments as an example of a person of exceptional intelligence who is nevertheless convinced by a phenomenon Hume takes it for granted his mostly-Protestant readers will dismiss.

The second mention of Pascal is lengthier, and more polite, but still very negative. We find it in a Dialogue that Hume appends to his *Enquiry Concerning the Principles of Morals* (*EM* Dialogue 342–3). The theme of this dialogue is the great variation in moral customs throughout the world, which leads people in one society to commend conduct as virtuous that would be condemned as vicious in other societies. The imaginary interlocutor who parades a variety of examples of this moral diversity is called Palamedes. Hume tells Palamedes that in spite of these variations, every human quality that is commended as virtuous is one that is judged to be either useful or agreeable, either to the person who has it, or to others: in a word, to have utility. Disagreements are all about what qualities are useful or agreeable; everyone agrees that it is usefulness and

[1] 'In short, the supernatural cure was so uncontestable, that it saved, for a time, that famous monastery from the ruin with which it was threatened by the Jesuits. Had it been a cheat, it had certainly been detected by such sagacious and powerful antagonists, and must have hastened the ruin of the contrivers. Our divines, who can build up such a formidable castle from such despicable materials; what a prodigious fabric could they have reared from these and any other circumstances, which I have not mentioned! How often would the great names of Pascal, Racine, Arnaud, Nicole, have resounded in our ears? But if they be wise, they had better adopt the miracle, as being more worth, a thousand times, than all the rest of their collection. Besides, it may serve very much to their purpose. For that miracle was really performed by the authentic touch of an authentic holy prickle of the holy thorn, which composed the holy crown, which, &c.' (*EU* x. n. 346).
[2] See Arnauld and Nicole 1965, 335–51; English version Arnauld 1964 edn., 337–54. See also Jones 1982, 44–76. I am indebted here to MacIntyre 1994; this essay deals with the parallels between Hume and Pascal that I explore below, parallels that MacIntyre alluded to previously in *After Virtue* (MacIntyre 1981, 52).

agreeableness that should be praised and cultivated. But Palamedes has a problem: this may well be true for the 'maxims of ordinary life and conduct', but what about '*artificial* lives and manners'? He explains that he is thinking of those whose lives are determined primarily by the influence of philosophical theory, or of religion. Philosophical theory led to eccentric moral attitudes in the ancient world; in modern times its place has been taken by religion, since philosophy has become a minority pastime. His ancient example of moral eccentricity is Diogenes; his modern example is Pascal, whom he chooses, he says, because he was a 'man of parts and genius . . . and perhaps, too, a man of virtue, had he allowed his virtuous inclinations to have exerted and displayed themselves'. Both these men showed contempt for common practices and values, yet both 'have met with general admiration in their different ages, and have been proposed as models of imitation. Where then', he continues, 'is the universal standard of morals, which you talk of?' Hume's cryptic answer to this question is that in these cases 'the natural principles of their mind play not with the same regularity, as if left to themselves, free from the illusions of religious superstition or philosophical enthusiasm'.

While it seems clear enough that Hume is less severe on Diogenes' philosophically motivated oddities than on Pascal's religiously motivated ones, we must not forget that one of the aspects of religion in his own time that most angered him was the fact that it had absorbed so much philosophy into it.[3] It is in part the very admixture of philosophy in Pascal's religious apologetic that makes it a formidable target for him. In the dialogue we are examining, however, the eccentricities he finds in Pascal are all of the superstitious and life-denying kind. Pascal, he says, was determined never to forget his 'wants and infirmities', showed a humility and 'hatred of himself', practiced austerities 'merely for their own sake', refused innocent pleasures 'even in private', and tried to cultivate an indifference even to those closest to him, 'and to love and speak well of his enemies'. He sums up Pascal's conduct by saying, 'The most ridiculous superstitions directed Pascal's faith and practice; and an extreme contempt of this life, in comparison of the future, was the chief foundation of his conduct,' (*EM* Dialogue 343).

---

[3] On this theme, see *NHR*, esp. sections VI–XIII, where Hume compares polytheism to monotheism, to the latter's disadvantage.

While these comments are not perhaps derisory, they are certainly as strongly negative as the judgements implied in Hume's remarks about the Holy Thorn. Certainly nothing here suggests Hume could have been *influenced* by the person he is describing, and Pascal's life and behaviour is used as a source of cautionary tales. So Hume seems to be following the estimate of Pascal that was common in his day, and that had been expressed most famously by Voltaire in his *Lettres Philosophiques*:

Il me paraît qu'en général l'esprit dans lequel M. Pascal écrivit ces *Pensées* était de montrer l'homme dans un jour odieux. Il s'acharne à nous peindre tous méchants et malheureux. Il écrit contre la nature humaine à peu près comme il écrivait contre les Jésuites . . . J'ose prendre le parti de l'humanité contre ce misanthrope sublime . . .[4]

On this view, Pascal's estimate of himself, and of others, was that of a scientific genius led astray by superstition into morbid estimates of our condition that could only be excused by the fact of his sickness. 'Hélas encore! hélas! Pascal, on voit bien que vous êtes malade.'[5]

So if we confine our attention to the two passages where Hume considers Pascal explicitly, it is tempting to suppose that he merely thinks of him as Voltaire does.[6] His comments could well have been based, as far as this evidence goes, either on Voltaire's very superficial

[4] 'It seems to me that in general the spirit in which M. Pascal wrote the *Pensées* was that of showing mankind in a hateful light. He incites himself to portray us all as wicked and wretched. He writes against human nature almost as he wrote against the Jesuits . . . I dare to take the side of humanity gainst this sublime misanthropist' (Voltaire 1956 edn., 141, my trans.). For a discussion of Voltaire's attack on Pascal, see Waterman 1970.
[5] Voltaire 1956 edn., 286. This comment comes from later remarks on the *Pensées*, dating from 1777, but they summarize perfectly the patronizing judgements of the earlier set.
[6] See Jones 1982, 198n. It is interesting to note that Hume's negative comments on Pascal in the first *Enquiry* drew fire from a Scottish source. George Anderson took exception to them in an anonymous volume entitled *An Estimate of the Profit and Loss of Religion,* published in Edinburgh in 1753. In a chapter called 'Of the Personal Advantages and Disadvantages of Religion', Anderson says that natural religion teaches the life to come is of more consequence than this one, but that this does not dectract from its value as a source of moral virtue; and adds the comment that Hume's own analysis of virtue as what leads to approbation is one that should lead him to ascribe it to Pascal because of his spiritual achievements. Anderson's attacks on Hume were among the causes of the unsuccessful attempts to have him formally censured by the General Assembly of the Church of Scotland in 1755 and 1756. See Mossner 1970, ch. 25.

criticisms, or on the information and comments in Bayle's article on
Pascal in his *Dictionary*. But I think there is reason to suppose Hume
had read and pondered Pascal for himself.


## II


We can, in the first instance, find strong Pascal-like overtones in one
of the most important and revealing parts of Hume's major work,
the *Treatise of Human Nature*. I refer to the concluding Section of
the first Book, where Hume describes the 'philosophical melancholy
and delirium' into which he is thrown by his sceptical reflections.
The popular image of Hume as a corpulent and rather frivolous
thinker who does not take philosophical questions with their proper
seriousness is as wide of the mark as the popular image of Pascal
that presents him as an other-wordly hater of society. Just as the
latter makes us overlook how much Pascal was involved in the world
of science and letters, and eagerly demanded his proper place in it,
in the period before his second conversion, so the popular picture
of Hume makes us overlook the fact that his lightness of manner and
emphasis on the limits of philosophy was a stance assumed deliberately by a person of somewhat depressive temperament, who had been
brought to the edge of breakdown by his philosophical enquiries.[7]
In the concluding Section of Book I of the *Treatise* he expresses the
anxiety at the heart of philosophical questioning in language that
Pascal may have taught him:

I am first affrighted and confounded with that forelorn solitude, in which
I am plac'd in my philosophy, and fancy myself some strange uncouth monster, who not being able to mingle and unite in society, has been expell'd
all human commerce, and left utterly abandon'd and disconsolate. Fain
wou'd I run into the crowd for shelter and warmth; but cannot prevail with
myself to mix with such deformity. I call upon others to join me, in order
to make a company apart; but no one will hearken to me. Every one keeps
at a distance, and dreads that storm, which beats upon me from every side.
(*T* I. iv. 7. 264)

Again:

---

[7] See the famous letter to an unnamed physician in *LDH* I, 12–18.

The *intense* view of these manifold contradictions and imperfections in human reason has so wrought upon me, and heated my brain, that I am ready to reject all belief and reasoning, and can look upon no opinion even as more probable or likely than another. Where am I, or what? From what causes do I derive my existence, and to what condition shall I return? Whose favour shall I court, and whose anger must I dread? What beings surround me? and on whom have I any influence, or who have any influence on me? I am confounded with all these questions, and begin to fancy myself in the most deplorable condition imaginable, inviron'd with the deepest darkness, and utterly depriv'd of the use of every member and faculty. (*T* I. iv. 7. 269)

To the modern reader of Pascal these make one think of the following very famous passage:

Quand je considère la petite durée de ma vie absorbée dans l'éternité précédente et suivante—*memoria hospitis unius diei praeteriuntis*—le petit espace que je remplis et même que je vois abîmé dans l'infinie immensitée des espaces que j'ignore et que m'ignorent, je m'effraye et m'étonne de me voir ici plutôt que là, car il n'y a point pourquoi ici plutôt que là, pourquoi à présent plutôt que lors. Qui m'y a mis? Par l'ordre et la conduite de qui ce lieu et ce temps a(-t) il été destiné à moi?[8]

This in turn makes us all recall the briefer and even more famous:

Le silence éternel de ces espaces infinis m'effraie (201/206).

So if we can concede that there is more philosophical bewilderment in Pascal's cosmic terrors, and more existential *angst* in Hume's epistemological perplexities, than the standard history-books tell us, it is not fanciful to think that the later thinker is echoing the earlier. With this is mind, a more specific echo can then strike us with some force. Both writers have occasion to offer critical estimates of the Hellenistic schools of Stoicism and Scepticism. We find this fragment in Pascal:

[8] 'When I consider the shortness of my life, absorbed into the eternity before and after it—the memory of a guest who stays only for a day—the small space I fill, and which I see swallowed up in the infinite immensity of spaces which I do not know and which do not know me, I am terrified and am astonished to find myself *here* rather than *there*; for there is no reason to find myself *here* rather than *there*, or *now* rather than *then*. Who has put me here? By whose order and command were this space and time destined for me?' *Pensées* 68/205. The first number is the one given the fragment in the Lafuma ordering, and the second is the number in the Brunschvicg ordering; hereafter cited parenthetically. I quote from *Pascal: Œuvres Complètes*, ed. Henri Gouhier 1963.

Stoïques.

Ils concluent qu'on peut toujours ce qu'on peut quelquefois et que puisque le désir de la gloire fait bien faire à ceux qu'il possède quelque chose, les autres le pourront bien aussi.[9]

In Part I of Hume's *Dialogues concerning Natural Religion* we find the following comment:

> In this view, there appears a great resemblance between sects of the Stoics and the Pyrrhonians, though perpetual antagonists. And both of them seem founded on this erroneous maxim, that what a man can perform sometimes, and in some dispositions, he can perform always, and in every disposition. (*D* I. 133)

Having opened up the possibility of making conjectures about influence, however, I must now refer to an obvious problem that faces any theory about Pascal's influence in the eighteenth century. His projected Apology for the Christian Religion was far from completion at the time of his death, and what we have in the *Pensées* are fragments assembled by a succession of editors. While the most recent presentations of his work may order these fragments in a way that approximates to Pascal's own intentions, in Hume's time they were available only in the version edited by some of his friends at Port-Royal, and published in 1670 and 1678. This version differs markedly from the more complete and authentic ones now available to us. So a thought that seems to find a parallel in the work of a writer in the century after Pascal's death is less likely to have exerted a direct influence if the fragment or fragments containing it did not appear in the Port-Royal edition. I have already supplied, deliberately, examples to illustrate the problem. The two famous fragments I quoted to show the metaphysical component in Pascal's expressions of human anxiety did not appear in any edition available to Hume. The comment about the Stoics, however, did appear there. So although Hume's remark about the Stoics and Pyrrhonians does make it likely that he read the Port-Royal edition, and did not depend for his understanding of Pascal on secondary

---

[9] 'Stoics. They conclude one can do all the time what one can do some of the time, and that since the desire for glory does indeed move those who have it to do this or that, the rest of us can do likewise.' This fragment appears in the Port-Royal edition of the *Pensées* at XXI.1. Port-Royal numbers are subsequently cited in parentheses, beginning in each case with the letters P-R. I have used the 1971 edition of Georges Couton and Jean Jehasse.

writings (of which there were, of course, a great many[10]), if his reflections on the philosophical predicament are in any way allusive to Pascal, they cannot be allusions to the fragments of which they most naturally remind *us*.

For reasons that were religious, political, and philosophical together, the Port-Royal editors arranged Pascal's fragments in a thematic order that was quite different from the order that Pascal himself had intended to follow, and which he had himself described to them.[11] Not only were they rearranged, and in the case of some of the longer and more finished ones shortened and even split up, but about half of those now in modern editions were omitted altogether. There appears to have been a deliberate policy of suppressing themes that are essential to an understanding of Pascal's intentions. His hostility to Descartes, with whom the editors sympathized quite strongly, was not allowed to show. His insistence on the valuelessness of attempting to prove the existence of God (a standard part of apologetics since Aquinas) was editorially excised. So was his qualified but quite emphatic endorsement of Pyrrhonian Scepticism, which includes a fragment that begins unambiguously with the assertion 'Le pyrrhonisme est le vrai' (691/432). This, too, is a vital phase in his apologetic strategy. (The famous Wager argument, for example, presupposes it.) The result of these heavy-handed editorial intrusions is a much-censored edition of Pascal's work, which is presented in an over-simplified and domesticated form that makes it harder to recognize how far he intended to depart from traditional apologetics.

But although this is important, its importance should not be exaggerated. Writing as powerful as Pascal's can still make its impact in spite of editorial obfuscations, and it does so many times over. We should also bear in mind that the Port-Royal editors put in a preface by Étienne Périer that included an account of the occasion when Pascal described the plan of his apologetic project to his friends; so although their editorial plan departs in major ways from that plan, this fact, however reprehensible it is, is not concealed, and it is possible for a reader to interpret what the edition contains in the light of Pascal's reported purposes. Furthermore, another important document, the *Entretien avec M. de Saci*, was published in 1728, and in this document Pascal comments at length on Epictetus and

---

[10] See Barker 1975.    [11] The authoritative study of this is Vamos 1972.

Montaigne, who represent Stoicism and Pyrrhonism for him; what is available here compensates to a modest degree for some of the philosophically important omissions in the Port-Royal text.

I think we can assume that although Hume would certainly not have been one of Pascal's more sympathetic readers, he would, nevertheless, have been one of his more discerning ones. If, therefore, we find important elements in his thought that either resemble distinctive themes in Pascal, or are manifest contrasts to them, I suggest this will be deliberate and not accidental. I shall be concerned here with two areas in which we do find this. The first is their understanding of human nature, and in particular the ways in which its non-intellectual elements contribute to the formation of our beliefs. The second, as we would expect, is their understanding of the nature of religious faith. In the first we find instructive similarities, and in the second instructive and deliberate contrast.

## III

I cannot enter into detailed discussion of Pascal's apologetic strategy; but it is, I think, uncontroversial now that the most important innovation in this strategy was his intention to begin with a depiction of human nature rather than a philosophical attempt to prove the reality of God. The portrayal of human nature that he planned, and partially executed, was one that would have the purpose of bringing about the reader's *acknowledgment* of the paradoxes of his or her own condition. The apologetic was designed to move the reader toward *conversion*, not mere philosophical enlightenment, and the self-knowledge that Pascal, in true Socratic manner, sought to induce, was a self-knowledge that would lead the reader to listen to God, not engage in philosophical analysis (see 131/434). This portrayal of human nature emphasizes both its wretchedness and its grandeur. (The appearance of misanthropy that so angered Voltaire derived in part at least from the fact that the editors, as true Augustinians, emphasized the wretchedness in their selections at the expense of the grandeur, giving the whole document an air of conventional gloom.) Pascal's vision combines the wretchedness and the grandeur in a paradoxical manner designed to cry out for special explanation and special cure: the explanation, of course, being the doctrine of the Fall and the cure being redemption through Christ.

The uneasy mixture of wretchedness and grandeur, Pascal tells us, has led thinkers like the Stoics to attempt to gain redemption through the use of reason. It has been the role of the Sceptics, such as the classical Pyrrhonists and their modern counterparts like Montaigne, to turn reason on itself and show that it is incapable of fulfilling this role. The role can only be fulfilled by faith; and Pascal tries to turn the reader from a recognition of his divided and anxious condition toward faith by urging him to take account of the signs of God's presence and his wish to redeem us that are available to us all, especially in the Scriptures. These signs, though always present, are hidden from those who are unwilling to acknowledge their need for them, and choose instead to seek distraction from their finitude and their sinfulness. For those willing to listen to God, the Scriptures are full of the signs of his redemption in Christ. Much of the latter part of the Apology was to have been devoted to a scrutiny of the Scriptures that showed these signs to those willing to seek for them. The editors obscured the strategy that Pascal had himself outlined to them by placing many of the passages dealing with scriptural interpretation toward the beginning of their edition, thus ignoring the important fact that the reader was to have been urged to see the signs the scriptures contained only after being brought to seek a cure for his condition, and not before.

The most important feature of Pascal's strategy, then, was the fact that it proceeded from the analysis of the human condition, through an attack on the attempt to cure that condition by philosophical reasoning, an attack that involved Pascal in accepting the philosophical correctness of Scepticism, to an examination of the signs of God's proffered redemption in the New Testament. It was a strategy that self-consciously dispensed with the attempt to prove the existence of God by philosophical means. For Pascal thinks such an attempt is spiritually *inappropriate*. I shall return to the reasons he gives for this judgement (reasons which are excised from the Port-Royal edition) at a later stage. The fact that he makes it, however, entitles us to place him firmly in the Fideist tradition of apologetic, and to see him as the most important ancestor of Kierkegaard, whom he anticipates in many ways.[12]

But Kierkegaard is not the only thinker he anticipates. For one might well state the anti-rationalist thrust of Pascal's apologetic

[12] This is recognized and developed in Patrick 1947.

strategy by saying that in his view, 'To be a philosophical sceptic is the first and most essential step towards being a sound, believing Christian.' That, as anyone familiar with him will immediately have recognized, is a quotation from Hume (*D* XII. 228). It is high time we returned to him.


# IV

While the differences between Hume's intentions and Pascal's could not be greater, they are precisely the sorts of difference that generate important parallels and similarities. I have already said that Pascal's evocation of human anxiety and finitude has a clear philosophical strand in it, and that Hume is a thinker who was not merely puzzled by philosophical problems but anxious in the face of their non-resolution. I will now go further, and say that just as the Sceptics of antiquity offered their arguments against the cosmic claims of Epicureans and Stoics as a cure for anxiety and not merely for intellectual display, so Hume is, like Pascal, offering his serious reader more than a journey through intellectual excitements. He is offering a saving way of life. It is, certainly, a self-consciously restricted, and to some no doubt enervating, way of life; but it is equally a response to the anxieties of the human condition. It is a deliberately secularizing response, because Hume sees religion as a major source of anxiety, not a cure for it. But it represents a systematic attempt to use an understanding of human nature as a basis for a way of life that will free us from those avoidable ills that are due to *mis*-understandings of it. Hume is in the Hellenistic, and therefore in the Socratic, tradition; and it is of the essence of his philosophical system (and he does not fail to have one merely because philosophy students are always encouraged to read him in anthologized bits) that it is in the secularized and scientific study of what our nature is really like that we can find the right ways of escaping human anxiety. It is also of the essence of that system that philosophy, like religion, has to have its proper place determined by that study if it is not to be a source of anxiety and social distress on its own account.

Given these likenesses between what Pascal and Hume are about, and their parallel inclinations toward philosophical scepticism, it is in no way a surprise that they should say remarkably similar things about the way the non-intellectual components in our natures determine the formation of our beliefs, and the structures of our social relationships. It is also, of course, to be expected that although they frequently tell the same story about human nature and its workings, their evaluation of the story they tell is almost always opposite.

It is high time for some illustrations.[13] The first general theme that is emphasized by both thinkers is the importance of the non-intellectual forces in human nature in the formation of our beliefs. There are two such forces on which both lay great stress. One is custom, and the other is imagination.

Pascal's dominant image for the role of custom (*coutume, habitude*) in our natures is the machine. Man is, as Descartes said, a machine as well as an intelligence; but in a way that Descartes ignored, this means that the human mind too is mechanical, that is, habitual, in its workings. Our beliefs are largely determined by this. To philosophers, the most famous passage in which Pascal makes use of this insight is near the close of the Wager argument, where the doubter is persuaded to induce belief in himself by becoming habituated through religious observances. 'Naturellement même cela vous fera croire et vous abêtira.' The fragment is partially reproduced in the Port-Royal text, but this thoroughly unCartesian sentence is omitted (418/233, *P-R* xxi. 2). There are, however, many other key fragments that emphasize the importance of custom.[14] In one of the most philosophically interesting to find its way into the Port-Royal text, Pascal contrasts the importance of custom in producing beliefs with the relative unimportance of proofs: who ever proved, he says, that it will dawn tomorrow, or that we will die? and what is more widely believed than these things? (821/252, *P-R* vii. 3). The anticipation of Hume could hardly be more direct. For everyone who knows about Hume at all knows that he tells us it is custom, and not reason, that assures us the sun will rise tomorrow. And just as Hume's conception of custom is far wider than that of internal habit, and embraces the social conventions on which the artificial virtues, particularly justice, depend; so Pascal attributes to custom in this wide sense the power that social institutions have

[13] In what follows, I make no attempt to do more than isolate some themes that appear in important fragments. Any general account of the psychology and epistemology of the *Pensées* would have to deal with matters there is no space for here; in particular, the doctrine of the Three Orders. For expositions of this see, for example, Broome 1966 and Hazelton 1974.

[14] See 419/419, 126/93 (*P-R* xxv. 15), 698/119, 663/121.

upon us. 'La justice est ce qui est établi; et ainsi toutes nos lois établies seront nécessairement tenues pour justes sans être examinées, puisqu'elles sont établies' (645/312).[15]

As with custom, so with the intimately allied faculty of imagination. For both writers, the imagination is the major force that determines the character of our life-world. Here, as elsewhere, it is only Hume who is systematic; for him the fundamental principle that determines the workings of the mind is the principle of association; this principle governs the imagination, that is, the faculty that creates *images* and supplies our experience with what direct perception and reasoning cannot supply.[16] In doing this, Hume tells us, the imagination will frequently *beguile* the reason, and will make us lazily acquiesce in many opinions it is convenient for us to believe, but for which the Sceptic can readily demonstrate we do not have evidence. (Among these beliefs are the confidence in the continuing existence of objects we no longer see or touch, or the universal regularity of the natural world.)

Pascal also paints the imagination as a power that beguiles us. It is a *puissance trompeuse*, a deceptive power: one that enables us, very particularly, to deceive ourselves. It is true that sometimes its power will overcome our inclinations and fill us with irrational fears— one thinks here of his famous example of the great philosopher on a plank over a precipice, who knows that the plank is quite wide enough to save him, but is still struck with terror by his imagination (44/82); but more commonly it beguiles us in ways we want—as when magistrates and physicians wear pompous garments in order to stimulate the imagination of their public and stifle their critical judgement.

A comparison between the relevant texts makes it instantly obvious that although Pascal often accords both custom and imagination the same functions that Hume does, his evaluation of those functions is far more negative. To Pascal, the fact that custom and imagination can entrench beliefs that philosophical criticism can show to have no rational foundation is a sign of human depravity and self-deception. But Hume tells the story of their powers in a wholly different tone of voice. For him, the fact that we come to believe

---

[15] 'Justice is that which is established; hence all our established laws will necessarily be considered just without examination, because they are established.'
[16] Most important here is the role given the imagination in the formation of our belief in the reality of the external world, in *T* I. iv. 2.

what we do through habit and convention is a merciful dispensation, for without it we would be sunk in practical paralysis. The fact that we are not rigorous analysts most of the time is a Darwinian provision, essential for our survival. He even says in one famous place that 'Carelessness and inattention alone can afford us any remedy. For this reason I rely entirely upon them' (*T* I. iv. 2. 218). This remark usually raises a smile; but Hume means it. Nevertheless, the story of how we come to believe in the reality of the physical world outside us is a story full of ascriptions of laziness and confusion that Pascal would have found congenial.

So Pascal and Hume are at one in regarding our beliefs as being, in Hume's language, 'more properly an act of the sensitive, than of the cogitative part of our natures' (*T* I. iv. 1. 183). Pascal would have said they are the work of the heart, rather than of the reason. They are even more clearly at one on the way in which, as they see it, our natures, so described, protect us against the effects of Sceptical argument. Both Pascal and Hume say that the *arguments* of the Pyrrhonian Sceptics are unanswerable: that is, no philosopher has been able to refute them. But both also say, quite explicitly, that the non-intellectual elements in our natures protect us against the despair and the inaction that would otherwise follow from this. In Pascal's case we find an interesting complication: while maintaining that our natures ensure that there can be no such thing as a thoroughly Pyrrhonian person in practice, he reserves his most extended and vitriolic attacks for those who seem, at least, to manage to live out the easy-going acceptance of our intellectual limits that the classical Pyrrhonists, such as Sextus Empiricus, proclaimed as the natural result of abandoning the search for knowledge. This seems to involve him in condemning as wickedly frivolous an attitude that he seems also to say our nature makes impossible for us. If it is impossible, why go on so much about how monstrous it is to adopt it? I think the answer is that Pascal thinks there are only *some* spheres in which our natures supply us with the beliefs we need to avoid sceptical anxiety: roughly, those of common sense and science. The apparent insouciance with which professed sceptics proclaim their doubts about deeper, cosmic matters is only assumed and not real. We can see this in the way in which they, like the rest of us, seek to distract ourselves from the fact of human finitude and weakness by vanities and diversions. Few things in the *Pensées* are better known than the passages in which Pascal tries to expose the self-deception

at the heart of play and recreation, which he sees as primarily a process of filling the soul with distracting rubbish that hides the self's
emptiness from it. The off-hand lightness of the Sceptic's tone is one
such game, designed, as all games are, to deceive all who take part
in it.[17]

Hume's attitude to Scepticism is in all key respects the same.
He thinks the doubts of the Pyrrhonian cannot be answered by
argument, in spite of the repeated efforts of philosophers. But no
one is affected in practice by this. The Sceptic's doubts are 'vain' or
impotent. They admit of no answer and produce no conviction.[18]
The scientific study of the imagination and its workings shows why:
it is because we are beings who are instinctively programmed to *believe.*
But although we are instinctively programmed to believe, and would
be driven to insanity by the Sceptic's arguments if this were not so,
the fact that there is no *refutation* of them of these arguments is
disturbing to the unhappy few who have a predilection for philosophical enquiry. Hume himself is such a person, and after a solid
dose of sceptical philosophy he fancies himself, he says, a strange
uncouth monster, racked by anxiety. This state is unnatural, but it
is real enough while it lasts. Hume joins Pascal in thinking that
Sceptical doubts do not lead to the peace of mind that the Greek
Sceptics said, but to anxiety, unless something can rescue us. What
can? Hume's answer is: distraction; play. 'I dine, I play a game of
back-gammon, I converse, and am merry with my friends; and
when after three or four hours' amusement, I wou'd return to these
speculations, they appear so cold, and strain'd, and ridiculous, that
I cannot find it in my heart to enter into them any farther' (*T* I. iv.
7. 269). Hume's cure for the ills of sceptical doubt involve him in
leaning on those very resources of feeling, instinct and social life that
Pascal has seen as *puissances trompeuses.* There are other aids too:
there are the intellectual distractions that can come from directing
one's rational faculties away from those worrying cosmic questions
that are beyond us, and on to history, or science. And there are the
protections that come from fighting those superstitions that generate their own brands of fear and anxiety, and weaken our social

---

[17] On vanities, or forms of self-inflation, see 627/150 (*P-R* xxxiv. 5), 597/455
(*P-R* xxix. 18), 668/457, 978/100. On diversions, see 136/139 (*P-R* xxvi. 1. 2. 3), 137/142
(*P-R* xxvi. 1), 138/166 (*P-R* xxxi. 3), 139/143 (*P-R* xxvi. 2) etc.
[18] Hume actually pronounces this verdict on Berkeley in a passage where he
claims Berkeley's arguments lead to sceptical conclusions (*EU* xii. 155n).

resources by turning us away from society and its nourishments for the spirit. It is Hume's turn to be vitriolic when he comments on 'celibacy, fasting, penance, mortification, self-denial, humility, silence, solitude, and the whole train of monkish virtues'. These, if we pursue them, *prevent* us from shoring one another up against the darts of anxiety and superstition. 'A gloomy, hair-brained enthusiast, after his death, may have a place in the calendar; but will scarcely ever be admitted, when alive, into intimacy and society, except by those who are as delirious and dismal as himself' (*EM* IX. 270).

I have argued so far that the opinions of Pascal and Hume on the relation between human nature and truth are largely mirror-images of one another. Hume's naturalism is often said by scholars to be developed in systematic opposition to rationalist interpretations of the human mind. This is indeed true. But Pascal's teachings are developed in opposition to rationalism also, in spite of his well-known remarks about the dignity of reason. They both give reason a *role* in human life; but each maintains that that role is more restricted than the rationalists from Plato to Descartes have maintained. I think we can understand Hume's naturalism better if we see it as being intended, in addition, as a systematic antidote to the sort of fideism that Pascal wanted to substitute for rationalism. To try to confirm this judgement, I shall conclude with some comments on how Hume responds to Pascal's philosophy of religion.

## V

I must begin this with an extract from one of the more substantial fragments of the *Pensées*—one that was included in the Port-Royal text:

De plus que personne n'a d'assurance, hors de la foi—s'il veille ou s'il dort, vu que durant le sommeil on croit veiller aussi fermement que nous faisons.[19]

This remark has an obvious target: the Descartes of the first *Meditation*. Pascal is insisting that sceptical doubts, such as Descartes' suggestion that we might, at any given time, be dreaming when we think we are awake, cannot be answered by reasoning

[19] Krailsheimer translates: 'Moreover, no one can be sure, apart from faith, whether he is asleep or waking, because when we are asleep we are just as firmly convinced we are awake as we are now', Pascal 1966 edn..

as Descartes believed. The assurance that we need is supplied not
by reason, but by the heart: by the instincts, as Hume was to say
later. We have already seen this major area of agreement between
them. But Pascal takes a further step that Hume could not take. To
Pascal the heart, that gives us this reassurance, is intended by God
to open itself to him. For, he says, it is the heart, not the reason,
that perceives God; indeed that is what faith is: God perceived by
the heart, not by the reason (424/278). Therefore the obstacles to
faith are not intellectual; they lie in our passions, and it is these that
we must tame before the signs of God's redemption can enter the
heart as he intends.

So to Pascal common sense conviction about our own immediate
environment, and faith in God, are epistemologically continuous. Both
come, if they come at all, from the heart, not the intellect. The fact
that so many have the one, but not the other, is not due to anyone's
intellectual limitations (for the intellect supplies neither), but to cor-
ruption and to pride. Therefore Pascal says that our common sense
convictions are as much a matter of faith as *faith* is.

Hume, of course, rejects this. But how *can* he reject it?[20] He tells
us with approval that the resources of instinct supply us with the
beliefs we need at the level of secular common sense, in spite of the
limitations of our reason; but he seems to think that the inability of
reason to generate or justify the claims of religious faith is a good
reason for not accepting those claims. Why should he accept the one
and not the other?

Hume has several answers to this challenge, as one would expect.
What is crucial for the understanding of his system, however, is
that he sees the need to produce them, and is occupied in doing so
throughout his philosophical career. His answers are meticulously
connected, and together they constitute a systematic naturalistic
response to Pascal's apologetic. I want to outline it; to do this I must
comment, very briefly, on three of his anti-religious writings.

I turn first to his short treatise, *The Natural History of Religion.*
In this rather neglected work, he begins by separating out the question of the justification of religious beliefs from the question of their
origins in human nature. He then addresses the second question, and
tells a story about why it is that people believe in gods, and come

[20] I have attempted to deal at length with the whole issue of the relationship between
scepticism and fideism in Penelhum 1983.

to believe in one supreme God—for he is convinced that religion begins as primitive polytheism, and only evolves into high theism much later. The story he tells is a story of mankind haunted by fears and anxieties in the face of natural dangers and calamities. As these calamities assault them, they reach for the only sort of explanations they can invent. They ascribe the disasters that befall them to the intervention of personal powers, and fill their imaginary world with spiritual agents that intervene in nature, and have to be appeased by worship and flattery. Much later, this polytheistic world is further darkened by the rivalries that result when the devotees of one such god seek his approval by insisting on his merits to such an extent that they reject the claims of all the others, and try to retain his favour by extremes of flattery. The inner logic of worship thus creates the omnipotent and all-knowing deity who cannot be admitted to have any moral failings, yet knows all our failings intimately and demands total obedience. Hume insists that, given these origins, the devotional stance that worshippers have toward such a God does not embody the certitude and consolation that Pascal proclaims as the fruit of faith, but is a condition that is insincere, ambivalent, and chronically anxious—a condition very like the state Pascal had said the human soul is in *without* the consolation of the presence of God. So he offers a naturalistic account of the power that the idea of God has. And it is a story about the power of the God of Abraham, Isaac and Jacob, not a story about the God of the philosophers from whom Pascal is so anxious to distinguish Him.

I turn now to the most famous of Hume's anti-religious writings, his Section 'Of Miracles' (*EU* x). Hume's argument here, which I shall not repeat, is designed to show that the supposedly revelatory signs of God to which Pascal urges us to be open are historically dubious, and only acceptable if we suspend the very dependence on custom and habit that is the sole antidote to Scepticism at the common sense level. His special hostile interest in the miracle story of Port-Royal is not an accident.

I turn, thirdly, to Hume's most important study of religion, the *Dialogues Concerning Natural Religion*. It deals, of course, with the attempt to prove the existence of God by reason. Pascal explicitly rejects this way of persuading his readers toward faith. He gives more than one reason for this rejection, and I am unsure how far the reasons he gives are fully consistent with each other. But his most telling comment is the assertion that such philosophical arguments can only lead to deism, which he says is almost as remote from the Christian religion as atheism is (449/556). The God to whom Pascal wishes to bring us is a God who fills the heart and soul; he intervenes in history with repeated acts of grace. The God of the deists did no such thing.[21] Now while Hume shares a low estimate of the attempts to prove the existence of God, and indeed many think he has destroyed them, he appears near the very end of the *Dialogues*, in passages that are the despair of commentators, to espouse, himself, a vague and minimal form of deism, and even to commend it as 'true religion'. His private opinions are hard to determine, and are artfully concealed beneath the dialogue form; but he seems to encourage, or at least to acquiesce in, the polite, philosophical apologetic that issues in the totally formal and unreligious acknowledgment of a wholly non-interventionist deity. This is a form of so-called religion that will bolster, and not disturb, the way of life that human beings in polite lettered society have developed for themselves. Such a God, unlike Pascal's, is only hidden in the sense that his presence or absence would make no difference at all to experience. While we cannot be sure how far Hume's protagonists in the *Dialogues* speak for him at the close, it seems clear, in my judgement, that this is largely a result of the fact that what is left at issue between them by then is not very important. Pascal had eschewed the attempt to prove the existence of God because such a proof was not worth providing, and gives the soul no religious nourishment. For this very same reason, Hume does not think such a proof is worth fighting. For the God of the philosophers never intervenes.

When faced with the silence and ambiguity of nature, Pascal was torn, and wrote, in a passage to which Hume had access, about the way in which his spirit was divided between what seemed to be signs that God was present and what seemed to be a vision of a world without God (429/229, *P-R* viii. 1). By the end of the *Dialogues*, Hume seems willing to concede a cause, or causes, of cosmic order that probably bears some remote analogy to human intelligence, and has

---

[21] Compare the famous recorded remark about Descartes: 'Je ne suis pardonner à Descartes: il voudrai bien, dans toute la philosophie, se pouvoir passer de Dieu; mais il n'a pus s'empècher de lui donner une chiquenaude pour mettre le monde en mouvement; après cela, il n'a plus faire de Dieu' ('I cannot forgive Descartes: through all his philosophy he would have liked to manage without God; but he could not stop himself giving him a flick of the fingers to start the world moving; after that he had no more use for God') (*Oeuvres Complètes*, 640).

'neither goodness nor malice'.[22] He describes his acquiescence as a 'plain, philosophical assent'. I have my doubts whether in private Hume assents even to this vague deistic position, but I am sure that if he does it is precisely because it is a position that is as far from Christian faith as Pascal says it is. And it is possible for Hume's reader to come to rest in this bland and religiously empty view because Hume has given an account of his competing theistic impulses that will make him distrust them, and has undermined his confidence in the reality of those revelatory events where he might be inclined to think God can be found.

The important fragment in which Pascal rejects the apologetic route of the theistic proofs is not in the Port-Royal edition, whose Cartesian editors would have found it distasteful. But even if Hume could not otherwise have inferred Pascal's estimate of the value of the theistic arguments, it is an estimate he was well able to reach on his own account. And having done so, he was able to commend the product of such argument for the very reason Pascal had given for condemning it.

Scholars have guessed that the personages in Hume's *Dialogues* can be identified with some of his predecessors, such as Samuel Clarke (Demea), Joseph Butler (Cleanthes) and Pierre Bayle (Philo).[23] Perhaps. But I do not doubt, myself, that although Hume took the measure of all these thinkers, he also saw himself as responding to someone who towered above them intellectually as well as religiously, and whose challenge he thought it much more important to meet.

## VI

I have tried to suggest that the two great men whose work I have been comparing agree in far more than is usually recognized, and that Hume is trying, however much or little we can trace his ideas to direct textual influence, to give an answer to Pascal's fideism, both in his philosophy of religion, and in his secular account of human nature and its instincts. If the thought of these two does indeed

---

[22] *D* XI. 212. Philo says that the facts of evil make this the most likely moral condition of the deity or deities responsible for the world.

[23] The first two identifications are by Mossner, the third by Anders Jeffner. See Mossner 1936 and Jeffner 1966.

mesh in the way I have suggested, their writings give us the two supreme expressions of anti-rationalist thought in early modern times. Neither has been bettered, in my view, as an exemplar of the stance he represents. By comparison with Pascal, for example, Kierkegaard is turgid; by comparison with Hume, Kant is ludicrously professorial and Russell merely frivolous. If one compares the systems, it becomes, in my view, clearer and clearer that each has resources that enable him to answer, and also to explain, the other. For over and over, they are each telling the same tale, in a different tone of voice. How are we lesser thinkers to decide between them?

My own view, for what it is worth, is that there is no way of doing so if we accept the starting point that they share: the belief that somehow we can discover the right stance to take towards our world by understanding our own natures and their needs. Pope took this from Pascal and put it into heroic couplets; but stating it in heroic couplets does not turn it into a deeper insight. The very deadlock that Pascal and Hume represent, when we place one against the other, suggests that it may be mistaken to suppose that we can understand ourselves and our needs without knowing the answers to some of those hard questions about what sort of cosmos we inhabit. If there is a God who wants to reach us, then our needs are likely to be rather different from what they would be if there is not. We seem to need to know whether or not this is so before we know what our real natures are.

But what about all those Sceptical arguments that suggest questions of this vast nature are beyond us? All I can say is that if they are indeed beyond us, then we are also incapable of understanding ourselves very fully. Scepticism does lead to indecision, because it stands in the way of self-knowledge.

# REFERENCES

AINSLIE, DONALD (1999), 'Scepticism about Persons in Book II of Hume's *Treatise*', *Journal of the History of Philosophy*, 37, 469–92; (2001), 'Hume's Reflections on the Simplicity and Identity of Mind', *Philosophy and Phenomenological Research*, 62, 557–78; 'Hume's Anti-Cogito', unpub. MS.

AMERIKS, KARL (1982), *Kant's Theory of Mind: An Analysis of the Paralogisms of Reason* (Oxford: Clarendon Press).

ANNAS, JULIA (1994), 'Hume and Ancient Scepticism', presented to Hume Society Congress, Rome; published version *Acta Philosophica Fennica*, 66, 2000, 271–85.

ANNAS, JULIA, and BARNES, JONATHAN (1985), *The Modes of Skepticism: Ancient Texts and Modern Interpretations* (Cambridge: Cambridge University Press).

ÁRDAL, PÁLL S. (1966), *Passion and Value in Hume's Treatise* (Edinburgh: Edinburgh University Press).

ARNAULD, ANTOINE and NICOLE, PIERRE (1964 edn.), *The Art of Thinking*, ed. James Dickoff and Patricia James (Indianapolis: Bobs-Merrill).

—— (1965 edn.), *La Logique, ou l'Art de Penser*, ed. Pierre Clair and Francois Girbal (Paris: Presses Universitaires de France).

ASHLEY, LAWRENCE, and STACK, MICHAEL (1974), 'Hume's Doctrine of Personal Identity', *Dialogue*, 13, 239–54.

BAIER, ANNETTE (1991), *A Progress of Sentiments: Reflections on Hume's Treatise* (Cambridge, Mass.: Harvard University Press).

BAKER, BRENDA (1974), 'Acting Under Duress', *Canadian Journal of Philosophy*, 3, 515–23.

BARKER, JOHN (1975), *Strange Contrarieties: Pascal in England during the Age of Reason* (Montreal: McGill University Press).

BASSON, A. H. (1958), *David Hume* (Harmondsworth: Penguin Books).

BECK, LEWIS WHITE (1978), *Essays on Kant and Hume* (New Haven: Yale University Press).

BELL, MARTIN, and MCGINN, MARIE (1990), 'Naturalism and Scepticism', *Philosophy*, 65, 399–418.

BOSWELL, JAMES (1906 edn.), *The Life of Samuel Johnson*, 2 vols. (London: J. M. Dent & Sons).

BRETT, NATHAN (1974), 'Scepticism and Vain Questions', *Dialogue*, 13, 657–73.

BRICKE, JOHN (1980), *Hume's Philosophy of Mind* (Princeton: Princeton University Press).

BRICKE, JOHN (1996), *Mind and Morality: An Examination of Hume's Moral Psychology* (Oxford: Clarendon Press).

BROOME, J. H. (1966), *Pascal* (New York: Barnes and Noble).

BURNS, R. M. (1981), *The Great Debate on Miracles: From Joseph Glanvil to David Hume* (Lewisburg: Bucknell University Press).

BURNYEAT, MYLES (ed.) (1983), *The Skeptical Tradition* (Berkeley: University of California Press).

BUTLER, JOSEPH (1897), *The Works of Bishop Butler*, ed. W. E. Gladstone, 2 vols. (Oxford: Clarendon Press).

—— (1900), *The Works of Bishop Butler*, ed. J. H. Bernard, 2 vols. (London: Macmillan).

BUTLER, R. J. (1960), 'Natural Belief and the Enigma of Hume', *Archiv für Geschichte der Philosophie*, 42, 73–100.

BYRNE, PETER (1989), *Natural Religion and the Nature of Religion: the Legacy of Deism* (London: Routledge).

CAPALDI, NICHOLAS (1975), *David Hume: The Newtonian Philosopher* (Boston: Twayne).

—— (1989), *Hume's Place in Moral Philosophy* (New York: Peter Lang).

CHAPPELL, V. C. (ed.), (1966), *Hume: A Collection of Critical Essays* (Garden City, NJ: Doubleday).

CHAZAN, PAULINE (1992), 'Pride, Virtue and Self-Hood: A Reconstruction of Hume', *Canadian Journal of Philosophy*, 22, 45–64.

CHISHOLM, RODERICK M. (1966), 'Freedom and Action', in Keith, Lehrer (ed.) 1966, 11–44.

—— (1976), *Person and Object: A Metaphysical Study* (La Salle: Open Court).

CICERO (1953 edn.), *De Divinatione*, trans. W. A. Falconer, Loeb Classical Library (London: Heinemann).

—— (1972 edn.), *The Nature of the Gods*, trans. Horace C. P. McGregor (Harmondsworth: Penguin Books).

CLARKE, SAMUEL (1978 edn.), *The Works of Samuel Clarke D. D.* (1738), 4 vols. (New York: Garland Publishing).

COLLINS, STEVEN (1982), *Selfless Persons: Imagery and Thought in Theravada Buddhism* (Cambridge: Cambridge University Press).

DESCARTES, RENÉ (1966 edn.), *Philosophical Writings*, ed. Elizabeth Anscombe and Peter Thomas Geach (London: Thomas Nelson).

EMERSON, ROGER L. (1994), 'The "Affair" at Edinburgh and the "Project" at Glasgow: the Politics of Hume's Attempts to Become a Professor', in M. A. Stewart and John P. Wright (eds.) 1–22.

FLEW, ANTONY G. N. (1949), ' "Selves" ', *Mind*, ns 59, 355–8.

—— (1961), *Hume's Philosophy of Belief: A Study of his First Inquiry* (London: Routledge and Kegan Paul).

—— (1986), *David Hume: Philosopher of Moral Science* (Oxford: Basil Blackwell).

—— (1990), 'Fogelin on Hume on Miracles', *Hume Studies*, 16, 141–44.

FOGELIN, ROBERT J. (1985), *Hume's Skepticism in the Treatise of Human Nature* (London: Routledge & Kegan Paul).

—— (1990), 'What Hume Actually Said About Miracles', *Hume Studies*, 16, 81–6.

FRANKFURT, HARRY (1971), 'Freedom of the Will and the Concept of a Person', *Journal of Philosophy*, 68, 5–20.

GARRETT, DON (1997), *Cognition and Commitment in Hume's Philosophy* (New York: Oxford University Press).

GASKIN, JOHN (1974), 'God, Hume, and Natural Belief', *Philosophy*, 49, 281–94.

—— (1978), *Hume's Philosophy of Religion*, 1st edn. (London: Macmillan).

—— (1988), *Hume's Philosophy of Religion*, 2nd edn. (London: Macmillan).

HOBBES, THOMAS (1909 edn.), *Leviathan*, with essay by W. G. Pogson Smith (Oxford: Clarendon Press).

HAKSAR, VINIT (1991), *Indivisible Selves and Moral Practice* (Delhi: Oxford University Press).

HANKINSON, R. J. (1995), *The Sceptics* (London: Routledge).

HAZELTON, ROGER (1974), *Blaise Pascal: The Genius of His Thought* (Philadelphia: Westminster Press).

HENDERSON, ROBERT S. (1990), 'David Hume on Personal Identity and the Indirect Passions', *Hume Studies*, 16, 33–44.

HUMBER, JAMES M. (1995), 'Hume's Invisible Self', *American Catholic Philosophical Quarterly*, 69, 485–501.

—— (1999), 'Hume on Liberty, Necessity, Morality and Religion', *Philosophical Inquiry*, 21, 17–31.

HUME, DAVID (1932 edn.), *The Letters of David Hume*, ed. J. Y. T. Greig (Oxford: Oxford University Press).

—— (1954 edn.), *New Letters of David Hume*, ed. Raymond Klibansky and Ernest C. Mossner (Oxford: Clarendon Press).

—— (1964), *Philosophical Works*, ed. T. H. Green and T. H. Grose, 4 vols. (reprint Scientia Verlag Aalen; 1st edn. London: Longmans Green, 1878).

—— (1965), *An Abstract of a Treatise of Human Nature 1740*, with Introduction by J. M. Keynes and P. Sraffa (reprint Hamden, Conn.: Archon Books; 1st edn. Cambridge: Cambridge University Press, 1938).

—— (1967 edn.), *A Letter from a Gentleman to His Friend in Edinburgh*, ed. Ernest C. Mossner and John V. Price (Edinburgh: Edinburgh University Press).

—— (1970 edn.), *Dialogues concerning Natural Religion*, edited and with commentary by Nelson Pike (Indianapolis: Bobbs-Merrill).

—— (1975 edn.), *Enquiries Concerning Human Understanding and Concerning the Principles of Morals*, ed. L. A. Selby-Bigge, 3rd edn. with text revised and notes by P. H. Nidditch (Oxford: Clarendon Press).

286      *References*

HUME, DAVID (1978 edn.), *A Treatise of Human Nature*, ed. L. A. Selby-Bigge, 2nd edn. with text revised and notes by P. H. Nidditch (Oxford: Clarendon Press).

—— (1980), *Dialogues Concerning Natural Religion*, ed. Norman Kemp Smith (reprint Indianapolis, Ind.: Bobbs-Merrill; 1st edn. Edinburgh: Thomas Nelson, 1947).

JACOBSON, NOLAN PLINY (1966), *Buddhism: The Religion of Analysis* (London: Allen & Unwin).

JEFFNER, ANDERS (1966), *Butler and Hume on Religion* (Stockholm: Diakonistyrelsens Bokforlag).

JONES, J. R. (1950), ' "Selves": A Reply to Mr. Flew', *Mind*, NS 59, 233–6.

JONES, PETER (1982), *Hume's Sentiments: Their Ciceronian and French Context* (Edinburgh: Edinburgh University Press).

KENNY, ANTHONY (1975), *Will, Freedom and Power* (Oxford: Basil Blackwell).

—— (1992), *The Metaphysics of Mind* (Oxford: Oxford University Press).

KYDD, RACHEL M. (1946), *Reason and Conduct in Hume's Treatise* (Oxford: Clarendon Press).

LEHRER, KEITH (1989), *Thomas Reid* (London: Routledge).

—— (1966), *Freedom and Determinism* (New York: Random House).

LEMAHIEU, D. L. (1976), *The Mind of William Paley* (Lincoln: University of Nebraska Press).

LIVINGSTON, DONALD W. (1998), *Philosophical Melancholy and Delirium: Hume's Pathology of Philosophy* (Chicago: University of Chicago Press).

LOCKE, JOHN (1970 edn.), *An Essay Concerning Human Understanding*, ed. Alexander Campbell Fraser (New York: Dover).

LOGAN, BERYL (1993), *A Religion Without Talking* (New York: Peter Lang).

MACINTOSH, J. J. and MEYNELL, H. A. (eds.), (1994), *Faith, Scepticism and Personal Identity* (Calgary: University of Calgary Press).

MACINTYRE, ALASDAIR (1981), *After Virtue* (London: Duckworth).

—— (1994), 'Hume, Testimony to Miracles, the Order of Nature, and Jansenism', in MacIntosh and Meynell (eds.), 1994.

MACNABB, D. G. C. (1951), *David Hume: His Theory of Knowledge and Morality* (London: Hutchinson).

MADELL, GEOFFREY (1981), *The Identity of the Self* (Edinburgh: Edinburgh University Press).

—— (1994), 'Personal Identity and Objective Reality', in MacIntosh and Meynell (eds.), 1994, 185–98.

MCINTYRE, JANE L. (1979a), 'Is Hume's Self Consistent?', in Norton, David *et al.*, 79–88.

—— (1979b), 'Further Remarks on the Consistency of Hume's Account of the Self', *Hume Studies*, 5, 55–61.

—— (1989), 'Personal Identity and the Passions', *Journal of the History of Philosophy*, 27, 545–57.

—— (1990), 'Character: A Humean Account', *History of Philosophy Quarterly*, 7, 193–206.

—— (1995), 'Hume's "New and Extraordinary" Account of the Passions', presented to Hume Society Conference, Park City, Utah.

—— (1996), 'Hume's Passions: Direct and Indirect', presented to Hume Society Conference, Nottingham.

MERCER, PHILIP (1972), *Sympathy and Ethics* (Oxford: Clarendon Press).

MERRILL, KENNETH R. and SHAHAN, ROBERT W. (eds.), (1976), *David Hume: Many-sided Genius* (Norman: University of Oklahoma Press).

MIJUSKOVIC, BEN LAZARE (1974), *The Achilles of Rationalist Arguments* (The Hague: Martinus Nijhoff).

MOORE, G. E. (1922), *Philosophical Studies* (London: Routledge & Kegan Paul).

MOSSNER, ERNEST C. (1936), 'The Enigma of Hume', *Mind*, 45, 334–49.

—— (1970), *The Life of David Hume* (reprint Oxford: Clarendon Press; 1st edn. Nelson and University of Texas Press, 1954).

—— (1971), *Bishop Butler and the Age of Reason* (reprint New York: Benjamin Blom; 1st edn. New York: Macmillan, 1936).

MOUNCE, H. O. (1999), *Hume's Naturalism* (London: Routledge).

NORTON, DAVID FATE (1982), *David Hume: Common-Sense Moralist, Sceptical Metaphysician* (Princeton: Princeton University Press).

—— (1994), 'How a Sceptic May Live Scepticism', in MacIntosh and Meynell (eds.), 119–39.

—— (1993), *The Cambridge Companion to Hume* (Cambridge: Cambridge University Press).

—— CAPALDI, NICHOLAS, and ROBISON, WADE (eds.), (1979), *McGill Hume Studies* (San Diego: Austin Hill Press).

NOXON, JAMES (1966), 'Hume's Agnosticism', in Chappell, 1966, 361–83.

—— (1969), 'Senses of Identity in Hume's *Treatise*', *Dialogue*, 8, 367–84.

PALEY, WILLIAM (1838), *The Works of William Paley*, 4 vols. (London: Longmans).

PARFIT, DEREK (1971*a*), 'On "The Importance of Self-identity"'. *Journal of Philosophy*, 68, 683–90.

—— (1971*b*), 'Personal Identity', *Philosophical Review*, 80, 3–27.

—— (1984), *Reasons and Persons* (Oxford: Clarendon Press).

PASCAL, BLAISE (1963 edn.), *Oeuvres Complètes*, ed. Henri Gouhier (Paris: du Seuil).

—— (1966 edn.), *Pensées*, trans. Alban Krailsheimer (Harmondsworth: Penguin).

—— (1971 edn.), *Pensées de M. Pascal sur la Religion* (Port-Royal edition (1670), presented by Georges Couton and Jean Jehasse); (Universités de la Région Rhone-Alpes).

PASSMORE, JOHN A. (1952), *Hume's Intentions* (Cambridge: Cambridge University Press).

PATON, H. J. (1951), 'Self-Identity', in *In Defence of Reason* (London: Hutchinson), 99–116.

PATRICK, DENZIL (1947), *Pascal and Kierkegaard*, 2 vols. (London: Lutterworth).

PAYNE, ROBERT (1960), *Hubris: A Study of Pride* (New York: Harper Torchbooks).

PENELHUM, TERENCE (1964), 'Pleasure and Falsity', *American Philosophical Quarterly*, 1, 81–91.

—— (1971a), 'The Importance of Self-identity', *Journal of Philosophy*, 68, 667–78.

—— (1971b), *Religion and Rationality* (New York: Random House).

—— (1975), *Hume* (London: Macmillan).

—— (1976), 'The Self in Hume's Philosophy', in Merrill and Shahan (eds.), 9–24.

—— (1983), *God and Skepticism* (Dordrecht: Reidel).

—— (1985), *Butler* (London: Routledge & Kegan Paul).

—— (1998), critical notice of Paul Russell's *Freedom and Moral Sentiment*, *Canadian Journal of Philosophy*, 28, 81–94.

PERRY, DAVID (1967), *The Concept of Pleasure* (The Hague: Mouton).

PIKE, NELSON (1967), 'Hume's Bundle Theory of the Self: A Limited Defense', *American Philosophical Quarterly*, 4, 159–65.

POPKIN, RICHARD (1951), 'Hume's Pyrrhonism and his Critique of Pyrrhonism', *Philosophical Quarterly*, 1, 385–407, reprinted in Chappell, 1966, 53–98.

—— (1979), *The History of Scepticism from Erasmus to Spinoza* (Berkeley: University of California Press).

—— (1980), *The High Road to Pyrrhonism*, ed. Richard Watson and James Force, (San Diego: Austin Hill Press).

REID, THOMAS (1969 edn.), *Essays on the Active Powers of the Human Mind*, introduction by Baruch A. Brody (Cambridge, Mass.: M. I. T. Press).

ROBISON, WADE (1973), 'Hume's Scepticism', *Dialogue*, 12, 87–99.

ROWE, WILLIAM L. (1991), *Thomas Reid on Freedom and Morality* (Ithaca: Cornell University Press).

RUSSELL, PAUL (1995), *Freedom and Moral Sentiment: Hume's Way of Naturalizing Responsibility* (New York: Oxford University Press).

RYLE, GILBERT (1949), *The Concept of Mind* (London: Hutchinson).

SANDERS, E. P. (1993), *The Historical Figure of Jesus* (Harmondsworth: Penguin).

SCHNEEWIND, J. B. (1984), 'The Divine Corporation and the History of Ethics', in *Philosophy in History*, ed. R. Rorty, J. B. Schneewind, and Q. Skinner (Cambridge: Cambridge University Press), 173–92.

SEXTUS EMPIRICUS (1967 edn.), *Sextus Empiricus*, with English translation by R. G. Bury, 4 vols., Loeb Classical Library (Cambridge, Mass.: Harvard University Press).

SHOEMAKER, SYDNEY (1996), *The First-Person Perspective and Other Essays* (Cambridge: Cambridge University Press).

SMART, NINIAN (1964), *Doctrine and Argument in Indian Philosophy* (London: George Allen & Unwin).

SMITH, NORMAN KEMP (1905), 'The Naturalism of Hume', *Mind*, NS 54, 149–53, 335–47.

—— (1918), *A Commentary to Kant's 'Critique of Pure Reason'* (London: Macmillan).

—— (1941), *The Philosophy of David Hume* (London: Macmillan).

SPRAGUE, ELMER (1967), 'Paley', in *Encyclopedia of Philosophy*, ed. Paul Edwards, vi, 19–20.

STACE, W. T. (1960), *Mysticism and Philosophy* (London: Macmillan).

STEVENSON, CHARLES L. (1944), *Ethics and Language* (New Haven: Yale University Press).

—— (1963), *Facts and Values* (New Haven: Yale University Press).

STEWART, JOHN B. (1963), *The Moral and Political Philosophy of David Hume* (New York: Columbia University Press).

STEWART, M. A. (1994), 'Hume's Historical View of Miracles', in M. A. Stewart and John P. Wright (eds.), 1994.

—— (1990), *Studies in the Philosophy of the Scottish Enlightenment* (Oxford: Clarendon Press).

—— (1994), *Hume and Hume's Connexions*, ed. M. A. Stewart and John P. wright (Edinburgh: Edinburgh University Press).

—— (1995), *The Kirk and the Infidel*, inaugural lecture, Lancaster University, 1994.

STOVE, DAVID (1975), 'Hume, the Causal Principle, and Kemp Smith', *Hume Studies*, 1, 1–22.

STRAWSON, P. F. (1959), *Individuals: An Essay in Descriptive Metaphysics* (London: Methuen).

STROUD, BARRY (1977), *Hume* (London: Routledge & Kegan Paul).

—— (1984), *The Significance of Philosophical Scepticism* (Oxford: Clarendon Press).

SUTHERLAND, STEWART R. (1983), 'Penelhum on Hume', *Philosophical Quarterly*, 33, 182–6.

SWINBURNE, RICHARD (ed.), (1989), *Miracles* (New York: Macmillan).

TAYLOR, A. E. (1927), *David Hume and the Miraculous* (Cambridge: Cambridge University Press).

TILLOTSON, JOHN (1735), *Works of the Most Reverend Dr. John Tillotson*, 5th edn., 3 vols. (London: James Knapton).

TINDAL, MATTHEW (1978), *Christianity as Old as the Creation* (1730) (New York: Garland Publishers).

VAMOS, MARIA (1972), 'Pascal's *Pensées* and the Enlightenment: The Roots of a Misunderstanding', *Studies on Voltaire and the Eighteenth Century*, 97, 7–145.

*References*

VOLTAIRE (1956 edn.), *Lettres Philosophiques: ou Lettres Anglaises*, ed. Raymond Naves (Paris: Garnier).

WATERMAN, MINA (1942), *Voltaire, Pascal, and Human Destiny* (New York: Octagon).

WILSON, FRED (1979), 'Hume's Theory of Mental Activity', in Norton, Capaldi and Robison (eds.), 101–20.

—— (1997), *Hume's Defence of Causal Reasoning* (Toronto: University of Toronto Press).

WOLFF, ROBERT PAUL (1960), 'Hume's Theory of Mental Activity', *Philosophical Review*, 69, reprinted in Chappell, 99–128.

WOOTTON, DAVID (1990), 'Hume's "Of Miracles": Probability and Irreligion', in M. A. Stewart (ed.) (1990), 191–229.

WRIGHT, JOHN P. (1983), *The Sceptical Realism of David Hume* (Manchester: Manchester University Press).

—— (1986), 'Hume's Academic Scepticism: A Reappraisal of His Philosophy of Human Understanding', *Canadian Journal of Philosophy*, 16, 407–36.

YANDELL, KEITH E. (1990), *Hume's 'Inexplicable Mystery': His Views on Religion* (Philadelphia: Temple University Press).

# INDEX